THE BEDFORD SERIES IN HISTORY AND CULTURE

Plessy v. Ferguson
A Brief History with Documents

Related Titles in
THE BEDFORD SERIES IN HISTORY AND CULTURE
Advisory Editors: Lynn Hunt, *University of California, Los Angeles*
David W. Blight, *Yale University*
Bonnie G. Smith, *Rutgers University*
Natalie Zemon Davis, *Princeton University*
Ernest R. May, *Harvard University*

THE BEDFORD SERIES IN HISTORY AND CULTURE

Plessy v. Ferguson

A Brief History with Documents

Edited with an Introduction by

Brook Thomas

University of California, Irvine

BEDFORD/ST. MARTIN'S   Boston ♦ New York

For Bedford/St. Martin's
President and Publisher: Charles H. Christensen
General Manager and Associate Publisher: Joan E. Feinberg
History Editor: Katherine E. Kurzman
Associate Developmental Editor: Richard Keaveny
Editorial Assistant: Charisse Kiino
Managing Editor: Elizabeth M. Schaaf
Production Editor: Maureen Murray
Copyeditor: Barbara G. Flanagan
Indexer: Steve Csipke
Text Design: Claire Seng-Niemoeller
Cover Design: Susan Pace
Cover Art: Negro Expulsion from Railway Car, Philadelphia. Library of Congress, LCUSZ6245698.

For information, write: Bedford/St. Martin's, 75 Arlington Street, Boston, MA 02116 (617-399-4000)

ISBN-10: 0–312–13743–5 (paperback)
0–312–16284–7 (hardcover)
ISBN-13: 978–0–312–13743–4 (paperback)
978–0–312–16284–9 (hardcover)

Acknowledgments

Charles W. Chesnutt, "The Courts and the Negro." Reprinted by permission of John C. Slade and the Fisk University Library.

Illustrations

Page 2: Negro Expulsion from Railway Car, Philadelphia. Library of Congress, LCUSZ6245698.
Page 6: Daniel Desdunes. Courtesy of The Amistad Research Center, Tulane University, New Orleans, La.
Page 20: Harper's Weekly, "Of Course He Wants to Vote the Democratic Ticket." Courtesy of the Boston Public Library.
Page 49: Albion W. Tourgée Courtesy of the Chautauqua County Historical Society, Westfield, N.Y.
Page 178: 1896 Supreme Court. Courtesy of the Collection of the Supreme Court of the United States.

Foreword

The Bedford Series in History and Culture is designed so that readers can study the past as historians do.

The historian's first task is finding the evidence. Documents, letters, memoirs, interviews, pictures, movies, novels, or poems can provide facts and clues. Then the historian questions and compares the sources. There is more to do than in a courtroom, for hearsay evidence is welcome, and the historian is usually looking for answers beyond act and motive. Different views of an event may be as important as a single verdict. How a story is told may yield as much information as what it says.

Along the way the historian seeks help from other historians and perhaps from specialists in other disciplines. Finally, it is time to write, to decide on an interpretation and how to arrange the evidence for readers.

Each book in this series contains an important historical document or group of documents, each document a witness from the past and open to interpretation in different ways. The documents are combined with some element of historical narrative — an introduction or a biographical essay, for example — that provides students with an analysis of the primary source material and important background information about the world in which it was produced.

Each book in the series focuses on a specific topic within a specific historical period. Each provides a basis for lively thought and discussion about several aspects of the topic and the historian's role. Each is short enough (and inexpensive enough) to be a reasonable one-week assignment in a college course. Whether as classroom or personal reading, each book in the series provides firsthand experience of the challenge — and fun — of discovering, re-creating, and interpreting the past.

Lynn Hunt
David W. Blight
Bonnie G. Smith
Natalie Zemon Davis
Ernest R. May

Preface

On May 18, 1896, the United States Supreme Court ruled that a Louisiana law mandating separate but equal accommodations for "whites" and "coloreds" on intrastate railroads did not violate the constitutional rights of Homer Plessy, who with one-eighth African blood was a "colored" person under state law. The Court's decision made possible a legal system of racial segregation in the United States until the ruling of *Brown v. Board of Education* in 1954. The aim of this volume is to allow students of the *Plessy* case to understand the Court's reasoning, the factors that made such a decision possible, and the effects of the decision.

The book is divided into three parts. The first part provides an introduction to the legal issues of the case. The second reprints the Court's opinion in full, including the dissent of Justice John Marshall Harlan, along with representative samples of different views on the "race question" of the time. It allows students to re-create a partial context of the complicated debates and conditions in which the decision took place. Part Two also reprints a variety of responses, direct and indirect, to the decision. The final section is a short summary of the strategy developed by the National Association for the Advancement of Colored People to have the decision overturned and of the consequences of the decision on racial politics in the United States today.

In addition to making the *Plessy* decision available, the volume prints for the first time a speech by the African American lawyer and novelist Charles W. Chesnutt. It also includes the original 1897 essay by W. E. B. Du Bois, "Strivings of the Negro People," with careful annotations of how he revised the essay to become the first chapter in *The Souls of Black Folk* (1903). These annotations allow students to see subtle changes in Du Bois's thought in the immediate post-*Plessy* era. It is precisely this time when he began to distance himself from Booker T. Washington, whose "Atlanta Exposition Address" of 1895 is also printed in full. The Washington, Du Bois, and Chesnutt selections allow students to compare the authors' positions as well as to contrast them with representative views on the "race problem" by a southern senator, a statistician who draws on the scientific racism of the time, and a northern minister.

The appendices include: (1) a brief profile of the members of the Supreme Court in 1896, which provides a glimpse into the backgrounds of the men who decided the case and gives students some insight into the politics of the Court; (2) a short chronology of important events connected with the case; (3) some questions to help students focus on important aspects of the material and to wrestle with the dilemmas that the decision raised, and continues to raise, about the role of law in confronting the racial diversity of the people of the United States; and (4) a selected bibliography.

ACKNOWLEDGMENTS

I owe a major debt to the students and instructional staff of Humanities Core Course at the University of California, Irvine, who gave important advice on how to teach the *Plessy* case over a number of years. The American Council of Learned Societies and the Woodrow Wilson Center helped to support me during a year in which I put the edition together. Robert Grossman provided excellent research assistance. Mills Thornton offered valuable suggestions. David Brodenhamer, William E. Montgomery, Linda Przybyszewski, Tinsley Yarbrough, Melvin Urofsky, and Daniel Littlefield read the manuscript for Bedford Books and collectively helped to improve it. Charles Christensen a nd Joan Feinberg supported the project throughout. Barbara Flanagan was an excellent copyeditor. Others at Bedford who deserve my thanks are Elizabeth Schaaf, Richard Keaveny, Maureen Murray, Charisse Kiino, and Katherine Kurzman. The memory of Hattie and Marshall sustained me during work on the project.

Brook Thomas

Contents

Plessy v. Ferguson

A Brief History with Documents

PART ONE

Introduction:
The Legal Background

In 1885 Samuel E. Courtney, an African American teacher in Alabama, and some other African American colleagues took a train to attend the wedding of two in their group. Describing their journey in a Boston newspaper, Courtney wrote, "We teachers happened to be riding on the first car of the train. All of us were mulattoes [people of mixed European and African blood], and would pass for white people in a pinch. Down there it is a criminal offence for a negro to ride on the same train with a white man, however." When the train stopped for refreshments, a group of "crackers" (poor whites in the South) surrounded the train.

"'There are three coons on that first class car,' one of them sung out.

"'Put 'em off,' said someone else."

Twelve white men carrying revolvers approached the group. One told Courtney:

"'Say, you look like an intelligent nigger. Don't you know better than to ride in a first-class car? Before we'll let you ride any further in that car we'll take you out there in the field and fill you with bullets.'"

For the rest of the trip the people in Courtney's group had to ride in the "Jim Crow" car, the car reserved for "colored" people. But their difficulties were not over. According to Courtney, "Later in the journey the bridegroom was arrested and fined $25 on some trumped up charge.

NEGRO EXPULSION FROM RAILWAY CAR, PHILADELPHIA.

Southern Jim Crow laws passed at the end of the nineteenth century had as models laws in northern states before the Civil War. This engraving from the *Illustrated London News*, September 27, 1856, shows a free black man being expelled from a whites-only car in Philadelphia.

We paid the fine, with costs, and then he was immediately rearrested by the County officers and fined $35 on another trumped up charge. After paying this we decided to go the remainder of the distance on horse back, and that night we drove 35 miles through the woods."[1]

This incident reveals the violent intimidation experienced by African Americans in the South at the end of the last century. Sometimes that intimidation arose spontaneously. Sometimes it was planned and organized by white supremacist groups like the Ku Klux Klan. The incident also reveals that rather than rely on the state for protection, African Americans knew that most government officials were themselves part of the system of repression, as illustrated by the fines levied on the bridegroom. Even worse, in a country that prided itself on a legal system in which all were treated equally, African American citizens were subject to laws that organized society along racial lines.

The Alabama law that made it illegal for African Americans to sit in cars with whites was one of many laws passed by southern states beginning in the 1880s that mandated racial segregation. These laws were in part modeled on similar ones that existed in the North prior to the Civil War. But the large number of blacks in the South made that region's late nineteenth-century laws more noticeable. The mulatto status of Courtney's group and its members' ability to pass as "white" point to one problem with such laws. They were designed to keep the races separate, yet already widespread racial mixture played havoc with efforts to divide the population into pure black and white categories. Nonetheless, the passage of "Jim Crow" laws created a world of separate railroad cars, schools, hospitals, cemeteries, restaurants, bathrooms, and even drinking fountains. Whereas officially facilities were supposed to be "separate but equal," in fact they rarely were equal. People learned their place in segregated society through the pervasive juxtaposition of clearly superior facilities marked "Whites Only" with inferior ones designated "Colored."

At the time of Courtney's ride, the Supreme Court had not yet ruled on the constitutionality of the laws that enforced segregation. But on May 18, 1896, it did so in the case of *Plessy v. Ferguson*. In June 1892, Homer Plessy had been arrested for violating section 2 of Act 111 passed by the Louisiana legislature in 1890. The law called for "equal but separate accommodations for the white and colored races" on all passenger railways within the state. Plessy's arrest was part of a planned challenge to the law by New Orleans African Americans. By September 1891 a small but influential group had formed a citizens' committee to devise a

---

[1] The Booker T. Washington Papers, ed. Louis R. Harlan (Urbana: University of Illinois Press, 1972), 2:273–74.

strategy to overturn the law. For the most part, members of the committee were Creoles — French-speaking people of mixed blood whose families had lived in Louisiana for generations.[2] The committee contacted the white lawyer and novelist Albion Winegar Tourgée, who in August 1891 had begun calling attention to separate-car laws in his newspaper column.

A resident of upstate New York, Tourgée was perhaps the leading white spokesman for people of color. Following service in the Union army, he moved to North Carolina after the Civil War, where he served as a judge. Tourgée provided the period's most vivid account of the experiences of a carpetbagger (a person from the North who moved South after the Civil War) in his popularly successful autobiographical novel, *A Fool's Errand by One of the Fools* (1879). Continuing his legal and literary career after he returned to New York, he worked to expose the Ku Klux Klan and campaigned for improved conditions for freedmen. Convinced that the only solution to the "race problem" in the United States was education — for whites to reduce racial prejudice and for freedmen to increase economic opportunity and to inform them as new citizens — Tourgée actively campaigned for federal money to wipe out illiteracy, which was especially high in the South. His proposal was, however, never adopted.[3] When the New Orleans citizens' committee contacted him, it had raised $1,412.70, but he agreed to represent the group at a distance for no fee. His aim was to get the United States Supreme Court to declare segregation laws unconstitutional.

Part of Tourgée's strategy was to have someone of mixed blood violate the law, since to do so would allow him to question the arbitrariness by which people were classified "colored." Homer Plessy agreed to be a test case. Plessy had been born free in 1862. His family was French-speaking. He had only one-eighth African blood and, according to his counsel, "the mixture [was] not discernible."[4] Most likely he could

[2] Rodolphe Lucien Desdunes, *Our People and Our History*, trans. Sister Dorothea Olga McCants (1911; reprint, Baton Rouge: Louisiana State University Press, 1973).

[3] Tourgée's proposal failed in part because of southern opposition and in part because of his unwillingness to compromise and support a different measure, the Blair Bill, which was opposed by the white supremacist Senator John Tyler Morgan. (See Morgan's essay "The Race Question in the United States" printed on p. 62 of this book.) We can only speculate on what the effects on United States society would have been if Tourgée's plan had been adopted or if he had compromised his position and helped pass the less than perfect Blair Bill.

[4] Charles A. Lofgren, *The Plessy Case: A Legal-Historical Interpretation* (New York: Oxford University Press, 1987), 41. My account of the *Plessy* case is especially indebted to Lofgren. It also relies on Otto H. Olsen, *Carpetbagger's Crusade: The Life of Albion Winegar Tourgée* (Baltimore: Johns Hopkins University Press, 1965); Otto H. Olsen, ed.,

have ridden in the white car without trouble, but the committee wanted a legal challenge. Its challenge received some silent support from railroad companies, which did not like the added expense of providing separate cars. By prearrangement, the railroad conductor and a private detective detained Plessy when he sat in the forbidden coach.

A month after his arrest Plessy came before a Louisiana district court presided over by Justice John Howard Ferguson. A native of Massachusetts, Ferguson was a carpetbagger who had stayed in the South, marrying the daughter of a prominent New Orleans attorney. Between Plessy's arrest and his trial, Ferguson had ruled on another test case in which Daniel F. Desdunes was arrested for traveling in the white car on an interstate train. Also someone who could pass as white, Desdunes was the twenty-one-year-old son of Rodolphe Desdunes, one of the leaders of the New Orleans citizens' committee. Ferguson ruled that the law was unconstitutional on interstate trains because of the federal government's power to regulate interstate commerce, and the committee celebrated. Plessy, however, was traveling on an intrastate train, and at his trial Ferguson upheld the law, arguing that a state had the power to regulate railroad companies operating solely within its borders. The constitutional challenge was under way; the decision was appealed to the state supreme court and eventually the United States Supreme Court.

The Louisiana Jim Crow law was possible only because the goals of Reconstruction after the Civil War had not been realized. Reconstruction had two primary goals, which are implied by its name. The first was to rebuild the South, whose buildings and industry had been devastated by the violence of war. The second was to reform southern society, which had been based on a slave economy. Reconstructing the South materially proved easier than reconstructing it socially.

There were two stages of Reconstruction: presidential and Radical or congressional. The first was led by Andrew Johnson, who assumed the presidency after the assassination of Abraham Lincoln in 1865, toward the end of the war. This stage was relatively uncontroversial and consisted mainly in using the federal government's power to enforce the Thirteenth Amendment, passed in 1865, which abolished slavery. Abolishing slavery, however, did not eliminate racial hierarchy. Most south-

---

The Thin Disguise: Plessy v. Ferguson (New York: Humanities Press, 1967); Owen M. Fiss, *Troubled Beginnings of the Modern State, 1888–1910,* vol. 8 of Holmes Devise, *History of the Supreme Court of the United States* (New York: Macmillan, 1993); and Keith Weldon Medley, "The Sad Story of How 'Separate but Equal' Was Born," *Smithsonian,* February 1994, 105–17.

Daniel F. Desdunes, with one-eighth African blood and seven-eighths European blood, was officially "colored" under Louisiana law. He volunteered to challenge Louisiana's "equal but separate" law on interstate travel and won.

ern states passed "black codes," which, although they granted African Americans the right to own property and bring suits in court, still forbade them from serving on juries, testifying against whites, or voting. Some black codes also kept former slaves, or freedmen, in a subservient economic position by requiring that they sign yearly labor contracts. Those who did not were subject to arrest and imprisonment as vagrants. Since in many states prisoners could in turn be leased out at minimal costs as laborers, the black codes allowed a form of disguised slavery.

This repression of freedmen sparked new efforts at reform from members of Congress, and in 1866 a Civil Rights Act was passed, effectively voiding practices mandated by black codes by making African Americans full United States citizens and guaranteeing certain rights of citizenship. To ensure the constitutionality of this act, Congress also passed the Fourteenth Amendment, which was ratified by the states in 1868. The passage of the 1866 Civil Rights Act and the Fourteenth Amendment marked the move toward Radical Reconstruction, which was extremely controversial. Shortly we will come to a more detailed explanation of the Civil Rights Act and the Fourteenth Amendment, but first we need to examine the controversy over the attempt to use them to expand the goals of Reconstruction.

A member of the 1866 Congress, future president James A. Garfield proclaimed that with the passage of both measures, "personal liberty and personal rights are placed in the keeping of the nation. . . . We must make American citizenship the shield that protects every citizen, on every foot of American soil."[5] But President Johnson and most southerners strongly disagreed with the wisdom of such action. Indeed, it violated two of their most sacred beliefs: white supremacy and states' rights. For them, African Americans were unworthy of United States citizenship. Furthermore, they resisted the federal government's intrusion into the internal affairs of the states. In heated and partisan debates they opposed both the Civil Rights Act and the Fourteenth Amendment.

Supporters of both countered by pointing out a historical inconsistency in their opponents' arguments against federal control. Recalling how the federal government had enforced a law passed in 1850 requiring the return to the South of slaves who had escaped to freedom in the North, Senator Lyman Trumbull of Illinois noted, "Surely we have the authority to enact a law as efficient in the interests of freedom, now that

---

[5] Quoted in Aviam Soifer. "Protecting Civil Rights: A Critique of Raoul Berger's History," *New York University Law Review* 54 (1979): 682.

freedom prevails throughout the country, as we had in the interest of slavery when it prevailed in a portion of the country."[6] Another senator found "poetic justice" in using constitutional powers previously used to support slavery to support the rights of freedmen.[7] But there was a danger in remedying past injustices by using the means of the past. When the federal government used its power to return fugitive slaves in the 1850s, many people evoked higher authority to disobey the law. Similarly, white southerners were prepared to appeal to higher law to resist what they felt were revengeful federal laws designed to punish the South for its rebellion. The Ku Klux Klan, for instance, claimed to serve the dictates of divine justice.

The white South felt particularly abused in 1867 when Congress passed the Reconstruction Act, which expanded the federal government's control by dividing the South into military zones and giving federal troops power to enforce regulations emanating from Washington. Johnson promptly vetoed this and other Reconstruction legislation. In response, the House voted to impeach Johnson for what it considered treasonable offenses. As provided in the Constitution, the Senate then tried Johnson, but its vote of thirty-five to nineteen fell one short of the two-thirds majority required to remove him from office. The only president ever to be impeached, Johnson remained in office, but he was virtually powerless for the remainder of his term. Congress continually overrode his vetoes, thus closing out the stage of presidential Reconstruction and instituting the second phase, of Radical Reconstruction.

Radical Reconstruction was implemented by a group of Republicans known as Radical Republicans, who controlled Congress in the period right after the Civil War. Radical Republicans passed laws designed to bring about a second American revolution, in which all citizens, including blacks, would enjoy equal civil and political rights. The presidential election of 1868 was in effect a referendum on their legislation. Democrats, who primarily supported the interests of white southerners and those white laborers in the North who feared competition from African American labor, nominated Horatio Seymour, the governor of New York. Republicans nominated Ulysses S. Grant, the hero of the North's military victory in the Civil War. The campaign produced vicious and simplistic attacks. Republicans frequently identified Democrats with

---

[6] Quoted in Robert J. Kaczorowski, "To Begin the Nation Anew: Congress, Citizenship, and Civil Rights after the Civil War," *American Historical Review* 92 (1987): 59.

[7] Quoted in Charles Fairman, *Reconstruction and Reunion, 1865–1888* vol. 6 of Holmes Devise, *History of the Supreme Court of the United States* (New York: Macmillan, 1971), 1170.

secession and treason, while Democrats had but one issue: opposition to Reconstruction. That opposition appealed to the racist sentiment of some white voters. For instance, Francis P. Blair, Seymour's vice presidential candidate, accused the Republicans of allowing the South to be controlled by a "semi-barbarous race of blacks who are worshippers of fetishes and poligamists" intent on subjecting "white women to their unbridled lust."[8]

Democrats also warned that the new rights granted to African Americans would force states in the North and the South to rescind antimiscegenation laws that prohibited marriages between whites and people from other races. In fact, debates over the Civil Rights Act indicate that few Republicans were egalitarian enough to support interracial marriage. Furthermore, as Tourgée pointed out, it was hypocritical to worry so much about interracial marriage when illicit sexual contact between the races, which had been widespread under slavery, continued in the South. Nonetheless, irrational fears of racial intermixture continued to capture the imaginations of a number of voters.

In the end, however, the Democrats' racist campaign did not succeed, and Grant won an overwhelming victory that he repeated in 1872. Radical Reconstruction was in effect during his two administrations. As many historians have pointed out, this stage of Reconstruction was not quite as radical as its name implies.[9] The Fifteenth Amendment, the third and last of the Civil War amendments to the Constitution, removed race and color as barriers to the vote for male citizens. But most supporters of Radical Reconstruction did not envision total social equality for African Americans. Furthermore, whereas its supporters tried to bring about a new social order in the South, they did not aim for a truly egalitarian society. Granted, freedmen were given political power and were provided economic and educational opportunities unimaginable a generation earlier. Nonetheless, the model for the new order was small-scale competitive capitalism in the North that celebrated the moral superiority of free labor. In that order African Americans were not treated as equals, and laborers were often exploited.

A new social order did arise in the South. But it was neither egalitarian nor a reflection of northern society. Instead, it was one in which the "color line" separating the races was honored as much as, if not more than, it had been under slavery. It was also one bound together by the resentful

---

[8] Quoted in Eric Foner, *Reconstruction* (New York: Harper and Row, 1988), 340.
[9] See especially John Hope Franklin, *Reconstruction after the Civil War* (Chicago: University of Chicago Press, 1960).

belief of most white southerners that the North had used military rule during Reconstruction to allow freedmen to lord over their former masters.

By all accounts Reconstruction was a failure. For most white southerners it was a failure because it was a misguided effort from the start and soon turned into a vehicle for the victorious North to seek revenge against the rebellious South by submitting southern whites to the rule of carpetbaggers and African Americans. This vision remained and even intensified in future generations. For instance, Thomas Dixon's racist 1905 novel *The Clansman,* which celebrates the Ku Klux Klan, is set during Reconstruction and demonizes both its congressional architects and freedmen who came to power at that time. The novel and film *Gone with the Wind* spread the South's vision of a corrupt Reconstruction to an even broader audience.

For those who shared the goals of Reconstruction, it was a failure because those goals were never realized. It failed in part because of corruption and unscrupulous opportunism by some carpetbaggers seeking to profit from the defeated condition of the South. But the major reason for its failure was the country's unwillingness to continue to pursue its goal of reconstructing the nation to provide political and civic, if not social, equality for African Americans. If pursuing those goals would have meant adjusting policies that were not working and correcting abuses that admittedly took place, it would also have meant refusing to compromise with those intent on keeping African Americans in a subservient position. But neither the country nor the Republican Party was able to maintain its resolve. The end of Reconstruction came with the election of 1876.

That election was very close. The Democrat Samuel Tilden received more popular votes than Republican Rutherford B. Hayes. Returns in Florida, Louisiana, Oregon, and South Carolina were disputed. In southern states, for instance, there were widespread claims that whites used violent intimidation to control black votes. Congress, where Republicans controlled the Senate and Democrats the House, had constitutional authority to resolve the dispute. It gave power to an election commission of eight Republicans and seven Democrats. A compromise was worked out in which Hayes was given a one-vote majority in the electoral college in return for an end to Reconstruction. Hayes was named president, and federal troops returned to their garrisons.

Reconstruction was over, but the three Civil War amendments remained the law of the land. Since an understanding of two of them is critical for an understanding of the *Plessy* case, we need to look at them and the 1866 Civil Rights Act more closely.

THE CIVIL WAR AMENDMENTS

As the *Plessy* case does not involve the Fifteenth Amendment, we can turn to it first.

AMENDMENT XV [1870]

Section 1. The right of citizens of the United States to vote shall not be denied or abridged by the United States or by any State on account of race, color, or previous condition of servitude.

Section 2. The Congress shall have power to enforce this article by appropriate legislation.

This amendment was necessary because of laws denying African Americans the right to vote. It did not guarantee all African Americans the right to vote, however; it simply kept states from denying someone the right to vote solely on the basis of race, color, or the fact that one was previously a slave. States were perfectly free to restrict voting by other criteria. For instance, in 1870 no state allowed women, white or black, to vote. Indeed, some people opposed the Fifteenth Amendment because it did not keep states from denying the right to vote on the basis of sex. Furthermore, because the amendment simply restricted the actions of states and did not provide a positive guarantee to African Americans, after Reconstruction clever legal minds quickly saw ways to adhere to the letter of the law while violating its spirit. For instance, some states gave only those men who passed a stringent literacy test the right to vote. In practice, illiterate white men were often given the answers beforehand. Another strategy was to levy a poll tax that most black men and poor white men could not afford. As a result of such laws and intimidation, by as late as the 1960s many southern counties with a majority of African American residents had virtually no African Americans registered to vote.

The Thirteenth Amendment, which was at issue in *Plessy*, reads:

AMENDMENT XIII [1865]

Section 1. Neither slavery nor involuntary servitude, except as a punishment for crime whereof the party shall have been duly convicted, shall exist within the United States, or any place subject to their jurisdiction.

Section 2. Congress shall have power to enforce this article by appropriate legislation.

The primary purpose of this amendment was to make slavery illegal and, as we have seen, its passage was relatively uncontroversial. But the amendment has a complicated history. Those who proposed it did not see it as the first of three amendments. Instead, they felt that it would be enough to give African Americans their rightful place in United States society. But people did not agree on what that place should be. Some, like President Johnson, felt that all the amendment was supposed to do was to free slaves. Others felt that it also banned any racial discrimination that, in marking blacks with a "badge of servitude," perpetuated the heritage of slavery.[10] Read this way, the amendment gave Congress power to enact legislation prohibiting most forms of discrimination.

But passage of black codes made it clear that, if prohibiting discrimination was the intention of the amendment, its language was not specific enough. The 1866 Civil Rights Act provided much more specific guarantees. To understand the importance of that act we need to understand how various people at the time distinguished civil rights from social and political rights.

Political rights are best imagined along a vertical axis. They are rights that we have in relationship to the political entity that governs over us. In contrast, social rights are best imagined along a horizontal axis. They are not rights in relation to a governing body but in relation to other human beings in society. The right to vote, for instance, is a political right. In contrast, unless the right to associate with whom we want is guaranteed by law, it is a social right. Political rights are secured by law; social rights are not.

What, then, are "civil" rights? Civil rights are the nonpolitical rights of citizens of a particular country. Civil rights, therefore, tend to occupy a middle ground between political and social rights. They are not to be equated with social rights because they, like political rights, are a product of human-made laws. They should not, however, be equated with political rights. Some people might mistakenly believe that the right to vote is a right guaranteed to each citizen, but it is not. It is a political, not a civil, right.[11] For example, today people under eighteen may be citizens of the United States but they do not have the right to vote.

[10] See Harold M. Hyman and William M. Wiecek, *Equal Justice under Law* (New York: Harper and Row, 1982). The point that legislation unfriendly to blacks constituted a "badge of servitude" and thus was unconstitutional was made by Senator Trumbull in debates over the 1866 Freedmen's Bureau Bill and Civil Rights Act. See Fairman, *Reconstruction and Reunion*, 1165, 1173.

[11] The important distinction between civil and political rights is being effaced. In the first edition of the College Edition of *Webster's New World Dictionary*, civil rights are defined as "those rights guaranteed to the individual by the 13th and 14th Amendments to the Constitution of the United States and by certain other acts of Congress; especially exemption from involuntary servitude and equal treatment of all people with respect to the enjoyment of life, liberty, and property and to the protection of the law." The second edition defines them as "those rights guaranteed to the individual by the 13th, 14th, 15th, and 19th Amendments to the Constitution of the United States and by other acts of Congress; esp., the right to vote, exemption from involuntary servitude, and equal treatment of all people with respect to the enjoyment of life, liberty, and property and to the protection of the law."

When Congress passes a civil rights act, it decides that some social rights are so important that they should receive legal protection. It might seem to make sense simply to declare all social rights civil rights. But governments do not do so because various social rights often come into conflict. For instance, people might consider it their right when seeking a hotel room not to be discriminated against on the basis of their race. At the same time, hotel owners can claim that it is their right to decide who stays in the property they own. To make both of these rights civil rights is not to resolve the potential conflict. Indeed, those skeptical of government sometimes argue that the state should not involve itself in such conflicts at all but should instead allow forces of the market to resolve them. Others, however, argue that some rights are so fundamental that the government should guarantee them for all citizens. Thus, in designating some social rights as civil rights Congress sets priorities about which rights it feels are most important. To be sure, conflicts can still arise among designated civil rights. In such cases, unless Congress has indicated that some rights have priority over others, disputes must be arbitrated by the courts.

The 1866 Civil Rights Act provided for African American citizenship and certain rights with the following language:

> All persons born in the United States and not subject to any foreign power, excluding Indians not taxed, are hereby declared to be citizens of the United States: and such citizens of every race and color [including former slaves], shall have the same right, in every State and territory of the United States, to make and enforce contracts, to sue, be parties, and give evidence, to inherit, purchase, lease, sell, hold, and convey real and personal property, and to full and equal benefit of all laws and proceedings for the security of person and property, as is enjoyed by white citizens, and shall be subject to like punishments, pains, and penalties, and to none other, any statute, ordinance, regulation, or custom, to the contrary notwithstanding.[12]

Many of these guaranteed civil rights, such as making and enforcing contracts and holding and conveying property, are economic rights that had previously been denied to slaves. Guaranteeing these rights to all citizens was part of the campaign to have the entire country adopt the northern economic system.

As fundamental as these rights may seem to us today, sponsors of the 1866 Civil Rights Act worried that its opponents might challenge its

---

[12] An early draft of the act declared: "That there shall be no discrimination in civil rights or immunities among the inhabitants of any State or Territory of the United States on account of race, color, or previous condition of slavery." But this language was deleted during debate in the House of Representatives.

constitutionality. Under the federal system of the United States, in which power is divided between the states and the federal government, such rights had traditionally been guaranteed by the states, which were responsible for protecting citizens within their jurisdictions. For Congress to guarantee these rights meant a fundamental change in the relationship between the federal government and the states. Thus, to ensure the constitutionality of its act, the 1866 Congress also proposed the Fourteenth Amendment, which, according to legal scholar Charles Wallace Collins, shifted "the court of final appeal from the State to the Federal Supreme Court."[13]

Defenders of states' rights passionately resisted that shift. Collins claimed that "so far as the records show not one single Democrat in a single State of the Union" voted for it. For most white southerners, the amendment was a partisan and undemocratic "attempt by one section of the country to force its political ideals upon another section."[14] Indeed, it was ratified by the states in 1868 only because southern states could not rejoin the Union without ratifying it. Careful attention to its language reveals why it was so controversial.

AMENDMENT XIV [1868]

Section 1. All persons born or naturalized in the United States, and subject to the jurisdiction thereof, are citizens of the United States and of the State wherein they reside. No State shall make or enforce any law which shall abridge the privileges or immunities of citizens of the United States; nor shall any State deprive any person of life, liberty, or property, without due process of law; nor deny to any person within its jurisdiction the equal protection of the laws. . . .

Section 5. The Congress shall have power to enforce, by appropriate legislation, the provisions of this article.

The wording of this amendment is much more complicated than that of either the Thirteenth or the Fifteenth Amendments. The first sentence defines the conditions of United States citizenship. It was necessary because, although the Thirteenth Amendment made slavery illegal, it did not explicitly guarantee former slaves citizenship. Indeed, in the infamous *Dred Scott* case (1857) the Supreme Court had denied United States citizenship to all African Americans, not just slaves. How it did so

[Handwritten margin notes: "right to be equal + called citizenship clause"; "not saying that everyone equal but that everyone deserves equal"; "means that the fed can"; "federal government can intervene"; "if rights are taken away"]

[13] Charles Wallace Collins, *The Fourteenth Amendment and the States* (Boston: Little, Brown, 1912), 151.
[14] Ibid., 144, 142–43.

is important for an understanding of the legal background of *Plessy v. Ferguson.*

As United States citizenship had not been defined in the Constitution, Chief Justice Roger B. Taney, writing for the majority in *Dred Scott,* offered an interpretation that linked citizenship with the famous phrase "We, the people of the United States." "The words 'people of the United States,' and 'citizens,'" Taney wrote, "are synonymous terms, and mean the same thing. They both describe the political body, who, according to our republican institutions, form the sovereignty, and who hold the power and conduct the government through their representatives. They are what we familiarly call the 'sovereign people,' and every citizen is one of this people, and a constituent member of this sovereignty." Taney's definition implied that there is only one class of citizens and citizens are those who constitute the sovereignty of the country. But Taney used this democratic-sounding definition to deny citizenship to African Americans. Allowing for only one class of citizens, he argued that the "deep and enduring marks of inferiority and degradation" implanted on blacks excluded them from the community that originally constituted the sovereign people of the nation.[15]

Despite this definition, Taney did admit that African Americans were citizens in some states. The issue, he felt, was whether or not their state citizenship granted them United States citizenship. His answer was no. Since, according to him, members of the "negro African race" were not part of the sovereign people who constituted the country, the only way for one of them to become a citizen of the United States would be through naturalization. But the Constitution had granted the power of naturalization to the national Congress, not to the individual states. Therefore, if an African American became a citizen in a state, he did not automatically become a United States citizen. "We must not confound the rights of citizenship, which a state may confer within its own limits, and the rights of citizenship as a member of the Union. It does not by any means follow, because he has all the rights and privileges of a citizen of a State, that he must be a citizen of the United States."[16]

The first sentence of the Fourteenth Amendment overturned Taney's ruling, making all people born in the United States citizens of the United

[15] 19 How. 393 at 404 and 416 (1857).

[16] 19 How. 393 at 405, 406, and 405 (1857). In *Dred Scott* Taney contradicted his earlier claim that "every citizen of a State is also a citizen of the United States" (7 How. 283 at 492).

States. Included, therefore, were almost all African Americans, whether former slaves or not.[17] In addition to guaranteeing citizenship, the amendment protects the rights of those who are citizens. Its second sentence makes it unconstitutional for any state to "make or enforce" laws that "shall abridge the privileges or immunities of citizens of the United States." This provision gave the federal government important power over the states. Guaranteeing *national* citizenship rights, it implies that if someone is a citizen in one state, he or she is automatically a citizen of the entire country, and that no state can abridge the "privileges or immunities" of that citizenship. Once again the language of the amendment was designed to overturn *Dred Scott*.[18]

The second clause of the second sentence is its "due process" clause. Most of its language simply repeats language from the Fifth Amendment. We might ask why this repetition is necessary. It is because of the addition of the words "any State." As in the first clause, the "due process" clause limits the power of individual states to restrict various rights. Emphasizing the transfer of power from the states to the federal government, it declares unconstitutional a state's effort to "deprive any person of life, liberty, or property, without due process of law." As similar as the second clause is to the first in giving the federal government control over states, an important change has occurred. The first clause protects "citizens;" the second, "any person." "Citizens" has a more restricted meaning than "person." All citizens of the United States are people, but not all people are citizens of the United States. The authors obviously wanted to make it clear that citizens of the United States have privileges and immunities *other than* the guaranteed protection of life, liberty, and property. This distinction is important to keep in mind when we move to the third clause of the second sentence, the "equal protection" clause. By guaranteeing "any person within its jurisdiction the equal protection of the laws," this clause might seem to grant all people within

[17] The phrase "and subject to the jurisdiction thereof" caused some confusion. Were, for instance, children born in the United States of foreign parents subject to United States jurisdiction or the jurisdiction of the parents' country? For African Americans the issue was irrelevant because, even though they were denied national citizenship by *Dred Scott*, they were not subject to any foreign power. But for other immigrant groups the issue was extremely important, especially for those not of European or African descent since they were not allowed to become naturalized citizens. The Supreme Court did not rule on the issue until *United States v. Wong Kim Ark* (1898), when it declared that the citizenship of parents was irrelevant.

[18] The first use of "privileges and immunities" in the constitutional history of the country is in the Articles of Confederation (1781). Article IV, section 2 of the Constitution states, "The citizens of each State shall be entitled to all Privileges and Immunities of Citizens in the several States."

a state absolute legal equality. But "equal protection of the laws" clearly does not mean that everyone is entitled to the "privileges and immunities" of United States citizenship. For instance, foreigners living in the United States do not have the rights of United States citizenship.

Both proponents and opponents acknowledged that the Fourteenth Amendment shifted the balance of power in favor of the federal government over the states. Nonetheless, a number of issues of importance for the *Plessy* case remained unresolved. One was how expansively the amendment should be interpreted to protect the rights of African Americans. Was it simply intended to prohibit states from abridging the privileges and immunities of citizenship enumerated in the 1866 Civil Rights Act, or should the scope of its protection be interpreted more widely? There is evidence for both a restricted and an expanded interpretation.[19]

Even if an expanded interpretation is granted, another issue presents itself. As legal scholar Alfred H. Kelley puts it, if the two amendments were designed to guarantee equality for African Americans, did the meaning of equality forbid separation by race if equal conditions were provided?[20] Once again there is evidence on both sides.[21] As we have seen, Democratic opponents of the 1866 Civil Rights Act and the Fourteenth Amendment warned that the two measures would bring about total integration of the races. At the same time, Senator Lyman Trumbull, who sponsored the Civil Rights Act, argued that it would not threaten state antimiscegenation laws because, even though such laws prevented integration, they treated blacks and whites the same. Both blacks and whites were forbidden from marrying someone from the other race and both were punished equally if they broke the laws.[22] Although prior to 1896 the Supreme Court established precedents determining whether it would adopt a restricted or expanded view of the Thirteenth and Fourteenth

[19] For restrictive interpretations, see Fairman, *Reconstruction and Reunion*; Herman Belz, *Emancipation and Equal Rights* (New York: Norton, 1978); and Raoul Berger, *Government by Judiciary* (Cambridge: Harvard University Press, 1977). For expansive interpretations, see Hyman and Wiecek, *Equal Justice under Law*; Kenneth L. Karst, *Belonging to America* (New Haven: Yale University Press, 1989); Jacobus tenBrock, *Equal under Law* (New York: Collier, 1965); Soifer, "Protecting Civil Rights"; and Aviam Soifer, "Status, Contract, and Promises Unkept," *Yale Law Journal* 96 (1987): 1916–59.

[20] Alfred H. Kelley, "The Fourteenth Amendment Reconsidered: The Segregation Question," *Michigan Law Review* 54 (1956): 1050. Kelley, writing in the wake of the Supreme Court's decision in *Brown v. Board of Education* (1954), concentrates on the Fourteenth Amendment.

[21] Lofgren, *The Plessy Case*, 64–67.

[22] Trumbull first made his argument about antimiscegenation laws during debates on the Freedmen's Bureau Bill of 1866, but he repeated it in debates on the Civil Rights Act. See Fairman, *Reconstruction and Reunion*, 1164–65, 1180.

Amendments, before *Plessy* it had not explicitly ruled on the issue of separate but equal on intrastate public transportation. Before turning to *Plessy*, however, we need to examine some of those important precedents.

THE *SLAUGHTER-HOUSE CASES* AND THEIR IMPLICATIONS

The first time the Court ruled on the Thirteenth and Fourteenth Amendments was in 1873 in the *Slaughter-House Cases*, which involved the rights of white butchers, not African Americans. In 1869 Louisiana passed a law restricting the slaughter of livestock in New Orleans to locations run by two companies. Its purpose was ostensibly to protect the public health by requiring all slaughterhouses to be below the point where their waste would run into the Mississippi River and the city's water supply. Indeed, all states had the right to exert their "police powers" to regulate slaughterhouses in the interest of protecting the public's health. But the butchers excluded by the law claimed that the real purpose was not to protect health but to grant a monopoly to the favored companies. They sued, claiming that their Thirteenth and Fourteenth Amendment rights had been violated.

The suit of the excluded butchers indicates how expansive the interpretation of the two amendments could be. After all, neither of the amendments seems to have been passed with the intention of protecting the rights of white butchers. Nonetheless, the butchers' lawyer argued that the two amendments had brought about a fundamental revolution that allowed the federal government to guarantee whatever is essential to liberty and proper to citizenship in the United States. He claimed, for instance, that the monopoly created by the state's action deprived other butchers of the liberty to pursue their calling. In doing so, it violated the Fourteenth Amendment by reducing the excluded butchers' potential to accumulate property. He also claimed that the Louisiana law violated the Thirteenth Amendment because to restrict a person's occupation was to institute a form of servitude common under feudalism but incompatible with a republican form of government.

Four justices agreed with the butchers, but the majority ruled against them. Writing for the majority, Justice Samuel Miller ruled that the two amendments had not brought about a revolution in the United States' system of federalism. The purpose of the Thirteenth Amendment was, he argued, very specific: to abolish the institution of Negro slavery. Similarly, the Fourteenth Amendment's purpose was to provide citizenship to African Americans and to protect those freedoms that were guaranteed by the federal government.

The majority's insistence that the two amendments were restricted to concerns about the condition of African Americans would seem to indicate a victory for people intent on protecting and affirming the rights of freedmen. But this was not necessarily the case. In fact, what advocates for African Americans needed was both an expanded and a restricted interpretation of the scope of the amendments. They needed an expanded interpretation because only such an interpretation would provide adequate federal protection for African Americans' claims to take a place in society as full and equal citizens. But they needed a restricted interpretation to make sure that the amendments' primary focus remained on combatting the nation's heritage of slavery and racial discrimination. The *Slaughter-House Cases* helped to create conditions by which African Americans got the worst of all possible interpretations.

Whereas the majority decision called attention to the amendments' purpose to protect African Americans, it restricted the scope of federal protection. For instance, Miller claimed that, if the authors of the Fourteenth Amendment had wanted to grant the federal government the power to be a "perpetual censor upon all the legislation of the States," they would have made it clear that they were bringing about such a revolution.[23] Not detecting specific language to that effect, Miller ruled that the amendment was designed to distinguish between national and state citizenship and did very little to alter what was previously considered state citizenship. For instance, the right to pursue an occupation of one's choice was a right that states, not the federal government, should protect. What the Fourteenth Amendment forbade, Miller argued, was simply state infringement on the privileges and immunities of United States citizenship, which, he implied, were narrow in scope. By restricting the scope of United States citizenship and the power of the federal government to guarantee its rights, Miller severely limited the power of the Fourteenth Amendment.

Although the case did not involve African American rights, the restraints the majority placed on the federal government meant that states had regained some of the power that white southerners thought the Fourteenth Amendment had taken away. As a result, it might seem that those intent on using federal power to protect African American rights would have had to turn to the dissenters to find a favorable interpretation. Indeed, both Justices Joseph P. Bradley and Stephen Field in

---

[23] 16 Wall. 36 at 78 (1873).

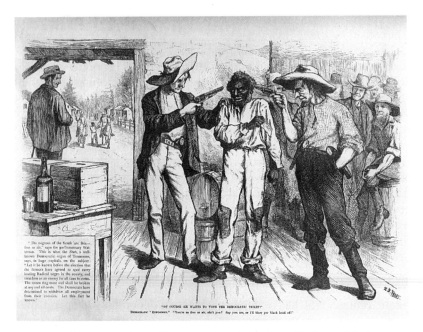

This 1876 *Harper's* cartoon illustrates the violent intimidation of black voters during the election of the same year. The caption reads: "'OF COURSE HE WANTS TO VOTE THE DEMOCRATIC TICKET.' /DEMOCRATIC 'REFORMER.' 'You're as free as air, ain't you! Say you are, or I'll blow yer black head off!'" The inset text reads: "'The negroes of the South are free — free as air,' says the parliamentary Watterson. This is what the *State*, a well-known Democratic organ of Tennessee, says, in huge capitals, on the subject: 'Let it be known before the election that the farmers have agreed to spot every leading Radical negro in the county, and treat him as an enemy for all time to come. The rotten ring must and shall be broken at any and all costs. The Democrats have determined to withdraw all employment from their enemies. Let this fact be known.'"

dissent argued for much more federal authority. But Bradley and Field were not intent on evoking the Fourteenth Amendment to protect the interests of freedmen. Instead, they saw the potential to use it to keep states from interfering with big businesses. For instance, in *Santa Clara County v. Southern Pacific Railroad Company* (1886) the Court, influenced by a circuit court decision by Field, ruled that corporations, as artificial legal "persons," come under the due process and equal protection clauses of the Fourteenth Amendment. As a result, numerous corporations drew on their vast financial resources to appeal to the Supreme Court when states passed laws trying to control corporate influence. When corporations were taxed at a higher rate than individuals, they argued that they had been deprived of property without due process of law. By 1911, the Supreme Court had heard 607 Fourteenth Amendment cases. Three hundred and twelve involved corporations; thirty involved issues related to the rights of African Americans.[24]

If rulings like *Santa Clara County* expanded the scope of the Fourteenth Amendment, but not for the benefit of freedmen, the period also saw a restriction in the scope of the Thirteenth Amendment. Its decline began with the *Slaughter-House Cases* when Miller proclaimed that the primary intention of the amendment was simply to abolish slavery. To be sure, he granted that it also prohibited other forms of involuntary servitude, such as peonage or coolie labor. Nonetheless, he suggested that the very existence of the Fourteenth Amendment indicates how narrow the Thirteenth Amendment is in scope. After all, he reasoned, if the Thirteenth Amendment provided wide protection of African American rights, a new amendment would have been unnecessary. Future decisions endorsed Miller's reasoning. The significance of this narrow interpretation of the Thirteenth Amendment comes into focus when we consider yet another restriction on the Fourteenth Amendment reinforced in *United States v. Cruikshank* (1876).

William J. Cruikshank was a member of a paramilitary group known as the White League that killed at least sixty-nine and as many as one hundred blacks in Colfax, Louisiana, as part of a campaign to keep blacks from participating in the political process. He was convicted under the Enforcement Act of 1870, which outlawed bands from intimidating or threatening any citizen from exercising rights or privileges guaranteed by the Constitution or laws of the United States. Represented by David Dudley Field, the brother of Supreme Court Justice Stephen Field, Cruikshank appealed his conviction by arguing that the second sentence of the Fourteenth Amendment protects various rights of citizens and persons against only state action. "No *State*," the amendment reads, "shall make or enforce any law which shall abridge the privileges or immunities of citizens of the United States" (emphasis added). The Court agreed with Field and ruled that the Fourteenth Amendment provided no federal protection against actions committed by one person against another.

---

[24] Collins, *The Fourteenth Amendment*, 145–46. I have slightly adjusted Collins's statistics because he leaves out two cases concerned with blacks and one concerned with the citizenship of Chinese Americans.

Instead, it prohibited state action alone. To be sure, people who felt that their rights had been violated by private parties could seek legal remedies, but they had to seek them in state, not federal, courts. The foundation for *Cruikshank* had been laid in Miller's *Slaughter-House* ruling. The Fourteenth Amendment may have shifted from state courts to the Supreme Court a final appeal for people worried about violations of various rights, but the appeal to the Supreme Court in the *Slaughter-House Cases* resulted in a ruling that restored to states the final appeal on many issues. If the *Slaughter-House Cases* did not involve black rights, *Cruikshank* did, and it illustrated the consequences of restricting federal enforcement powers for freedmen. Given the racial sentiment in the white South, to grant states the responsibility for protecting most rights of citizenship was to create conditions in which the rights of newly freed slaves might well be circumscribed. Of course, when *Cruikshank* was decided, racial sentiment in the South was still held somewhat in check by Reconstruction policies. But a year later Reconstruction ended, and the defenders of black rights confronted the irony of having the Thirteenth Amendment's restricted scope confirmed by the passage of the Fourteenth Amendment at the same time that the Fourteenth Amendment was itself severely restricted in its power to protect black rights.

If the Thirteenth Amendment had been granted an expanded scope, it would have been an effective protection against racial discrimination because potentially it posed neither of the problems presented by the Fourteenth Amendment. Because its primary intention was to abolish slavery, it was much more difficult to expand its scope for some while limiting it for African Americans. Furthermore, unlike the Fourteenth Amendment, it has no language limiting its prohibitions to states. Thus, it clearly grants the federal government the power to intervene when private individuals, not states, are involved. The question facing the Court was how to decide whether an action perpetuates slavery or involuntary servitude. Did the Thirteenth Amendment simply abolish slavery or was it intended to eliminate all discrimination that threatened to perpetuate what Justice Taney had called the "deep and enduring marks of inferiority and degradation"[25] that slavery had stamped on African Americans? Following Miller's suggestions in the *Slaughter-House Cases*, the Court, as we have seen, opted for a narrow interpretation.

Nonetheless, not all Supreme Court decisions were defeats for blacks. In *Strauder v. West Virginia* (1880) the Court established that to try

[25] 19 How. 393 at 416 (1857).

blacks by juries that excluded blacks was to violate the Fourteenth Amendment. The construction of a jury is, after all, a state action and thus comes under the Court's restricted interpretation of the amendment. But even in *Strauder* not all of the justices agreed. Justices Field and Nathan Clifford dissented. Their reason was made clear in Field's dissent in another jury case: The right to serve on a jury, for Field, was a political, not a civil right, and the Fourteenth Amendment protected only civil rights. According to Field, if the Fourteenth Amendment guaranteed political rights, the Fifteenth Amendment would have been unnecessary. Indeed, in the case of *Minor v. Happersett* (1875), when a female United States citizen claimed that a law forbidding her to vote violated her Fourteenth Amendment rights, the Supreme Court denied her appeal, explicitly declaring that the right to vote is not a civil right. Stressing the importance of distinguishing among various rights, Field added that the Fourteenth Amendment "has no more reference to [political rights] than it does to social rights and duties, which do not rest upon any positive law, though they are more potential in controlling the intercourse of individuals."[26] The majority in *Strauder* did not disagree with Field on the Fourteenth Amendment's restriction to the field of civil rights. It simply disagreed with him as to how to categorize the right to serve on juries.

THE *CIVIL RIGHTS CASES* AND THEIR CONSEQUENCES

With the distinction among various rights and the Court's previous rulings in mind, we can turn to the decision that most directly affected the rights of freedmen prior to the *Plessy* decision. In the early 1870s, the Massachusetts Republican senator Charles Sumner unsuccessfully proposed a new civil rights bill. But in a lame-duck session in 1875, motivated by Sumner's death in 1874 and major losses in the 1874 election, the Republican-controlled Congress finally passed the new bill. It declared, among other things, full and equal enjoyment by all people within the jurisdiction of the United States of accommodations, public transportation on land and water, theaters, and other places of public amusement. By 1883 five challenges to its various parts reached the Supreme Court. They were decided together in the *Civil Rights Cases*

---

[26] *Ex parte Virginia,* 100 U.S. 339 at 367–68 (1880).

when an eight-to-one majority declared most of the provisions of the
1875 Civil Rights Act unconstitutional.

Justice Bradley's decision reflected the Court's growing reluctance
to use the power of government to regulate people's behavior, even if
that reluctance meant sacrificing the rights of freedmen. For the federal
government to try to "cover the whole domain of rights appertaining to
life, liberty, and property" would, Bradley declared, "establish a code of
municipal law regulative of all private rights between man and man in
society." For Bradley, in other words, most rights of private citizens
should remain social rights and not be elevated to the status of civil
rights. Furthermore, he expanded on the Court's earlier rulings that the
Fourteenth Amendment was limited to protecting actions by states, not
those by private parties. Declaring that most of the provisions in the
1875 Civil Rights Act regulated the actions of private parties, he ruled
that they did not come under Fourteenth Amendment protection. In
strong language Bradley also dismissed appeals based on the Thirteenth
Amendment. Mere discrimination on the basis of race or color did not,
he emphasized, stamp blacks with a badge of servitude linked to the
institution of slavery. After all, *free* blacks in the antebellum period
had also experienced discrimination. Declaring an end to what he saw
as the federal government's paternal protection of freedmen, he pronounced:

> When a man has emerged from slavery, and by aid of beneficient legis-
> lation has shaken off the inseparable concomitants of that state, there
> must be some stage in the progress of his elevation when he takes the
> ranks of a mere citizen, and ceases to be the special favorite of the law,
> and when his rights as a citizen or a man are to be protected in the
> ordinary modes by which other men's rights are protected.[27]

The majority opinion elicited a powerful dissent from Justice John
Marshall Harlan, the only southerner on the Court at the time and a
former slaveholder. The dissent did not come easily, however. Noticing
the difficulty that her husband was having writing, Harlan's wife placed
Taney's inkstand — a prized memento belonging to the couple — in a
noticeable position on his desk. The memory of the role that Taney's
inkstand had played in *Dred Scott* seemed to motivate Harlan, who
overcame his writer's block and soon finished his dissent.[28] In it he

---

[27] 109 U.S. 3 at 13 and 25 (1883).
[28] Loren P. Beth, *John Marshall Harlan: The Last Whig Justice* (Lexington: University
of Kentucky Press, 1992), 229.

basically (handwritten annotation top left)

14th amendment — reinterpreting (handwritten annotation left margin)

argued that through "subtle and ingenious verbal criticism" Bradley had sacrificed the "substance and spirit of the recent amendments."[29]

Harlan insisted on an expansive interpretation of the Thirteenth Amendment. Pointing out that the majority itself assumed that the amendment prohibited not only the institution of slavery but also "badges of servitude," he reminded the Court that the amendment gives Congress power to enact appropriate legislation of enforcement. To bolster his point he evoked the antebellum case of *Prigg v. Pennsylvania* (1842), which gave the federal government, not states, power to enforce the fugitive slave law, even though the Constitution, while providing for enactment of a fugitive slave law, does not designate who would have power to enforce it.[30] If the Court had earlier ruled that Congress had power to enact legislation to protect the institution of slavery, it certainly should rule that Congress had power to enact legislation guaranteeing rights to freedmen to undo its effects.

Harlan found additional support in the Fourteenth Amendment for Congress to enact the 1875 Civil Rights Act. That amendment was not designed simply to prohibit states from infringing upon preexisting rights. It also created new affirmative rights for United States citizens. In overturning *Dred Scott* the amendment's first sentence, according to Harlan, created a new national citizenship. The new citizenship wiped out the vestiges of feudalism in the country and created a new right that is fundamental to "*citizenship* in a republican government": the right to be exempt from "discrimination based on race or color, in respect of civil rights." The amendment did more than establish a new form of national citizenship; in its fifth section it grants "express power in Congress by legislation, to enforce the constitutional provision from which it is derived."[31] To be sure, as the majority pointed out, the second sentence of the amendment prohibits only state action. But, Harlan argued, the enforcement clause refers to the *first* sentence as well. The Civil Rights Act of 1875 was constitutional because it enforced the affirmative rights implied by the new national citizenship created by that sentence.

Though Harlan granted that the second sentence of the amendment prohibits only state action, he was not willing to concede that its limited scope meant that it did not authorize Congress to pass the 1875 Civil Rights Act. Almost all of the places in which racial discrimination was prohibited were recognized as public or quasi-public spaces. Railroads

---

[29] 109 U.S. 3 at 26 (1883).

[30] Article IV, section 2 of the Constitution provides for a fugitive slave law. It still exists in the document. The Thirteenth Amendment simply deprived it of any force.

[31] 109 U.S. 3 at 56 and 56 (1883).

received state charters and were considered public highways. "Other places of public amusement" were clearly public spaces, licensed by the state. Thus, state action was involved, and even the prohibitive clauses of the Fourteenth Amendment applied.

Despite his powerful arguments, Harlan recognized that he was a lone dissenter when, after referring to *Dred Scott*, he warned that to accept the majority ruling was to "enter upon an era of constitutional law, when the rights of freedom and American citizenship cannot receive from the nation that efficient protection which heretofore was unhesitatingly accorded to slavery and the rights of the master."[32]

If Harlan warned against entering such an era, many southern states gladly entered it, especially because 1884 saw the election of Grover Cleveland, the first Democratic president since the Civil War. Some of the consequences of the decision in the *Civil Rights Cases* and that election are indicated by the title of a famous essay published in *Century Magazine* in 1885. "The Freedman's Case in Equity" is by George Washington Cable, a well-known novelist, a friend of Mark Twain's, and a former southerner who had fought in the Confederate army. His essay received wide attention and helped to articulate the terms of a national debate over the country's responsibility to freedmen. Making a poignant plea for the South to treat blacks fairly, he summarized his argument as follows: "The question has reached a moment of special importance. The South stands on her honor before the clean equities of the issue. It is no longer whether constitutional amendments, but whether the eternal principles of justice, are violated."[33] Equity, we need to remember, is defined by Aristotle as the "sort of justice which goes beyond the written law."[34] It is traditionally associated with universal law that stands above the fallibility of merely human-made law. Cable was forced to advocate "the duty, necessity, and value of planting society firmly upon universal justice and equity"[35] because the decision in the *Civil Rights Cases* made it increasingly difficult to depend on written law to guarantee equal rights for freedmen. But his plea did not have the effect he hoped for. More persuasive was a response published by the *Century* written by Henry W. Grady, which represented the white southern position.

[32] 109 U.S. 3 at 57 (1883).

[33] George Washington Cable, "The Freedman's Case in Equity," *Century Magazine* 29 (1884–85): 418.

[34] Aristotle, *The Rhetoric and Poetics of Aristotle*, trans. W. Rhys Roberts (New York: Modern Library, 1954), 80 (bk. 1, chap. 13).

[35] Cable, "The Freedman's Case in Equity," 409.

Grady, who was from Atlanta, was an advocate of the New South, the South that had emerged from the Civil War and looked to the future rather than looking nostalgically at a never-to-be-recovered Old South. Grady responded to Cable by reassuring his audience that the South would indeed provide an equitable solution to the "Negro Question." But as his title, "In Plain Black and White," indicates, his sense of how a society should be planted on an equitable foundation was different from Cable's.

Grady thought of Radical Reconstruction as a revolution in three steps imposed on the South by the North while it was in control of the government after the Civil War. The first tried to establish equal economic rights for African Americans by abolishing slavery. The second worked for equal political rights by eliminating race as a barrier to suffrage. The third, through the Civil Rights Act of 1875, attempted to guarantee equal social and civil rights. Grady fully endorsed the first step. No one in the New South, he asserted, wanted a return to slavery. He was even willing to grant freedmen the right to vote, although he feared that doing so might prove unwise. But when the North tried to legislate the freedman's "social and civil rights," he recalled, "here for the first time the revolution faltered. . . . The third [step], wrong in purpose, has failed in execution. It stands denounced as null by the highest court, as inoperative by general confession, and as unwise by popular verdict." Indeed, by leaving protection of blacks' civil rights to the states, the Supreme Court granted the South all that Grady claimed it wanted. The South, he declared, simply said, "'Leave this problem to my working out. I will solve it in calmness and deliberation, without passion or prejudice, and with full regard for the unspeakable equities it holds.'"[36]

Since, according to Grady, there was a natural difference between blacks and whites, an equitable solution to the "Negro Question" was to maintain a strict separation between the races in all social affairs. He argued,

> In the segregation of the races blacks as well as whites obey a natural instinct, which, always granting that they get justice and equal advantages, they obey without the slightest ill-nature or without any sense of disgrace. They meet the white people in all avenues of business. They work side by side with the white bricklayer or carpenter in perfect accord and friendliness. When the trowel or the hammer is laid aside, the laborers part, each going his own way. Any attempt to carry the comradeship of the day into private life would be sternly resisted by both parties in interest.

[36] Henry W. Grady, "In Plain Black and White," *Century Magazine* 29 (1884–85): 910, 917.

As an example of an equitable law that respected the economic rights of blacks while accounting for their natural social differences from whites, Grady cited a law in Georgia that "requires all public roads or carriers to provide equal accommodation for each race, and failure to do so is made a penal offense."[37]

The Georgia Jim Crow law cited by Grady was one of many passed after the *Civil Rights Cases*. It was very similar to the one passed in Louisiana in 1890 and challenged by Homer Plessy. In the *Civil Rights Cases* the Supreme Court ruled that the federal government had authority to pass laws prohibiting only discriminatory actions by states, not those by private citizens. But a law mandating equal but separate accommodations on intrastate railroads was clearly a state action. The question facing the Court in *Plessy v. Ferguson* was whether the Louisiana law violated rights afforded to African Americans by the Thirteenth and Fourteenth Amendments. In 1892 Judge Ferguson ruled that it did not. His judgment was confirmed by the state supreme court. The next step was the United States Supreme Court.

To improve Plessy's chances for victory, Tourgée purposely delayed moving the case forward, hoping for changes in the Court's makeup and a more favorable political climate. He even advised a journalistic campaign to mobilize public opinion and put pressure on the justices to decide in Plessy's favor. "The court," he wrote, "has always been the foe of liberty until forced to move on by public opinion. . . . [I]f we can get the ear of the Country, and argue the matter fully *before the people first*, we may incline the wavering to fall on our side when the matter comes up."[38]

But from 1892 to 1896 the country's ear was turned elsewhere. Even an event that was considered by many to be a triumph for blacks tended to work against Plessy. In 1895 the African American leader Booker T. Washington was given the honor of addressing the Atlanta Exposition. In his speech he argued for the mutual dependence of blacks and whites in the South by employing the metaphor of a hand: "In all things that are purely social we can be as separate as the fingers, yet one as the hand in all things essential to mutual progress."[39] Although Washington himself was not in favor of equal-but-separate laws, his metaphor helped to confirm arguments for segregation.

But even if the mood of the country was not favorable, Tourgée could not postpone the trial indefinitely. In April 1896 the case came before

---

[37] Ibid., 914, 914–15.

[38] Olsen, *Thin Disguise*, 78–79.

[39] Booker T. Washington, *Up from Slavery* (New York: Doubleday, Page, 1901), 219–20. See page 119 of this book for Washington's speech and a brief description of its circumstances.

the Supreme Court. In it Plessy was the plaintiff in error, making a complaint against Judge Ferguson and his original ruling. Plessy's case was argued by Tourgée, James C. Walker, and Samuel F. Phillips. Walker was a New Orleans attorney who had been involved in the case from the start. Phillips, then in private practice in Washington, D.C., was an old friend of Tourgée's and as United States solicitor general had unsuccessfully argued the government's side in the *Civil Rights Cases* in 1883. Some of the important elements of Harlan's dissent came from Phillips's presentation at that time.

PLESSY'S ARGUMENT BEFORE THE COURT

Louisiana argued that its law was a constitutionally mandated use of a state's police powers to secure the public good by preserving the peace and the health of the community. Plessy, of course, disagreed. For instance, in his brief to the Court Tourgée argued that the law deprived Plessy of his equal protection rights under the Fourteenth Amendment by pointing to a provision that exempted nurses attending children of the other race. That provision, he argued, proved that there could not be any health reasons for keeping blacks and whites separate. "The exemption of nurses," Tourgée asserted, "shows that the real evil lies not in the color of the skin but in the relation the colored person sustains to the white. If he is a dependent it may be endured; if he is not, his presence is insufferable." The real intention of the law was not, according to Tourgée, to promote the public good but to promote the happiness of whites at the expense of blacks. To do so was not to provide equal protection for both races. "Justice," he declared, "is pictured as blind and her daughter, the Law, ought at least to be color-blind."[40]

As important as this argument was, its practical effect was limited because the provision about nurses could be eliminated without substantially altering the law. Tourgée's due process argument, however, had widespread implications. It exploited the fact that Plessy had only one-eighth African blood to point to the arbitrariness of racial classifications. Racial mixing was so prevalent that it was virtually impossible to

[40] Quoted in Olsen, *Thin Disguise*, 90. Harlan borrowed the color-blind metaphor in his dissent. In a novel Tourgée made a different use of the blindfold on justice that reveals a fairly traditional attitude toward women. "As [Justice] is always represented as blindfolded we may infer she is not particular about her appearance and doesn't care who sees her; — though it seems inconsistent to speak of her as a woman if that is the case." (*Pactolus Prime* [New York: Cassell, 1890], 91). For more on Tourgée's use of the color-blind metaphor, see the Conclusion, "In the Wake of *Plessy*," on page 169 of this book.

determine race in any equitable manner. Indeed, determination of who was "colored" varied from state to state. Such a difficult determination, Tourgée argued, should not be left up to a railroad conductor as allowed under the Louisiana law.

Tourgée also argued that the reputation of belonging to one race or the other was a form of property. "How much would it be *worth* to a young man entering upon the practice of law," he asked, "to be regarded as a *white* man rather than a colored one? Six-sevenths of the population are white. Nineteen-twentieths of the property of the country is owned by white people. . . . Under these conditions, is it possible to conclude that the *reputation of being white* is not property? Indeed, is it not the most valuable sort of property, being the master-key that unlocks the golden door of opportunity?"[41] In allowing a conductor to assign Plessy to the colored car, the Louisiana law deprived him of a reputation as a white man and thus took away property without due process of law.

Some people have criticized this argument as the defense of the nearly white man, not the black. But given widespread racial mixing, if it had been successful, it would have played havoc with all laws designed to make distinctions, as Grady had put it, based on categories of plain black and white.

A less ambitious but potentially effective line of argument was developed by Phillips in his brief. Aware that segregated schools existed in Washington, D.C., which was ruled by the same Congress that passed the Thirteenth and Fourteenth Amendments, Phillips claimed that a state's power to exercise its regulatory police powers differed when applied to railroad cars and to schools. Education, he asserted, was an extension of the institutions of marriage and the family. Because the fate of future generations depended on such institutions, a state had a much more valid right to police them, as various states did by forbidding interracial marriages.[42] But the fate of future generations in no way depended on seating in railroad cars. Thus, arguments based on the existence of segregated schools did not apply to Plessy's case.

[41] Quoted in Olsen, *Thin Disguise*, 83. Tourgée imagined this argument in *Pactolus Prime*, his 1890 novel about a black who can pass as white.

[42] For Tourgée the prohibition of intermarriage "is not to prevent miscegenation, but to protect and encourage illegitimacy by making the plea of seduction under promise of marriage impossible." (*Daily Inter Ocean*, September 5, 1891, 4.) He does not, however, advocate a direct legal challenge to segregated schools. In *Pactolus Prime*, a senator comments, "We cannot compel the Southern states to admit colored children to their white schools." A black character, who mouths Tourgée's views on education, responds, "That is very true; and if you had the power it would be folly to attempt to exercise it. Prejudice, whether right or wrong, can rarely be legislated out of existence, and the schools of the South would be valueless to the colored population if they were opened by compulsion to them" (117–18).

If this strategy strikes modern readers as hopelessly conservative, Tourgée's most impassioned plea clearly was not. In addition to pointing out how the law violated Fourteenth Amendment guarantees to equal protection and due process, Tourgée tried to establish, as Harlan had tried to do in his *Civil Rights Cases* dissent, that the Thirteenth and Fourteenth Amendments created affirmative rights. The assortment of people according to race, Tourgée argued, violated the Thirteenth Amendment by perpetuating the essential features of slavery. Furthermore, contrary to the ruling in the *Slaughter-House Cases*, the Fourteenth Amendment made state citizenship "incidental to and coextensive with *national* citizenship in every State. . . . The United States having granted *both* stands pledged to protect and defend both." For Tourgée, the Fourteenth Amendment "*creates* a *new* citizenship of the United States embracing new rights, privileges and immunities, derivable in a *new* manner, controlled by *new* authority, having a *new* scope and extent, depending on national authority for its existence and looking to national power for its preservation."[43] If the Court had reversed itself and accepted all aspects of Tourgée's expanded interpretation of the Thirteenth and Fourteenth Amendments, the equal-but-separate law would indeed have been unconstitutional. But the majority was not convinced by his argument.

Only eight of the nine justices participated in the decision. Justice David J. Brewer, who missed the argument, withheld judgment. Henry Billings Brown, a resident of Michigan who was born in Massachusetts, wrote the majority opinion, which was delivered on May 18, 1896.

The official record of the case, reprinted in this book, begins with a brief summary of the ruling and a description of the case. It then turns to Brown's majority decision, followed by Harlan's dissent.

THE MAJORITY DECISION

Brown began by rehearsing the facts of the case. He then quickly disposed of the Thirteenth Amendment appeal by citing the strict interpretation of the amendment in the *Slaughter-House Cases* and the *Civil Rights Cases*. Admitting that the Fourteenth Amendment appeal was

---

[43] Quoted in Olsen, *Thin Disguise*, 86. When Tourgée argued that the affirmative provisions of the Fourteenth Amendment constituted "the *magna charta* of the American citizen's rights" (87), he recalled Representative William Lawrence, who made a similar argument about the 1866 Civil Rights Act. See Fairman, *Reconstruction and Reunion*, 1202. The losing attorney in the *Slaughter-House Cases* made a similar comparison, referring to the Fourteenth Amendment as "the Magna Charta" of the people's "rights and liberty" (16 Wall. 36 at 55 [1873]).

more complicated, he addressed it by evoking the *Slaughter-House* distinction between national and state citizenship. He then asserted,

> The object of the amendment was undoubtedly to enforce the absolute equality of the two races before the law, but in the nature of things it could not have been intended to abolish distinctions based upon color, or to enforce social, as distinguished from political equality, or a commingling of the two races upon terms unsatisfactory to either.[44]

This sentence is extremely important for an understanding of the majority's logic. First, it relies on the distinction between political and social equality.[45] Second, it reveals that the majority assumed that the social difference between races had a foundation "in the nature of things."

To support his contention that it had been general practice to allow legislation separating the races socially without infringing on the political rights of blacks, Brown cited the common practice, not disputed by Plessy's attorneys, of having segregated schools. His primary example was *Roberts v. City of Boston*, an 1849 case in Massachusetts decided by Herman Melville's father-in-law, Chief Justice Lemuel Shaw. Ruling against the argument advanced by Charles Sumner, Roberts's attorney, Shaw declared that segregated schools did not violate the Massachusetts constitution's guarantee of equality before the law.[46] Brown's use of Shaw was shrewd for two reasons. First, Massachusetts was the northern state most famous for its abolitionist sentiment. If Massachusetts could justify segregated schools, the Louisiana law looked less like an unreasonable product of southern racial prejudice. Second, Shaw was an expert on the use of police powers. Since what was at issue was Louisiana's use of its police powers, to evoke Shaw's name was to enlist his authority for the majority's point of view.[47]

Admitting that any police measure will interfere with someone's freedom, Brown also cited antimiscegenation laws as proof of the "universally recognized" power of states to enact ordinances separating the races. He then evoked numerous precedents justifying separate but equal accommodations on trains, including the *Civil Rights Cases*. None-

---

[44] 163 U.S. 537 at 544 (1896).

[45] Brown's implication that the Fourteenth Amendment protects political as well as civil rights seems to be a slight adjustment of earlier rulings.

[46] For more on *Roberts*, see Leonard W. Levy and Douglas L. Jones, *Jim Crow in Boston* (New York: DaCapo Press, 1974).

[47] The risk of citing *Roberts* was that it ruled against Sumner, who was a driving force behind the Fourteenth Amendment. At the same time, the Civil Rights Act of 1875 was designed by Sumner and most of it had already been declared unconstitutional. Since Brown did not have to identify Sumner in his opinion, but does so in parentheses, he might have wanted to evoke his name to link Plessy's argument with it.

theless, he did admit that a provision exempting the train's conductor from civil liability was questionable. But like the provision for nurses, this one could be dropped without affecting the main purpose of the law.

Tourgée's argument that the Jim Crow law deprived Plessy of his reputation as a white man and thus of property attracted Brown's attention. He did not deny that reputation can be property, but he did point out that Tourgée would be right only if Plessy were indeed white. Under Louisiana law he was black. To be sure, it might seem peculiar that definitions of "colored" varied from state to state. But at the very end of his decision, Brown came back to this inconsistency and concluded that definition of race was a state, not a federal, matter.

Having disposed of the property claim, Brown focused on what he saw as the crucial issue: whether the law was a reasonable use of the state's police powers. To determine this question he invoked the principle established in *Yick Wo v. Hopkins* (1886). *Yick Wo* involved a San Francisco ordinance that regulated laundries in the name of the public good. Although the law never mentioned the Chinese, in its administration it was shown to be aimed against them. Thus it was, in fact, a police measure intent on discriminating against one group, not on protecting the public health. Such a measure, the Court declared, was not reasonable. But, according to Brown, the law passed by the Louisiana legislature was. "In determining the question of reasonableness [the state legislature] is at liberty to act with reference to the established usages, customs and traditions of the people, and with a view to the promotion of their comfort, and the preservation of the public peace and good order."[48] An equal-but-separate law did not, he ruled, violate that standard.

In his next-to-last paragraph Brown listed the major problems with Plessy's Fourteenth Amendment claim. His first point relied on the fact that the law did not simply mandate separate facilities. It also mandated equal facilities. Therefore, the "underlying fallacy" of Plessy's argument, he asserted, was the "assumption that the enforced separation of the two races stamps the colored race with a badge of inferiority. If this be so, it is not by reason of anything found in the act, but solely because the colored race chooses to put that construction upon it."[49] Since a white was as forbidden from sitting in a black car as a black was from sitting in a white car and facilities in both were supposed to be equal, whites and blacks were, he reasoned, treated equally under the law.

[48] 163 U.S. 537 at 550 (1896).
[49] 163 U.S. 537 at 551 (1896).

A second fallacy of Plessy's argument, according to Brown, was the assumption "that social prejudices may be overcome by legislation, and that equal rights cannot be secured to the negro except by an enforced commingling of the two races." Disputing this assumption, Brown argued, "If the two races are to meet upon terms of social equality, it must be the result of natural affinities, a mutual appreciation of each other's merits and a voluntary consent of individuals." In conclusion he remarked, "If the civil and political rights of both races be equal one cannot be inferior to the other civilly or politically. If one race be inferior to the other socially, the Constitution of the United States cannot put them upon the same plane."[50]

Brown's harping on the limits of legal remedies is not surprising, since the *Plessy* Court was populated by laissez-faire judges who advocated minimal government interference in people's lives. What is surprising is that his argument came in a case in which the Court *upheld* the right of a state to interfere in people's lives by policing where they could sit in railroad cars. We can understand his logic only if we remember a crucial part of laissez-faire thought at the time. Laws were undesirable when they interfered with the "natural" operation of various forces, such as the "natural" law of supply and demand. It was, after all, folly to legislate against nature. But when a law conformed to nature, it made perfect sense. Since for the majority the social differences between blacks and whites were rooted in nature, Jim Crow laws made sense, so long as they did not violate constitutional guarantees of political and civil equality. What did not make sense were attempts to establish social equality by legislation. "In the nature of things" the Fourteenth Amendment "could not have been intended to abolish distinctions based on color, or to enforce social, as distinguished from political equality."[51] Justice Harlan did not agree.

HARLAN'S DISSENT

For Justice Harlan, the majority decision violated rather than affirmed the Constitution. A crucial difference between his mode of interpretation and Brown's is that Brown relied on his sense of "the nature of things" to decide what the Constitution meant, whereas Harlan tried his best to stick to the words as written and not impose on the document his sense of the

[50] 163 U.S. 537 at 551 and 551–52 (1896).
[51] 163 U.S. 537 at 544 (1896).

natural order. An exchange between the two a few years later highlighted this difference. In 1901 the Court was faced with the difficult question of deciding the rights of people in the territories that the United States had acquired as a result of the Spanish-American War. Writing for a majority that gave Congress power over the territories without granting the new subjects full and explicit Bill of Rights protections, Brown addressed fears that "an unrestrained possession of power on the part of Congress may lead to unjust and oppressive legislation, in which the natural rights of territories, or their inhabitants, may be engulfed in a centralized despotism." He tried to assure opponents that "[t]here are certain principles of natural justice inherent in the Anglo-Saxon character which need no expression in constitution or statute to give them effect."[52]

Skeptical of guarantees of justice that relied on natural law or on notions of reasonableness rather than on the written word, Harlan responded in his dissent, "The glory of our American system of government is that it was created by a written constitution which protects the people against the exercise of arbitrary, unlimited power." The limits imposed by the Constitution, he adds, cannot be violated by "the government it created, or by any branch of it, or even by the people who ordained it, except by amendment or change of its provisions." As for Brown's reassurance that a sense of natural justice inherent in the Anglo-Saxon character would suffice to avoid the abuse of power, he noted,

> The wise men who framed the Constitution, and the patriotic people who adopted it, were unwilling to depend for their safety upon such inherent principles. They proceeded upon the theory — the wisdom of which experience has vindicated — that the only safe guaranty against government oppression was to withhold or restrict the power to oppress. They well remembered that Anglo-Saxons across the ocean had attempted, in defiance of law and justice, to trample on the rights of Anglo-Saxons on this continent.[53]

In *Plessy* Harlan tried to keep Anglo-Saxons from passing legislation that trampled on the rights of their fellow black citizens.

Harlan's dissent began by describing the effect of the Louisiana law as he saw it, which was to regulate the "use of a public highway by citizens of the United States solely upon the basis of race."[54] He then set out to prove that such a law was unconstitutional. Spending a paragraph reasserting his demonstration in the *Civil Rights Cases* that railroads are

---

[52] *Downes v. Bidwell*, 182 U.S. 244 at 280, 280 (1901).
[53] *Downes v. Bidwell*, 182 U.S. 244 at 380–81, 381, and 381 (1901).
[54] 163 U.S. 537 at 553 (1896).

p 36 be strong

i need factual evidence

public highways, he pointed out that the Civil War amendments guaranteed crucial rights for all United States citizens. The Jim Crow law, he declared, "is inconsistent not only with that equality of rights which pertains to citizenship, National and State, but with the personal liberty enjoyed by every one within the United States." It is because, despite its guarantee of equal conditions, "[e]very one knows that the statute in question had its origin in the purpose, not so much to exclude white persons from railroad cars occupied by blacks, as to exclude colored people from coaches occupied by or assigned to white persons."[55]

Harlan bolstered his argument by borrowing from Tourgée's brief. In a point noted by many commenting on the case, he worried that, if the Court condoned laws separating citizens by race, it opened the door for states to pass laws mandating separation by religion or other criteria. He then confronted the majority's claim that the crucial issue was whether or not such laws were reasonable. In a paragraph that is somewhat confusing, Harlan asserted that the Court's task was to rule on constitutionality, not reasonableness. For Harlan the issue facing the Court was quite simple: Is the law in question constitutional or is it not? The Louisiana law, he argued, is clearly not constitutional, since for him, once again borrowing from Tourgée, "[o]ur Constitution is color-blind, and neither knows nor tolerates classes among citizens."[56]

But Harlan did not stop with that declaration. He went on to add a warning about the consequences of the majority's ruling. Comparing the decision to *Dred Scott*, he feared that it would allow legislation that, far from promoting the public good, would "arouse race hate" and "perpetuate a feeling of distrust" between the two races. "The thin disguise of 'equal' accommodations for passengers in railroad coaches," he concluded, "will not mislead any one, nor atone for the wrong this day done."[57]

As prophetic as Harlan's dissent was, it was also a product of its time. Harlan, for instance, tended to subscribe to the belief that the white race was the "dominant race" in the country "in prestige, . . . in education, in wealth and in power."[58] Also, to bolster his argument for blacks, he made

[55] 163 U.S. 537 at 555 and 557 (1896).
[56] 163 U.S. 537 at 559 (1896).
[57] 163 U.S. 537 at 560 and 562 (1896).
[58] 163 U.S. 537 at 559 (1896). Compare Harlan's language with the words Tourgée puts in the mouth of a fictional southerner who, like Harlan, abandons earlier convictions to support the rights of freedmen: "'It had always been claimed,' he said, 'that a white man is by nature and not merely by the adventitious circumstances of the past, innately and inherently, and he would almost add infinitely, the superior of the colored man. In intellectual culture, experience, habits of self-government and command, this was unquestionably true. Whether it were true as a natural and scientific fact was, perhaps, yet to be decided. But could it be possible that a people, a race priding itself on its superiority, should be unwilling or afraid to see the experiment [of equal rights] fairly tried?'" (*Bricks without Straw* [New York: Fords, Howard, and Hulbert, 1880], 412.)

statements at the expense of the Chinese, whom he called "a race so different from our own that we do not permit those belonging to it to become citizens of the United States."[59] Indeed, two years later Harlan dissented when the Court ruled by a six-to-two majority that the Fourteenth Amendment guaranteed citizenship to children born in this country of Chinese descent even if their parents were not citizens.[60]

But it is easy in retrospect to judge the limitations of people in the past. One of the reasons for reading the *Plessy* case today is to understand better the conditions that made W. E. B. Du Bois prophetic when, soon after the decision, he announced that the problem of the twentieth century would be the problem of the color line. As Harlan warned, the guarantee of equality proved but a thin disguise for instituting a regime of repressive racial segregation. For instance, in a 1945 book Du Bois cited a 1942 description of the so-called equal educational facilities provided for African American children in Atlanta:

> Of the 70,894 Atlanta children of school age 26,528 are Negroes; 44,456 are whites. There is one school for every 855 white children but one school for every 2,040 Negro children. We invest in school land and buildings $2,156 for each white pupil but $887 for each Negro pupil. In 1942, we expended for education $108.70 for each white pupil but $37.80 for each Negro pupil. The double session is the black market of public education for Negroes in Atlanta. The white child goes to school 6 ½ hours a day from nine A.M. until three-thirty P.M. The Negro child goes to school 3 ½ hours a day from nine A.M. until twelve-thirty P.M. or twelve-thirty P.M. until four P.M. The Negro pupil thus loses at least 2,700 class-hours during the first six years of his elementary school education.
>
> The results are unsupervised leisure hours; ineffective compulsory education laws; irregular attendance, retardation, delinquency; reduced efficiency of overburdened teachers. The Negro pupil lacks: teachers; the teachers have an average of forty pupils in each class compared with twenty in white classes; library facilities, an average of 1.4 books per pupil compared with 6.5 for whites; vocational training facilities; only a few ill-equipped shops at Booker T. Washington High School; kindergarten, no Negro school has one; clerical help, no Negro elementary school has any clerical help.[61]

As we look back a hundred years and try to learn from the case that helped create the conditions for such inequality, we need not only to

---

[59] 163 U.S. 537 at 561 (1896). Harlan would prove to be wrong about how southern Jim Crow laws would apply to people of Chinese ancestry. In *Gong Lum v. Rice* (1927) the Supreme Court upheld Mississippi's ruling that Chinese Americans were members of the "colored races" and could not attend white schools.

[60] See note 17 for a brief description of this Chinese citizenship case.

[61] W. E. B. Du Bois, *Color and Democracy* (New York: Harcourt and Brace, 1945), 90–91.

judge the decision but also to ask ourselves how people a hundred years in the future will look back and judge how effectively the actions of our generation addressed the problems of race, which is in part a legacy of the *Plessy* era. Will the positions we take on today's issues be seen as advancing positions taken by Plessy, Tourgée, and Harlan or those taken by the *Plessy* majority? A careful reading of the *Plessy* case should make us more aware of the consequences of the positions we take.

PART TWO

The Documents

1

Plessy v. Ferguson
May 18, 1896

Mr. Justice Brown, after stating the case, delivered the opinion of the court.

This case turns upon the constitutionality of an act of the General Assembly of the State of Louisiana, passed in 1890, providing for separate railway carriages for the white and colored races. Acts 1890, No. 111, p. 152.

The first section of the statute enacts "that all railway companies carrying passengers in their coaches in this State, shall provide equal but separate accommodations for the white, and colored races, by providing two or more passenger coaches for each passenger train, or by dividing the passenger coaches by a partition so as to secure separate accommodations: *Provided,* That this section shall not be construed to apply to street railroads. No person or persons, shall be admitted to occupy seats in coaches, other than, the ones, assigned, to them on account of the race they belong to."

By the second section it was enacted "that the officers of such passenger trains shall have power and are hereby required to assign each passenger to the coach or compartment used for the race to which such passenger belongs; any passenger insisting on going into a coach or compartment to which by race he does not belong, shall be liable to a fine of twenty-five dollars, or in lieu thereof to imprisonment for a period of not more than twenty days in the parish[1] prison, and any officer of any railroad insisting on assigning a passenger to a coach or compartment other than the one set aside for the race to which said passenger belongs, shall be liable to a fine of twenty-five dollars, or in lieu thereof to imprisonment for a period of not more than twenty days in the parish

---

[1]A parish is a district in Louisiana like a county in other states.

prison; and should any passenger refuse to occupy the coach or compartment to which he or she is assigned by the officer of such railway, said officer shall have power to refuse to carry such passenger on his train, and for such refusal neither he nor the railway company which he represents shall be liable for damages in any of the courts of this State."

The third section provides penalties for the refusal or neglect of the officers, directors, conductors, and employés of railway companies to comply with the act, with a proviso that "nothing in this act shall be construed as applying to nurses attending children of the other race." The fourth section is immaterial.

The information filed in the criminal District Court charged in substance that Plessy, being a passenger between two stations within the State of Louisiana, was assigned by officers of the company to the coach used for the race to which he belonged, but he insisted upon going into a coach used by the race to which he did not belong. Neither in the information nor plea was his particular race or color averred.

The petition for the writ of prohibition averred that petitioner was seven eighths Caucasian and one eighth African blood; that the mixture of colored blood was not discernible in him, and that he was entitled to every right, privilege and immunity secured to citizens of the United States of the white race; and that, upon such theory, he took possession of a vacant seat in a coach where passengers of the white race were accommodated, and was ordered by the conductor to vacate said coach and take a seat in another assigned to persons of the colored race, and having refused to comply with such demand he was forcibly ejected with the aid of a police officer, and imprisoned in the parish jail to answer a charge of having violated the above act.

The constitutionality of this act is attacked upon the ground that it conflicts both with the Thirteenth Amendment of the Constitution, abolishing slavery, and the Fourteenth Amendment, which prohibits certain restrictive legislation on the part of the States.

1. That it does not conflict with the Thirteenth Amendment, which abolished slavery and involuntary servitude, except as a punishment for crime, is too clear for argument. Slavery implies involuntary servitude — a state of bondage; the ownership of mankind as a chattel, or at least the control of the labor and services of one man for the benefit of another, and the absence of a legal right to the disposal of his own person, property and services. This amendment was said in the *Slaughter-house cases*, 16 Wall. 36, to have been intended primarily to abolish slavery, as it had been previously known in this country, and that it equally forbade Mexican peonage or the Chinese coolie trade, when

they amounted to slavery or involuntary servitude, and that the use of the word "servitude" was intended to prohibit the use of all forms of involuntary slavery, of whatever class or name. It was intimated, however, in that case that this amendment was regarded by the statesmen of that day as insufficient to protect the colored race from certain laws which had been enacted in the Southern States, imposing upon the colored race onerous disabilities and burdens, and curtailing their rights in the pursuit of life, liberty and property to such an extent that their freedom was of little value; and that the Fourteenth Amendment was devised to meet this exigency.

So, too, in the *Civil Rights cases*, 109 U. S. 3, 24, it was said that the act of a mere individual, the owner of an inn, a public conveyance or place of amusement, refusing accommodations to colored people, cannot be justly regarded as imposing any badge of slavery or servitude upon the applicant, but only as involving an ordinary civil injury, properly cognizable by the laws of the State, and presumably subject to redress by those laws until the contrary appears. "It would be running the slavery argument into the ground," said Mr. Justice Bradley, "to make it apply to every act of discrimination which a person may see fit to make as to the guests he will entertain, or as to the people he will take into his coach or cab or car, or admit to his concert or theatre, or deal with in other matters of intercourse or business."

A statute which implies merely a legal distinction between the white and colored races — a distinction which is founded in the color of the two races, and which must always exist so long as white men are distinguished from the other race by color — has no tendency to destroy the legal equality of the two races, or reëstablish a state of involuntary servitude. Indeed, we do not understand that the Thirteenth Amendment is strenuously relied upon by the plaintiff in error in this connection.

2. By the Fourteenth Amendment, all persons born or naturalized in the United States, and subject to the jurisdiction thereof, are made citizens of the United States and of the State wherein they reside; and the States are forbidden from making or enforcing any law which shall abridge the privileges or immunities of citizens of the United States, or shall deprive any person of life, liberty or property without due process of law, or deny to any person within their jurisdiction the equal protection of the laws.

The proper construction of this amendment was first called to the attention of this court in the *Slaughter-house cases*, 16 Wall. 36, which involved, however, not a question of race, but one of exclusive privileges. The case did not call for any expression of opinion as to the exact rights it was intended to secure to the colored race, but it was said generally that its main purpose was to establish the citizenship of the negro; to give definitions of citizenship of the United States and of the States, and to protect from the hostile legislation of the States the privileges and immunities of citizens of the United States, as distinguished from those of citizens of the States.

The object of the amendment was undoubtedly to enforce the absolute equality of the two races before the law, but in the nature of things it could not have been intended to abolish distinctions based upon color, or to enforce social, as distinguished from political equality, or a commingling of the two races upon terms unsatisfactory to either. Laws permitting, and even requiring, their separation in places where they are liable to be brought into contact do not necessarily imply the inferiority of either race to the other, and have been generally, if not universally, recognized as within the competency of the state legislatures in the exercise of their police power. The most common instance of this is connected with the establishment of separate schools for white and colored children, which has been held to be a valid exercise of the legislative power even by courts of States where the political rights of the colored race have been longest and most earnestly enforced.

One of the earliest of these cases is that of *Roberts v. City of Boston*, 5 Cush. 198, in which the Supreme Judicial Court of Massachusetts held that the general school committee of Boston had power to make provision for the instruction of colored children in separate schools established exclusively for them, and to prohibit their attendance upon the other schools. "The great principle," said Chief Justice Shaw, p. 206, "advanced by the learned and eloquent advocate for the plaintiff," (Mr. Charles Sumner,) "is, that by the constitution and laws of Massachusetts, all persons without distinction of age or sex, birth or color, origin or condition, are equal before the law. . . . But, when this great principle comes to be applied to the actual and various conditions of persons in society, it will not warrant the assertion, that men and women are legally clothed with the same civil and political powers, and that children and adults are legally to have the same functions and be subject to the same treatment; but only that the rights of all, as they are settled and regulated by law, are equally entitled to the paternal consideration and protection of the law for their maintenance and security." It was held that the powers of the committee extended to the establishment of separate schools for children of different ages, sexes, and colors, and that they might also establish special schools for poor and neglected children, who have become too old to attend the primary school, and yet have not acquired the rudiments of learning, to enable them to enter the ordinary schools. Similar laws have been enacted by Congress under its general power of legislation over the District of Columbia, Rev. Stat. D. C. §§ 281, 282, 283, 310, 319, as well as by the legislatures of many of the States, and have been generally, if not uniformly, sustained by the courts. *State* v. *McCann*, 21 Ohio St. 198; *Lehew* v. *Brummell*, 15 S. W. Rep. 765; *Ward* v. *Flood*, 48 California, 36; *Bertonneau* v. *School Directors*, 3 Woods, 177; *People* v. *Gallagher*, 93 N. Y. 438; *Cory* v. *Carter*, 48 Indiana, 327; *Dawson* v. *Lee*, 83 Kentucky, 49.

Laws forbidding the intermarriage of the two races may be said in a technical sense to interfere with the freedom of contract, and yet have been universally recognized as within the police power of the State. *State* v. *Gibson*, 36 Indiana, 389.

The distinction between laws interfering with the political equality of the negro and those requiring the separation of the two races in schools, theatres and railway carriages has been frequently drawn by this court. Thus in *Strauder* v. *West Virginia*, 100 U. S. 303, it was held that a law of West Virginia limiting to white male persons, 21 years of age and citizens of the State, the right to sit upon juries, was a discrimination which implied a legal inferiority in civil society, which lessened the security of the right of the colored race, and was a step toward reducing them to a condition of servility. Indeed, the right of a colored man that, in the selection of jurors to pass upon his life, liberty and property, there shall be no exclusion of his race, and no discrimination against them because of color, has been asserted in a number of cases. *Virginia* v. *Rives*, 100 U. S. 313; *Neal* v. *Delaware*, 103 U. S. 370; *Bush* v. *Kentucky*, 107 U. S. 110; *Gibson* v. *Mississippi*, 162 U. S. 565. So, where the laws of a particular locality or the charter of a particular railway corporation has provided that no person shall be excluded from the cars on account of color, we have held that this meant that persons of color should travel in the same car as white ones, and that the enactment was not satisfied by the company's providing cars assigned exclusively to people of color, though they were as good as those which they assigned exclusively to white persons. *Railroad Company* v. *Brown*, 17 Wall. 445.

Upon the other hand, where a statute of Louisiana required those engaged in the transportation of passengers among the States to give to all persons travelling within that State, upon vessels employed in that business, equal rights and privileges in all parts of the vessel, without distinction on account of race or color, and subjected to an action for damages the owner of such a vessel, who excluded colored passengers on account of their color from the cabin set aside by him for the use of whites, it was held to be so far as it applied to interstate commerce, unconstitutional and void. *Hall* v. *De Cuir*, 95 U. S. 485. The court in this case, however, expressly disclaimed that it had anything whatever to do with the statute as a regulation of internal commerce, or affecting anything else than commerce among the States.

In the *Civil Rights case*[s], 109 U. S. 3, it was held that an act of Congress, entitling all persons within the jurisdiction of the United States to the full and equal enjoyment of the accommodations, advantages, facilities and privileges of inns, public conveyances, on land or water, theatres and other places of public amusement, and made applicable to citizens of every race and color, regardless of any previous condition of servitude, was unconstitutional and void, upon the ground that the Fourteenth Amendment was prohibitory upon the States only, and the legislation authorized to be adopted by Congress for enforcing it was not direct legislation on matters respecting which the States were prohibited from making or enforcing certain laws, or doing certain acts, but was corrective legislation, such as might be necessary or proper for counteracting and redressing the effect of such laws or acts. In delivering the opinion of the court Mr. Justice Bradley observed that the Fourteenth Amendment "does not invest Congress with power to legislate upon subjects that are within the domain of state legislation; but to provide modes of relief against state legislation, or state action, of the kind referred to. It does not authorize Congress to create a code of municipal law for the regulation of private rights; but to provide modes of redress against the operation of state laws, and the action of state officers, executive or judicial, when these are subversive of the fundamental rights specified in the amendment. Positive rights and privileges are undoubtedly secured by the Fourteenth Amendment; but they are secured by way of prohibition against state laws and state proceedings affecting those rights and privileges, and by power given to Congress to legislate for the purpose of carrying such prohibition into effect; and such legislation must necessarily be predicated upon such supposed state laws or state proceedings, and be directed to the correction of their operation and effect."

Much nearer, and, indeed, almost directly in point, is the case of the *Louisville, New Orleans &c. Railway* v. *Mississippi*, 133 U. S. 587, wherein the railway company was indicted for a violation of a statute of Mississippi, enacting that all railroads carrying passengers should provide equal, but separate, accommodations for the white and colored races, by providing two or more passenger cars for each passenger train, or by dividing the passenger cars by a partition, so as to secure separate accommodations. The case was presented in a different aspect from the one under consideration, inasmuch as it was an indictment against the railway company for failing to provide the separate accommodations, but the question considered was the constitutionality of the law. In that case, the Supreme Court of Mississippi, 66 Mississippi, 662, had held that the statute applied solely to commerce within the State, and, that being the construction of the state statute by its highest court, was accepted as conclusive. "If it be a matter," said the court, p. 591, "respecting commerce wholly within a State, and not interfering with commerce between the States, then, obviously, there is no violation of the commerce clause of the Federal Constitution. . . . No question arises under this section, as to the power of the State to separate in different compartments interstate passengers, or affect, in any manner, the privileges and rights of such passengers. All that we can consider is, whether the State has the power to require that railroad trains within her limits shall have separate accommodations for the two races; that affecting only commerce within the State is no invasion of the power given to Congress by the commerce clause."

A like course of reasoning applies to the case under consideration, since the Supreme Court of Louisiana in the case of the *State ex rel. Abbott* v. *Hicks, Judge, et al.*, 44 La. Ann. 770, held that the statute in question did not apply to interstate passengers, but was confined in its application to passengers travelling exclusively within the borders of the State. The case was decided largely upon the authority of *Railway Co.* v. *State*, 66 Mississippi, 662, and affirmed by this court in 133 U. S. 587. In the present case no question of interference with interstate commerce can possibly arise, since the East Louisiana Railway appears to have been purely a local line, with both its termini within the State of Louisiana. Similar statutes for the separation of the two races upon public conveyances were held to be constitutional in *West Chester &c. Railroad* v. *Miles*, 55 Penn. St. 209; *Day* v. *Owen*, 5 Michigan, 520; *Chicago &c. Railway* v. *Williams*, 55 Illinois, 185; *Chesapeake &c. Railroad* v. *Wells*, 85 Tennessee, 613; *Memphis &c. Railroad* v. *Benson*, 85 Tennessee, 627; *The Sue*, 22 Fed. Rep. 843; *Logwood* v. *Memphis &c. Railroad*, 23 Fed. Rep. 318; *McGuinn* v. *Forbes*, 37 Fed. Rep. 639; *People* v. *King*, 18 N. E. Rep. 245; *Houck* v. *South Pac. Railway*, 38 Fed. Rep. 226; *Heard* v. *Georgia Railroad Co.*, 3 Int. Com. Com'n, 111; *S. C.*, 1 Ibid. 428.

While we think the enforced separation of the races, as applied to the internal commerce of the State, neither abridges the privileges or immunities of the colored man, deprives him of his property without due process of law, nor denies him the equal protection of the laws, within the meaning of the Fourteenth Amendment, we are not prepared to say that the conductor, in assigning passengers to the coaches according to their race, does not act at his peril, or that the provision of the second section of the act, that denies to the passenger compensation in damages for a refusal to receive him into the coach in which he properly belongs, is a valid exercise of the legislative power. Indeed, we understand it to be conceded by the State's attorney, that such part of the act as exempts from liability the railway company and its officers is unconstitutional. The power to assign to a particular coach obviously implies the power to determine to which race the passenger belongs, as well as the power to determine who, under the laws of the particular State, is to be deemed a white, and who a colored person. This question, though indicated in the brief of the plaintiff in error, does not properly arise upon the record in this case, since the only issue made is as to the unconstitutionality of the act, so far as it requires the railway to provide separate accommodations, and the conductor to assign passengers according to their race.

It is claimed by the plaintiff in error that, in any mixed community, the reputation of belonging to the dominant race, in this instance the white race, is *property*, in the same sense that a right of action, or of inheritance, is property. Conceding this to be so, for the purposes of this case, we are unable to see how this statute deprives him of, or in any way affects his right to, such property. If he be a white man and assigned to a colored coach, he may have his action for damages against the company for being deprived of his so called property. Upon the other hand, if he be a colored man and be so assigned, he has been deprived of no property, since he is not lawfully entitled to the reputation of being a white man.

In this connection, it is also suggested by the learned counsel for the plaintiff in error that the same argument that will justify the state legislature in requiring railways to provide separate accommodations for the two races will also authorize them to require separate cars to be provided for people whose hair is of a certain color, or who are aliens, or who belong to certain nationalities, or to enact laws requiring colored people to walk upon one side of the street, and white people upon the other, or requiring white men's houses to be painted white, and colored men's black, or their vehicles or business signs to be of different colors, upon the theory that one side of the street is as good as the other, or that a house or vehicle of one color is as good as one of another color. The reply to all this is that every exercise of the police power must be reasonable, and extend only to such laws as are enacted in good faith

Albion W. Tourgée, the lawyer/novelist who served as Homer Plessy's chief attorney. The writing, in Tourgée's hand, reads: "Ignorance and neglect are the mainsprings of misrule."

for the promotion for the public good, and not for the annoyance or oppression of a particular class. Thus in *Yick Wo* v. *Hopkins*, 118 U. S. 356, it was held by this court that a municipal ordinance of the city of San Francisco, to regulate the carrying on of public laundries within the limits of the municipality, violated the provisions of the Constitution of the United States, if it conferred upon the municipal authorities arbitrary power, at their own will, and without regard to discretion, in the legal sense of the term, to give or withhold consent as to persons or places, without regard to the competency of the persons applying, or the propriety of the places selected for the carrying on of the business. It was held to be a covert attempt on the part of the municipality to make an arbitrary and unjust discrimination against the Chinese race. While this was the case of a municipal ordinance, a like principle has been held to apply to acts of a state legislature passed in the exercise of the police power. *Railroad Company* v. *Husen*, 95 U. S. 465; *Louisville & Nashville Railroad* v. *Kentucky*, 161 U. S. 677, and cases cited on p. 700; *Daggett* v. *Hudson*, 43 Ohio St. 548; *Capen* v. *Foster*, 12 Pick. 485; *State ex rel. Wood* v. *Baker*, 38 Wisconsin, 71; *Monroe* v. *Collins*, 17 Ohio St. 665; *Hulseman* v. *Rems*, 41 Penn. St. 396; *Orman* v. *Riley*, 15 California, 48.

So far, then, as a conflict with the Fourteenth Amendment is concerned, the case reduces itself to the question whether the statute of Louisiana is a reasonable regulation, and with respect to this there must necessarily be a large discretion on the part of the legislature. In determining the question of reasonableness it is at liberty to act with reference to the established usages, customs and traditions of the people, and with a view to the promotion of their comfort, and the preservation of the public peace and good order. Gauged by this standard, we cannot say that a law which authorizes or even requires the separation of the two races in public conveyances is unreasonable, or more obnoxious to the Fourteenth Amendment than the acts of Congress requiring separate schools for colored children in the District of Columbia, the constitutionality of which does not seem to have been questioned, or the corresponding acts of state legislatures.

We consider the underlying fallacy of the plaintiff's argument to consist in the assumption that the enforced separation of the two races stamps the colored race with a badge of inferiority. If this be so, it is not by reason of anything found in the act, but solely because the colored race chooses to put that construction upon it. The argument necessarily assumes that if, as has been more than once the case, and is not unlikely to be so again, the colored race should become the dominant power in the state legislature, and should enact a law in precisely similar terms, it would thereby relegate the white race to an inferior position. We imagine that the white race, at least, would not acquiesce in this assumption. The argument also assumes that social prejudices may be overcome by legislation, and that equal rights cannot be secured to the negro except by an enforced commingling of the two races. We cannot accept this proposition. If the two races are to meet upon terms of social equality, it must be the result of natural affinities, a mutual appreciation of each other's merits and a voluntary consent of individuals. As was said by the Court of Appeals of New York in *People* v. *Gallagher*, 93 N. Y. 438, 448, "this end can neither be accomplished nor promoted by laws which conflict with the general sentiment of the community upon whom they are designed to operate. When the government, therefore, has secured to each of its citizens equal rights before the law and equal opportunities for improvement and progress, it has accomplished the end for which it was organized and performed all of the functions respecting social advantages with which it is endowed." Legislation is powerless to eradicate racial instincts or to abolish distinctions based upon physical differences, and the attempt to do so can only result in accentuating the difficulties of the present situation. If the civil and political rights of both races be equal one cannot be inferior to the other civilly or politically. If one race be inferior to the other socially, the Constitution of the United States cannot put them upon the same plane.

It is true that the question of the proportion of colored blood necessary to constitute a colored person, as distinguished from a white person, is one upon which there is a difference of opinion in the different States, some holding that any visible admixture of black blood stamps the person as belonging to the colored race, (*State* v. *Chavers*, 5 Jones, [N. C.] 1, p. 11); others that it depends upon the preponderance of blood, (*Gray* v. *State*, 4 Ohio, 354; *Monroe* v. *Collins*, 17 Ohio St. 665); and still others that the predominance of white blood must only be in the proportion of three fourths. (*People* v. *Dean*, 14 Michigan, 406; *Jones* v. *Commonwealth*, 80 Virginia, 538.) But these are questions to be determined under the laws of each State and are not properly put in issue in this case. Under the allegations of his petition it may undoubtedly become a question of importance whether, under the laws of Louisiana, the petitioner belongs to the white or colored race.

The judgment of the court below is, therefore,

Affirmed.

Mr. Justice Harlan dissenting.

By the Louisiana statute, the validity of which is here involved, all railway companies (other than street railroad companies) carrying passengers in that State are required to have separate but equal accommodations for white and colored persons, "by providing two or more passenger coaches for each passenger train, *or* by dividing the passenger coaches by a *partition* so as to secure separate accommodations." Under this statute, no colored person is permitted to occupy a seat in a coach assigned to white persons; nor any white person, to occupy a seat in a coach assigned to colored persons. The managers of the railroad are not allowed to exercise any discretion in the premises, but are required to assign each passenger to some coach or compartment set apart for the exclusive use of his race. If a passenger insists upon going into a coach or compartment not set apart for persons of his race, he is subject to be fined, or to be imprisoned in the parish jail. Penalties are prescribed for the refusal or neglect of the officers, directors, conductors and employés of railroad companies to comply with the provisions of the act.

Only "nurses attending children of the other race" are excepted from the operation of the statute. No exception is made of colored attendants travelling with adults. A white man is not permitted to have his colored servant with him in the same coach, even if his condition of health requires the constant, personal assistance of such servant. If a colored maid insists upon riding in the same coach with a white woman whom she has been employed to serve, and who may need her personal attention while travelling, she is subject to be fined or imprisoned for such an exhibition of zeal in the discharge of duty.

While there may be in Louisiana persons of different races who are not citizens of the United States, the words in the act, "white and colored races," necessarily include all citizens of the United States of both races residing in that State. So that we have before us a state enactment that compels, under penalties, the separation of the two races in railroad passenger coaches, and makes it a crime for a citizen of either race to enter a coach that has been assigned to citizens of the other race.

Thus the State regulates the use of a public highway by citizens of the United States solely upon the basis of race.

However apparent the injustice of such legislation may be, we have only to consider whether it is consistent with the Constitution of the United States.

That a railroad is a public highway, and that the corporation which owns or operates it is in the exercise of public functions, is not, at this day, to be disputed. Mr. Justice Nelson, speaking for this court in *New Jersey Steam Navigation Co.* v. *Merchants' Bank*, 6 How. 344, 382, said that a common carrier was in the exercise "of a sort of public office, and has public duties to perform, from which he should not be permitted to exonerate himself without the assent of the parties concerned." Mr. Justice Strong, delivering the judgment of this court in *Olcott* v. *The Supervisors*, 16 Wall. 678, 694, said: "That railroads, though constructed by private corporations and owned by them, are public highways, has been the doctrine of nearly all the courts ever since such conveniences for passage and transportation have had any existence. Very early the question arose whether a State's right of eminent domain could be exercised by a private corporation created for the purpose of constructing a railroad. Clearly it could not, unless taking land for such a purpose by such an agency is taking land for public use. The right of eminent domain nowhere justifies taking property for a private use. Yet it is a doctrine universally accepted that a state legislature may authorize a private corporation to take land for the construction of such a road, making compensation to the owner. What else does this doctrine mean if not that building a railroad, though it be built by a private corporation, is an act done for a public use?" So, in *Township of Pine Grove* v. *Talcott*, 19 Wall. 666, 676: "Though the corporation [a railroad company] was private, its work was public, as much so as if it were to be constructed by the State." So, in *Inhabitants of Worcester* v. *Western Railroad Corporation*, 4 Met. 564: "The establishment of that great thoroughfare is regarded as a public work, established by public authority, intended for the public use and benefit, the use of which is secured to the whole community, and constitutes, therefore, like a canal, turnpike or highway, a public easement." It is true that the real and personal property, necessary to the establishment and management of the railroad, is vested in the corporation; but it is in trust for the public."

In respect of civil rights, common to all citizens, the Constitution of the United States does not, I think, permit any public authority to know the race of those entitled to be protected in the enjoyment of such rights. Every true man has pride of race, and under appropriate circumstances when the rights of others, his equals before the law, are not to be affected, it is his privilege to express such pride and to take such action based upon it as to him seems proper. But I deny that any legislative body or judicial tribunal may have regard to the race of citizens when the civil rights of those citizens are involved. Indeed, such legislation, as that here in question, is inconsistent not only with that equality of rights which pertains to citizenship, National and State, but with the personal liberty enjoyed by every one within the United States.

The Thirteenth Amendment does not permit the withholding or the deprivation of any right necessarily inhering in freedom. It not only struck down the institution of slavery as previously existing in the United States, but it prevents the imposition of any burdens or disabilities that constitute badges of slavery or servitude. It decreed universal civil freedom in this country. This court has so adjudged. But that amendment having been found inadequate to the protection of the rights of those who had been in slavery, it was followed by the Fourteenth Amendment, which added greatly to the dignity and glory of American citizenship, and to the security of personal liberty, by declaring that "all persons born or naturalized in the United States, and subject to the jurisdiction thereof, are citizens of the United States and of the State wherein they reside," and that "no State shall make or enforce any law which shall abridge the privileges or immunities of citizens of the United States; nor shall any State deprive any person of life, liberty or property without due process of law, nor deny to any person within its jurisdiction the equal protection of the laws." These two amendments, if enforced according to their true intent and meaning, will protect all the civil rights that pertain to freedom and citizenship. Finally, and to the end that no citizen should be denied, on account of his race, the privilege of participating in the political control of his country, it was declared by the Fifteenth Amendment that "the right of citizens of the United States to vote shall not be denied or abridged by the United States or by any State on account of race, color or previous condition of servitude."

These notable additions to the fundamental law were welcomed by the friends of liberty throughout the world. They removed the race line from our governmental systems. They had, as this court has said, a common purpose, namely, to secure "to a race recently emancipated, a race that through many generations have been held in slavery, all the civil rights that the superior race enjoy." They declared, in legal effect, this court has further said, "that the law in the States shall be the same for the black as for the white; that all persons, whether colored or white, shall stand equal before the laws of the States, and, in regard to the colored race, for whose protection the amendment was primarily designed, that no discrimination shall be made against them by law because of their color." We also said: "The words of the amendment, it is true, are prohibitory, but they contain a necessary implication of a positive immunity, or right, most valuable to the colored race — the right to exemption from unfriendly legislation against them distinctively as colored — exemption from legal discriminations, implying inferiority in civil society, lessening the security of their enjoyment of the rights which others enjoy, and discriminations which are steps toward reducing them to the condition of a subject race." It was, consequently, adjudged that a state law that excluded citizens of the colored race from juries, because of their race and however well qualified in other respects to discharge the duties of jurymen, was repugnant to the Fourteenth Amendment. *Strauder* v. *West Virginia*, 100 U. S. 303, 306, 307; *Virginia* v. *Rives*, 100 U. S. 313; *Ex parte Virginia*, 100 U. S. 339; *Neal* v. *Delaware*, 103 U. S. 370, 386; *Bush* v. *Kentucky*, 107 U. S. 110, 116. At the present term, referring to the previous adjudications, this court declared that "underlying all of those decisions is the principle that the Constitution of the

United States, in its present form, forbids, so far as civil and political rights are concerned, discrimination by the General Government or the States against any citizen because of his race. All citizens are equal before the law." *Gibson* v. *Mississippi*, 162 U. S. 565.

The decisions referred to show the scope of the recent amendments of the Constitution. They also show that it is not within the power of a State to prohibit colored citizens, because of their race, from participating as jurors in the administration of justice.

It was said in argument that the statute of Louisiana does not discriminate against either race, but prescribes a rule applicable alike to white and colored citizens. But this argument does not meet the difficulty. Every one knows that the statute in question had its origin in the purpose, not so much to exclude white persons from railroad cars occupied by blacks, as to exclude colored people from coaches occupied by or assigned to white persons. Railroad corporations of Louisiana did not make discrimination among whites in the matter of accommodation for travellers. The thing to accomplish was, under the guise of giving equal accommodation for whites and blacks, to compel the latter to keep to themselves while travelling in railroad passenger coaches. No one would be so wanting in candor as to assert the contrary. The fundamental objection, therefore, to the statute is that it interferes with the personal freedom of citizens. "Personal liberty," it has been well said, "consists in the power of locomotion, of changing situation, or removing one's person to whatsoever places one's own inclination may direct, without imprisonment or restraint, unless by due course of law." 1 Bl. Com. *134. If a white man and a black man choose to occupy the same public conveyance on a public highway, it is their right to do so, and no government, proceeding alone on grounds of race, can prevent it without infringing the personal liberty of each.

It is one thing for railroad carriers to furnish, or to be required by law to furnish, equal accommodations for all whom they are under a legal duty to carry. It is quite another thing for government to forbid citizens of the white and black races from travelling in the same public conveyance, and to punish officers of railroad companies for permitting persons of the two races to occupy the same passenger coach. If a State can prescribe, as a rule of civil conduct, that whites and blacks shall not travel as passengers in the same railroad coach, why may it not so regulate the use of the streets of its cities and towns as to compel white citizens to keep on one side of a street and black citizens to keep on the other? Why may it not, upon like grounds, punish whites and blacks who ride together in street cars or in open vehicles on a public road or street? Why may it not require sheriffs to assign whites to one side of a court-room and blacks to the other? And why may it not also prohibit the commingling of the two races in the galleries of legislative halls or in public assemblages convened for the consideration of the political questions of the day? Further, if this statute of Louisiana is consistent with the personal liberty of citizens, why may not the State require the separation in railroad coaches of native and naturalized citizens of the United States, or of Protestants and Roman Catholics?

The answer given at the argument to these questions was that regulations of the kind they suggest would be unreasonable, and could not, therefore, stand before the law. Is it meant that the determination of questions of legislative power depends upon the inquiry whether the statute whose validity is questioned is, in the judgment of the courts, a reasonable one, taking all the circumstances into consideration? A statute may be unreasonable merely because a sound public policy forbade its enactment. But I do not understand that the courts have anything to do with the policy or expediency of legislation. A statute may be valid, and yet, upon grounds of public policy, may well be characterized as unreasonable. Mr. Sedgwick correctly states the rule when he says that the legislative intention being clearly ascertained, "the courts have no other duty to perform than to execute the legislative will, without any regard to their views as to the wisdom or justice of the particular enactment." Stat. & Const. Constr. 324. There is a dangerous tendency in these latter days to enlarge the functions of the courts, by means of judicial interference with the will of the people as expressed by the legislature. Our institutions have the distinguishing characteristic that the three departments of government are coördinate and separate. Each must keep within the limits defined by the Constitution. And the courts best discharge their duty by executing the will of the law-making power, constitutionally expressed, leaving the results of legislation to be dealt with by the people through their representatives. Statutes must always have a reasonable construction. Sometimes they are to be construed strictly; sometimes, liberally, in order to carry out the legislative will. But however construed, the intent of the legislature is to be respected, if the particular statute in question is · valid, although the courts, looking at the public interests, may conceive the statute to be both unreasonable and impolitic. If the power exists to enact a statute, that ends the matter so far as the courts are concerned. The adjudged cases in which statutes have been held to be void, because unreasonable, are those in which the means employed by the legislature were not at all germane to the end to which the legislature was competent.

The white race deems itself to be the dominant race in this country. And so it is, in prestige, in achievements, in education, in wealth and in *should used quotes man*

Constitution see color

power. So, I doubt not, it will continue to be for all time, if it remains true to its great heritage and holds fast to the principles of constitutional liberty. But in view of the Constitution, in the eye of the law, there is in this country no superior, dominant, ruling class of citizens. There is no caste here. Our Constitution is color-blind, and neither knows nor tolerates classes among citizens. In respect of civil rights, all citizens are equal before the law. The humblest is the peer of the most powerful. The law regards man as man, and takes no account of his surroundings or of his color when his civil rights as guaranteed by the supreme law of the land are involved. It is, therefore, to be regretted that this high tribunal, the final expositor of the fundamental law of the land, has reached the conclusion that it is competent for a State to regulate the enjoyment by citizens of their civil rights solely upon the basis of race.

In my opinion, the judgment this day rendered will, in time, prove to be quite as pernicious as the decision made by this tribunal in the *Dred Scott case*. It was adjudged in that case that the descendants of Africans who were imported into this country and sold as slaves were not included nor intended to be included under the word "citizens" in the Constitution, and could not claim any of the rights and privileges which that instrument provided for and secured to the citizens of the United States; that at the time of the adoption of the Constitution they were "considered as a subordinate and inferior class of beings, who had been subjugated by the dominant race, and, whether emancipated or not, yet remained subject to their authority, and had no rights or privileges but such as those who held the power and the government might choose to grant them." 19 How. 393, 404. The recent amendments of the Constitution, it was supposed, had eradicated these principles from our institutions. But it seems that we have yet, in some of the States, a dominant race — a superior class of citizens, which assumes to regulate the enjoyment of civil rights, common to all citizens, upon the basis of race. The present decision, it may well be apprehended, will not only stimulate aggressions, more or less brutal and irritating, upon the admitted rights of colored citizens, but will encourage the belief that it is possible, by means of state enactments, to defeat the beneficient purposes which the people of the United States had in view when they adopted the recent amendments of the Constitution, by one of which the blacks of this country were made citizens of the United States and of the States in which they respectively reside, and whose privileges and immunities, as citizens, the States are forbidden to abridge. Sixty millions of whites are in no danger from the presence here of eight millions of blacks. The destinies of the two races, in this country, are indissolubly linked together, and the interests of both require that the common government of all shall not permit the seeds of race hate to be planted under the sanction of law. What can more certainly arouse race hate, what more certainly create and perpetuate a feeling of distrust between these races, than state enactments, which, in fact, proceed on the ground that colored citizens are so inferior and degraded that they cannot be allowed to sit in public coaches occupied by white citizens? That, as all will admit, is the real meaning of such legislation as was enacted in Louisiana.

The sure guarantee of the peace and security of each race is the clear, distinct, unconditional recognition by our governments, National and State, of every right that inheres in civil freedom, and of the equality before the law of all citizens of the United States without regard to race. State enactments, regulating the enjoyment of civil rights, upon the basis of race, and cunningly devised to defeat legitimate results of the war, under the pretence of recognizing equality of rights, can have no other result than to render permanent peace impossible, and to keep alive a conflict of races, the continuance of which must do harm to all concerned. This question is not met by the suggestion that social equality cannot exist between the white and black races in this country. That argument, if it can be properly regarded as one, is scarcely worthy of consideration; for social equality no more exists between two races when travelling in a passenger coach or a public highway than when members of the same races sit by each other in a street car or in the jury box, or stand or sit with each other in a political assembly, or when they use in common the streets of a city or town, or when they are in the same room for the purpose of having their names placed on the registry of voters, or when they approach the ballot-box in order to exercise the high privilege of voting.

There is a race so different from our own that we do not permit those belonging to it to become citizens of the United States. Persons belonging to it are, with few exceptions, absolutely excluded from our country. I allude to the Chinese race. But by the statute in question, a Chinaman can ride in the same passenger coach with white citizens of the United States, while citizens of the black race in Louisiana, many of whom, perhaps, risked their lives for the preservation of the Union, who are entitled, by law, to participate in the political control of the State and nation, who are not excluded, by law or by reason of their race, from public stations of any kind, and who have all the legal rights that belong to white citizens, are yet declared to be criminals, liable to imprisonment, if they ride in a public coach occupied by citizens of the white race. It is scarcely just to say that a colored citizen should not object to occupying a public coach assigned to his own race. He does not object, nor, perhaps, would he object to separate coaches for his race, if his rights under the law were recognized. But he objects, and ought never to cease objecting to the proposition, that citizens of the white and black races can be adjudged criminals because they sit, or claim the right to sit, in the same public coach on a public highway.

The arbitrary separation of citizens, on the basis of race, while they are on a public highway, is a badge of servitude wholly inconsistent with the civil freedom and the equality before the law established by the Constitution. It cannot be justified upon any legal grounds.

If evils will result from the commingling of the two races upon public highways established for the benefit of all, they will be infinitely less than those that will surely come from state legislation regulating the enjoyment of civil rights upon the basis of race. We boast of the freedom enjoyed by our people above all other peoples. But it is difficult to reconcile that boast with a state of the law which, practically, puts the brand of servitude and degradation upon a large class of our fellow-citizens, our equals before the law. The thin disguise of "equal" accommodations for passengers in railroad coaches will not mislead any one, nor atone for the wrong this day done.

The result of the whole matter is, that while this court has frequently adjudged, and at the present term has recognized the doctrine, that a State cannot, consistently with the Constitution of the United States, prevent white and black citizens, having the required qualifications for jury service, from sitting in the same jury box, it is now solemnly held that a State may prohibit white and black citizens from sitting in the same passenger coach on a public highway, or may require that they be separated by a "partition," when in the same passenger coach. May it not now be reasonably expected that astute men of the dominant race, who affect to be disturbed at the possibility that the integrity of the white race may be corrupted, or that its supremacy will be imperilled, by contact on public highways with black people, will endeavor to procure statutes requiring white and black jurors to be separated in the jury box by a "partition," and that, upon retiring from the court room to consult as to their verdict, such partition, if it be a moveable one, shall be taken to their consultation room, and set up in such a way as to prevent black jurors from coming too close to their brother jurors of the white race. If the "partition" used in the court room happens to be stationary, provision could be made for screens with openings through which jurors of the two races could confer as to their verdict without coming into personal contact with each other. I cannot see but that, according to the principles this day announced, such state legislation, although conceived in hostility to, and enacted for the purpose of humiliating citizens of the United States of a particular race, would be held to be consistent with the Constitution.

I do not deem it necessary to review the decisions of state courts to which reference was made in argument. Some, and the most important, of them are wholly inapplicable, because rendered prior to the adoption of the last amendments of the Constitution, when colored people had very few rights which the dominant race felt obliged to respect. Others were made at a time when public opinion, in many localities, was dominated by the institution of slavery; when it would not have been safe to do justice to the black man; and when, so far as the rights of blacks were concerned, race prejudice was, practically, the supreme law of the land. Those decisions cannot be guides in the era introduced by the recent amendments of the supreme law, which established universal civil freedom, gave citizenship to all born or naturalized in the United States and residing here, obliterated the race line from our systems of governments, National and State, and placed our free institutions upon the broad and sure foundation of the equality of all men before the law.

I am of opinion that the statute of Louisiana is inconsistent with the personal liberty of citizens, white and black, in that State, and hostile to both the spirit and letter of the Constitution of the United States. If laws of like character should be enacted in the several States of the Union, the effect would be in the highest degree mischievous. Slavery, as an institution tolerated by law would, it is true, have disappeared from our country, but there would remain a power in the States, by sinister legislation, to interfere with the full enjoyment of the blessings of freedom; to regulate civil rights, common to all citizens, upon the basis of race; and to place in a condition of legal inferiority a large body of American citizens, now constituting a part of the political community called the People of the United States, for whom, and by whom through representatives, our government is administered. Such a system is inconsistent with the guarantee given by the Constitution to each State of a republican form of government, and may be stricken down by Congressional action, or by the courts in the discharge of their solemn duty to maintain the supreme law of the land, anything in the constitution or laws of any State to the contrary notwithstanding.

For the reasons stated, I am constrained to withhold my assent from the opinion and judgment of the majority.

Mr. Justice Brewer did not hear the argument or participate in the decision of this case.

2

Selected Views on the "Race Question" at the Time of *Plessy*

In the second half of the nineteenth century the "race question," along with the "woman question" and the "labor question," taxed the imagination of many people in the United States. The Louisiana law mandating separate but equal facilities on intrastate railroads was one state's legal solution. The *Plessy* decision was the judiciary's response to that solution. To understand how the Supreme Court could have considered Jim Crow laws reasonable, we need to look at views of the "race question" from other areas of life at the time. Proposed solutions were often quite different from those advocated today. Nonetheless, they were not all the same, as indicated by the 1885 debate referred to in the introduction between George Washington Cable and Henry Grady. Whereas no short selection can represent the full range of responses, this chapter reproduces a variety. Included are pieces by John Tyler Morgan, a noted Alabama politician; Frederick L. Hoffman, who compiled a statistical analysis of scientific studies on the characteristics of African Americans; Henry M. Field, a liberal northern minister; and Booker T. Washington, a well-known African American educator. Also included is a short excerpt from a law review on separate-coach laws. These selections should be contrasted with reactions to the case in the next chapter, especially with those by W. E. B. Du Bois and Charles W. Chesnutt, who offered very different views on the "race question."

JOHN TYLER MORGAN

The Race Question in the United States

September 1890

John Tyler Morgan (1824–1907) was born in the eastern hills of Tennessee. He grew up in rural Alabama where his father had established squatter's rights to unsurveyed Indian land. He had little formal education. His mother, the daughter of an Episcopal minister, gave him strong religious convictions. Morgan read for the law and was admitted to the bar at twenty-one. He began his legal career as a member of the Whig Party, the forerunner of the Republican Party, briefly switched to the Know-Nothing Party, and then became a Democrat. A passionate secessionist, he served in the Confederate army, beginning as a private and ending as a brigadier general. Receiving a pardon after the Civil War, he began a political career as a Redeemer, intent on "redeeming" the South from northern control. In 1876 he was elected to the Senate where he claimed that the Northeast sought to colonize the South and turn it into the Ireland of the American Union.

In 1890 Morgan was instrumental in defeating two important post-Reconstruction bills: the Blair and Force Bills. The Blair Bill committed federal education funds to the states to combat illiteracy. Although most of the money would have gone to the South, where illiteracy among both blacks and whites was highest, Morgan opposed the bill because he thought it would lead to overeducation of blacks and unwarranted federal intrusion into state affairs. The Force Bill responded to efforts to deny blacks the vote through intimidation and fraud by providing for federal supervision of elections. Fiercely opposed to black suffrage, Morgan worked tirelessly to defeat the bill. By 1901 he helped to bring about a state constitutional convention with the goal of disfranchising blacks in Alabama as much as possible. The measures passed were extremely effective. In 1900 about 180,000 blacks were eligible to vote in Alabama. In 1903 only 2,980 were registered. As difficult as it is for us to imagine, the campaign against black voter rights was seen by many as a reformist, progressive measure aimed at restoring the political realm to qualified and responsible voters. Morgan was also considered a progressive in his economic policy, which advocated the growth of industry and trade in the South. His vision of an

John J. Morgan, "The Race Question in the United States," *The Arena* 10 (1890): 385–98.

industrial South, not dependent on the North, led him to advocate construction of the Panama Canal and to support the imperialist policy of the United States, which resulted in the annexation of the Philippines and Puerto Rico after the Spanish-American War.

The 1890 essay included here was part of Morgan's journalistic campaign to defeat the Blair and Force Bills. It followed an 1889 essay entitled "Shall Negro Majorities Rule?" The major premise of the essay is that those of African descent are naturally inferior to whites. Evoking a commonplace religious argument of the day, Morgan claims that the differences between the races "have been arranged by the hand of the Creator." These God-created differences, he argues, generate a natural aversion between the races. Whereas Albion W. Tourgée, Plessy's lawyer, attributed racial tension to the history of slavery, Morgan claims that abolition actually increased the natural tendency of the races to conflict with one another. Such conflict was further increased by what Morgan sees as the unnatural effort to elevate blacks by granting them the vote. Playing on white fears of racial mixture, he links the effort to secure black suffrage with the attempt to demand social equality. He praises the family as the foundation of American society and warns against the "unwelcome intrusion of the negro race into the white family circle." Concluding that it is as unnatural to incorporate blacks into the country's body politic as into white families, he sees the only solution to the race problem to be the voluntary return of blacks to Africa.

Through a lifetime of scholarship, the African American W. E. B. Du Bois proved false such statements as Morgan's about the lack of African achievements in "art, science, or enterprise." Nonetheless, Morgan's racist attitudes, as extreme as they seem, were not as intense as those of others writing at the time, such as the minister-turned-novelist Thomas Dixon, who stressed the bestiality of blacks and the threat of the black rapist. Furthermore, Morgan did not officially demand the forceable removal of blacks from American shores. Even so, his views should help to place in perspective the decision of the Plessy court, which in contrast seems moderate. After all, that decision rests on acknowledging blacks' legitimate claim to the very political equality that Morgan spent his career trying to dismantle.

After the ratification of the 13th Amendment of the Constitution, it was, in the opinion of the abolitionists, necessary to further amend it, so as to provide against the effect of "race, color, and previous condition of servitude," upon the capacity of the negro race to rise to social and political equality with the white race in this country.

Something was needed, beyond any native virtues or powers of the negro, to lift him up to the full enjoyment of his liberty.

It was conceded by the measures that were adopted for this purpose that our negroes, trained and educated under the southern slave code, were well prepared for citizenship and the ballot in this great Republic.

This movement also ignored that declaration in the Constitution that this government was ordained "to secure the blessings of liberty to ourselves and our posterity;" or else it was determined that the negro race should become the posterity of the white race.

The 14th and 15th amendments furnish a strong support for the contention of the negro race that it was the purpose of these amendments to give them higher and more definite security for their liberties than was provided for the white race.

If that contention was true in theory, as it is in fact, it proves that it was considered necessary to save the negroes from the natural decay of their new-born liberties, which would result, necessarily, from their natural inability to preserve their freedom, and to enjoy its blessings.

If, as is asserted by some, the purpose of these amendments was to protect the negro race from the active hostility of the white race, it is obvious, in either case, that a race question was recognized in the very language of those amendments. In the first proposition, the race question appeared in the admitted inferiority of the negroes, as a race; and, in the other case, it appeared in the admitted aversion between the races.

The stringent prohibition of the action of the States, in denying them the power to discriminate against the political privileges of the negroes, confessed the existence of race aversion and prejudice, in such degree, that it could only be held in check by the organic law of the land.

It was expected that the citizenship conferred upon the negroes by these amendments and the peculiar protection guaranteed to their political powers, would carry with it, as a necessary incident, an equality of social privileges with the white race.

It was impossible to express this incidental class of privileges in the body of these amendments, because it would have been impossible to define them, or to enjoin their enforcement in the courts, or to compel obedience to their commands in the social relations and conduct of the people. They were, therefore, left as mere incidents of political power, to be worked out through the influence the negro race would exert in the government of the country.

This fruitful cause of strife has invited constant but futile effort on the part of the negro race and their political masters to force them, by political pressure and by acts of Congress, upon the white race as equals and associates in their domestic relations.

At whatever line their leaders may intend to fix the limits of this intrusion, the negroes have intended that the invasion shall not cease until the races become homogeneous through complete admixture. Not that the highest class of white people shall consort with the lowest class of negroes, but, that, where the conditions of wealth, education, culture, and position are equal, discriminations against the negro race shall cease.

The social and political questions connected with the African race, in the United States, all relate to and depend upon the essential differences between the negro and the white man, as they have been arranged by the hand of the Creator.

Amongst these differences, the color of the skin, while it distinguishes the races unmistakably, is the least important. The mental differences and differing traits, including the faculty of governing, forecast, enterprise, and the wide field of achievement in the arts and sciences, are accurately measured by the contrast of the civilization of the United States, with the barbarism of Central Africa.

If the negroes in the United States were not descended from a people who enslaved them and sold them into foreign bondage, and who are still engaged in the same traffic; if they had been invited to this country to become citizens and to contribute what talents and virtues they have to the conduct of our complex system of government, — the race question would still be as much a vital and unvoidable issue, political and social, as it is under the existing and widely different conditions.

It is the presence of seven or eight millions of negroes in this country and the friction caused by their political power and their social aspirations, and not the fact that they were recently in slavery, that agitates and distresses the people of both races. If they were not in the United States, there would be perfect peace and harmony amongst the people.

There is a decided aversion between the white race and the Indian, — a race who has never submitted to enslavement. The difference in color and in social traits sufficiently accounts for this aversion, which exists in spite of our admiration for them as a brave and independent race. Has it been long persistence in a course of injustice and ill usage that has caused this aversion, or is it the race aversion that has caused the ill usage and retaliations that have filled the fairest valleys of our country with massacre and havoc? Whether it was the one or the other, it was not slavery, nor the lack of manly independence or of fortitude, on the part of the Indians, that has engendered the constant collisions between the two races. In the history of the Indians we find the most conclusive proofs that no race, inferior in capacity and intelligence, can co-exist with the white race, in the same government, and preserve its distinctive traits, or social organization. If the two races cannot merge, and sink their individuality, by a commingling of blood, the inferior race will be crushed.

In some respects the North American Indians have a remarkable history which entitles them to great respect. They are the only race of people known to history, who have never enslaved their own people.

They might, with a show of reason, despise a man who had been a slave, or had descended from a slave parentage; while such a pretension would be filial ingratitude in Britons, English, Irish, French, Germans, Russians, Romans, Greeks or Chinese, and in all Oriental nations, all of whom have enslaved and made merchandise of their own kindred, as well as of all strangers who have come within their power. In the introduction to the work of Mr. Cobb, on Slavery, that great lawyer and statesman says: —

"A detailed and minute inquiry into the history of slavery would force us to trace the history of every nation of the earth; for the most enlightened have, at some period within their existence, adopted it as a system; and no organized government has been so barbarous as not to introduce it amongst its customs. It has been more universal than marriage, and more permanent than liberty."

The perishing of the Indian races in North America and the West India Islands, has been the result of their stubborn resistance to the dominance of races of superior knowledge and power. If they had yielded, as the negro has always done, to the *vis major,*[1] they would have increased in numbers and in useful knowledge; and they would have taken the places that the white people have accorded to the negroes, in citizenship, with greatly superior endowment of intellect, and of every great virtue. But the Indians, while they eagerly acquired the ownership of negro slaves, refused the bondage of slavery for their race, and have perished, rather than submit to such humiliation. Our history is full of records to prove this fact, and, in one of the Spanish American Islands, then known as Hispanolia (Santo Domingo), it is stated by eminent historians, that a population of 3,000,000 Indians

[1] Literally, "greater strength" in Latin.

shrunk to 1200 souls in the reign of Charles V. of Spain. This exter-
mination was the result of the efforts of the white race to enslave them.

In Irving's "Columbus,"[2] it is stated that whole villages of Indians
committed suicide to escape the bondage of slavery and invited other
Indians to join them in that dreadful work.

As a slave, the Indian has always perished, while, in all other races,
except the negroes, the slave has, at last, worked out his own deliverance. The African slaves have not yet made such an effort, either here
or in Africa. Their emancipation has always resulted from the benevolence of white people. They still assist in the slave trade with Asia, despite
the earnest endeavors of great nations to prevent that traffic.

Slavery continues in Africa without modification, or abatement. Slavery has always been the common law of the negro race in Africa, and
its abolishment there as a domestic institution is a very remote expectation.

In the experience of all the great nations, slavery has been a rudi-
mentary condition — the first exercise of political government, after the
family government, and no nation or race is to be despaired of because
its government was first rooted in slavery. The organization of the Congo
Free State has secured to the negro race the free and unobstructed
opportunity, with the aid of all the great powers, to prove, if they can do
so, that they are capable of breaking the chains of slavery riveted on
their limbs, by their own kindred, under a slave code ordained by their
own free will.

All the other nations have, with good cause, regarded the negroes as
an inferior race, aside from all the physical distinctions by which they
are separated from all other races of men. It was this estimate of their
condition that led the great powers of Europe to enter into the Berlin
Conference, which fixed the boundaries of the Congo Free State,[3] — a
vast and beautiful country abounding in natural resources, — and secure
to the negro race immunity from foreign invasion, that they might become a civilized people. The negro race, in their native land, have never
made a voluntary and concerted effort to rise above the plane of slavery;
they have not contributed a thought, or a labor, except by compulsion,

[2] U.S. author Washington Irving (1783–1859) wrote (besides "Rip Van Winkle" and other
tales) a popular history about Columbus.

[3] At the Berlin Conference of 1884, European powers recognized the Congo Free State
in Africa as a sovereign state with Leopold II of Belgium as its head. Claiming to "civilize"
the region, Leopold in fact allowed exploitative and repressive practices to rule. With his
death in 1908, the entire territory, which is now the country of Zaire, became a colony of
Belgium.

to aid the progress of civilization. Nothing has emanated from the negroes of Africa, in art, science, or enterprise that has been of the least service to mankind. Their own history, at home, demonstrates their inferiority when compared with that of other peoples.

They have been, for ages, the possessors of a fertile country, where they have bred in myriads, and no foreign power has attempted to subjugate them. The result of their contributions to the wealth of the world is limited to slaves, and the natural productions of the forests. They have no agricultural implement, except a rude, iron hoe; no ships for the seas and no beasts of burden. Their social development has never risen so high as to repress human sacrifices and cannibalism; while their religion is a witchcraft that is attended with every brutal crime.

The inferiority of the negro race, as compared with the white race, is so essentially true, and so obvious, that, to assume it in argument, cannot be justly attributed to prejudice. If it is prejudice, it is rare prejudice, which affects nearly all of the white race, and proves the existence of a deep-seated race aversion. This aversion is not a result of slavery. If it were, we could not take pride in the race of English and Saxon masters and slaves from whom we are descended. Whether the law that created this aversion is natural, or contrary to nature; whether it is of human or divine origin; whether it is wicked, or good, — it equally affects and controls both races in all their relations, and it is immutable, — grounded in convictions and sentiments that neither race can yield.

The negro race has but a slight hold on other races through the marriage relation.

Marriages have seldom occurred between Chinese, or Malays, or Indians, and the negro race; and, by the universal decree of the white race, such marriages are prohibited. No expression of race aversion could be more distinct than this.

This race aversion has been greatly increased in this country by the abolition of slavery. The trust and confidence felt by the slaves towards their former masters has been largely supplanted by a feeling of resentment, which politicians are rapidly converting into hatred and revenge. This condition would not have been so pronounced, if the negro race had not been forced, unprepared and disqualified, into the exercise of the full rights and powers incident to citizenship. That unwise and unnecessary decree has caused the aversion between the races to infuse its virus into the social and political affairs of the country, where it will be, forever, a rankling poison. It has intensified into a race conflict all political questions, in localities where there are large negro populations. It is discussed and voted upon everywhere, from the national capital to the ballot box; exciting the most acrimonious debate and extreme measures of legislation. Politicians deny, in vain, that it is an open question, and demand the execution, to the letter, of the provisions of the constitutional amendments; while the people, in all parts of the country, continue its discussion and refuse to lend the support of public opinion to the enforcement of the organic law.

The race conflict in the United States is, essentially, a social controversy, aggravated by its union with the government of the country.

Race conflicts have attended the entire history of English-speaking people. Having, as they believe, a mission and leadership in the civilization of barbarous people and in all the progress of mankind, they have not permitted the inferior races to check their movements.

Our North American history is filled with illustrations of this unrelenting progress. By the destruction of the implacable Indian, we have possessed ourselves of his inheritance, — the fairest and richest in the world. He would not be a slave, and we drove him out and filled his place with negroes found in bondage in their native land, and imported as slaves. The patient, thrifty Chinaman was found to be depraved. He was invited to come here under guarantees of full protection. When he became the successful rival of our laboring classes and encumbered our industries with a competition that starved the people who refused to admit him to their family circles as an equal, we summarily decreed his banishment.[4]

It was alleged by great statesmen who were endeavoring to account for the evil of the presence of the negro in our country that there was "an irrepressible conflict between free labor and slave labor." They demanded the abolition of slavery as the only remedy. This illogical conclusion was based on a thorough misconception of the truth, and the remedy was as mistaken as the supposed conflict of slave and free labor.

The alleged competition did not exist in any branch of human industry, except in servile and menial labor which the negro was alone fitted to perform and still monopolizes. The great body of negro slaves grew cotton and sugar in the South, while the producers of grain, provisions, wool, hemp, flax, and hay, occupied other latitudes. The South furnished them their nearest and best market for their supplies of food, draught animals, and machinery, and they were, in the aggregate, as much benefited by the labor of the negro slaves as their owners were.

---

[4] In 1882 Congress passed a law forbidding all Chinese, with a few exceptions, to enter the country. At the same time, no person of Asian descent could become a naturalized citizen. The only possibility for citizenship was, therefore, through birth in the United States, and even that possibility was disputed and not resolved by the Supreme Court until 1898.

Instead of there having been competition between slave and free labor, the two systems, separated by isothermal and commercial lines, but adjoining each other, were mutual contributors to the prosperity of the labors of both, and of the country at large. It was not labor competition, but political and sectional rivalry in the struggle for power, and deep seated race aversion, that caused the alleged "irreconcilable conflict."

In the adjoining fields, in the South, where white men and negro slaves grew cotton, there was no conflict, competition, or rivalry, the reason being that there was never an overproduction of cotton. There was never a moment when cotton was not ready sale, for cash. The production, however great, was always in demand. The slave laws held the negro to his daily work; made him temperate;[5] enforced subordination; repressed crime and misdemeanor; and made him a safe and harmless neighbor. There was no cause for social or political rivalry with the white people, who labored, or with any other class, and, while the slave did not aspire to such an attitude, the white man did not condescend to it. While the slaves were under the strict dominion of their masters, no class of people were better secured against interference, by other persons, with their rights, of any kind. The result was that there was neither rivalry nor friction between the laboring classes in the South.

There was instinctive race aversion between them, which nothing could prevent, or modify, except the inferior position of the negro, which neutralized all personal jealousies. This inferiority and dependence excited, in all classes of white people, that sort of Christian benevolence that compassionates, always, the poorest and least attractive of the human family. The Christian training of the negro race in the South is the undesirable proof of this state of sentiment towards them.

When this race aversion was excited by the apprehensions of the non-slaveholders, of the possibility of the future social equality, or union of the races, under political pressure, it flamed up into angry abhorrence, and has become a settled antagonism, as these apprehensions have been realized. It was this apprehension, and not any coercion, or other fear of consequences that, above all other considerations, incited, armed, fed with the bread earned by the toil of women in the fields, clothed with their skill, and sent to the Southern armies, the sturdiest and most resolute of that wonderful body of citizen soldiery. Knowing all that this political movement meant and fully comprehending its results, these men felt that any sacrifice they could make, to prevent race equality in

---

[5] That is, kept him from indulging in alcohol.

the South, could not outweigh their duty to their families, their race, and their country.

This race question has been a foot-ball for politicians, and a stumbling block for statesmen, since we began to organize into a federal union. In the beginning, the repression of the slave trade was obstinately resisted by northern and southern States interested in the profits, and a compromise, written into the constitution, was the necessary result.[6] Another compromise was made in relation to the rendition of fugitive slaves.[7] Another and more important compromise secured the enumeration of three fifths of the slave population in the basis of representation in Congress and in the electoral colleges.[8] Slavery and politics were thus linked in perpetual association and made the cause of perpetual strife.

Our fathers had more faith in our dutiful obedience to the constitution than we deserved, when they planted this temptation in the body of that instrument. There was inequality in that basis of representation; founded on a principle that warred against the theory of our government. It was not too much for the people of the free States to say that the property of the slave States should not, in justice, furnish in part, a basis of representation, while their own property was denied that influence. Still, the South entered the Union upon that agreement, and it was not too much for them to say, that the sworn compact should be observed.

In this condition of the subject, political controversy was bound up with the question of slavery, so closely and inevitably, that it has clung to the negro race since their emancipation, and has become the leading and controlling influence in their destiny.

It was the hope and expectation of the abolitionists who, as humanitarians, were also enthusiasts, that the emancipation of the negro would cure the alleged conflict between free and slave labor; that freedom would qualify the negro race for unobstructed social intercourse with the white race; and that the ballot would force them into such political influence as to compel the abolition, also, of race aversion and social discrimination. The ballot in the hands of the negro race has had just the contrary effect. It has been relied upon as a substitute for personal worth, industry, and good conduct, to lift the inferior race to the same

[6] Article I, section 9, paragraph 1 of the Constitution forbade restriction of the slave trade until 1808.
[7] Article IV, section 2, paragraph 3 of the Constitution allowed for the return of fugitive slaves.
[8] Article I, section 2, paragraph 3 of the Constitution implies that three-fifths of the slave population was to be added to the free population for determining representation in the House of Representatives and for apportioning direct taxes among states according to population.

plane with the superior race; but it has constantly exposed the negro race to organized political opposition, and has chilled the hopes and balked the efforts of those who most desired to help the negroes to profit by their freedom.

The negroes have uniformly used the ballot as a means of inflicting the penalties of resentment and race animosity upon southern people. They seem incapable of conceiving that their political power has any other valuable use than as an expression of hatred and ill will towards their former owners. The history of Hayti and Jamaica, on the other hand, has not been forgotten in the southern States. The people there understand that prudence has restrained the excesses that destroyed, or drove out, the white race, from these and other islands of the West Indies, for the same reasons that now animate the negroes and unite them, in solid political movement, in hostility to the white race. This strenuous and constant antagonism of the negro race towards the white people of the South, has compelled them, also, to unite on race lines for security.

The first movement of the negro party in the South, and of their white leaders there and in Congress, was directed to the vital point of securing race equality, in social as well as political privileges, by the compulsion of law. The negro race, flattered by this effort, with the hope, that is most keenly indulged by every negro of mixed blood, of being foisted into the white families, freely contributed its entire political power to assist in such robbery of States and people, as never before was practised under the authority of law. The warnings of that experience cannot be ignored or forgotten. It is impossible to divide the negro race on any political question, and whatever measures they will support or oppose will first be tested by the race issue.

Natural race instinct and caste is the controlling force in this movement.

The negro race has reason to know that the great body of the white people, in the northern section of the country, oppose the influence of their political power, elsewhere than in "the States lately in rebellion." Congress has stricken down all suffrage in the District of Columbia, for the sole purpose of disfranchising the negro voter; and in the northern States negroes are practically excluded from holding office, either under State or federal authority. Those who oppose negro influence in politics, in the States where small numbers of that race are found, can have no other reason than race aversion for their course. This feeling is quite as common in the northern States as in the South, where the people are brought into contact with the negroes in social intercourse, or into competition with their labor, or into party conflict with them in the elections.

With these facts, and many others in view, we must admit that there is a deep and immovable cause for the almost inflexible law of exclusion, that shuts out the negro race, through the pressure of public opinion, from all opportunity to rise to the level of the white race, in political and social affairs.

What is the cause of this condition of the negro race in the United States, which their power and political influence has not been able to remove, but has only aggravated? The answer is recorded in the home history of every white family in the United States. The negro race cannot be made homogeneous with the white race. It is the abhorrence that every white woman in our country feels towards the marriage of her son or daughter with a negro, that gives the final and conclusive answer to this question. Wealth, character, abilities, accomplishments and position, have no effect to modify this aversion of the white woman to a negro-marital alliance. Men may yield to such considerations, or to others of a baser sort; but the snows will fall from heaven in sooty blackness, sooner than the white women of the United States will consent to the maternity of negro families. It will become more and more the pride of the men of our race to resist any movement, social or political, that will promote the unwelcome intrusion of the negro race into the white family circle.

This is the central and vital point in the race question. If the negroes, being our equals in political privileges, could be absorbed into our race, as equals, there would be no obstacle to our harmonious and beneficent association, in this free country, but neither laws, nor any form of constraint, can force the doors to our homes and seat them at our firesides.

The voting power is the only reliance of the negro for lifting his race to the level of social union or equality with the white race. The race jealousy that the exertion of that power inflames, has united the white race on the color line, in every State where there is a dense negro population, and has moved other communities, that have no fear of negro domination, to feel for those who are threatened with this calamity, the warmest sympathy.

There is a reason for this condition of public sentiment, that is fatal to the movement for negro political domination in the southern States, — a reason existing in the very organism of our government; a feature that cannot be ignored.

Ours is a representative government, with sovereignty residing in the people; and those who exert the powers of sovereignty are chosen for that purpose, not by the people at large, but by qualified voters. One in about every five of our population is qualified by the law to represent himself and the four other persons in the group, in voting at elections. This arbitrary arrangement imposes no restraint upon the voter, as to how he will represent his group, except his sense of justice, his friendship for the race he represents, or his natural affections and love of country. He has no other than a remote, moral responsibility to his non-voting constituency: and he measures his duty to them by his more direct allegiance to his party. Four fifths of the people of the United States are thus arbitrarily represented in the ballot box, by the one fifth who are qualified voters.

This seemingly dangerous power of the voter is based upon the theory of the representation in the ballot box of that sacred relation which inspires the honest and intelligent voter with the most dutiful and quickened sense of trust and natural affection, — the family relation. Controlled by such influences, this voting power becomes the most conservative and the best element in a government for the people. But the danger of injecting into the voting power a feeling of race aversion, or class hostility, is obvious. It could scarcely be over-stated. It cannot be too carefully avoided in the government of the country. The family is the real unit of our power in free government.

While the families of the country are homogeneous, there is little danger that the voters who represent them will war upon their security, or fail to be loyal to their best interests. But where the voters, who represent one fifth of the political power of the entire country (and, in some of the States, have a majority), are excluded by reason of race, or caste, or their previous slavery, from family relationships with the minority, it is certain that resentment, prejudice, and hostility will animate them; and they will vote to humiliate and destroy that part of their constituency. Without extending the argument on this point over a wider field, it seems to be clear, that there is extreme danger, under existing conditions, in confiding to negro voters the representation of white families in the ballot box.

This is the real race question, in politics, that has vexed our people from the beginning; that has afflicted the country with a terrible civil war; and still calls for the wisest statesmanship and the most patient forbearance, in its settlement.

If the emancipated slaves had been of our own race, as were the English villeins, and as the Russian serfs and Mexican peons were of those races, they would have been clothed with the political powers of citizenship without any injurious consequences; because they would have been incorporated, without social disturbance, into the families of the country. It is this race difficulty that confronts the negro, and it will, while it continues, resist and obstruct his political power.

The practical phase of the question is, whether the white race can be made to include the negro race in a free and honest welcome into their families, as "men and brethren." There are some enthusiasts, claiming to be exalted humanitarians, who advocate the solution of this difficulty by raising the negro race to the social level of the white race through legislative expedients that look to the mingling of the blood of the races; but this is far from being the sentiment of the great body of the people of the United States. They understand the impossibility of such a result. The full-blooded negroes also understand it, and hesitate, if they do not refuse, to make this effort. "The Afro-Americans," as the mulattoes describe themselves, believe that a precedent has been set, by their foremost man, which they can follow, with the aid of the politicians, that will secure their incorporation, by marriage, into the white families of the country. These vain expectations will be followed with the chagrin of utter disappointment, and will increase their discontent.

Every day the distance increases between these races, and they are becoming more jealous and intolerant of each other. This condition is disclosed in the schools, churches, and in every industrial pursuit. The field for negro labor, except in the heaviest drudgery and in menial occupations, is constantly narrowing, until their presence is not tolerated in the higher commercial pursuits, or in the use of important corporate franchises. This is more distinctly the result of race aversion than is the exclusion of the Chinese from our country. The political power given to the negro race, no matter how they may use it, only increases race antagonism. That power has, so far, greatly aggravated the opposition to them. It can never make their presence in this country, which has always been a cause of dissension, welcome to the white people.

The separation of the races under different governments will alone cure this flagrant evil, by giving to the negro race an opportunity for self government; and to the white race an unobstructed course in the accomplishment of their high destiny. The feeling of unrest among the negroes, which has made them homeless, and sweeps them in revolving eddies from one State to another, is a plain indication that they are preparing for a general exodus.

As soon as they have determined the way they would go, and have, in their own free will, concluded to depart to some other country, justice

to them and ourselves, and the behests of peace and prosperity to both
races, will call forth freely the financial aid of our people and government,
for their deliverance.

For a great deliverance it will be!

FREDERICK L. HOFFMAN

Race Amalgamation

August 1896

*Frederick Ludwig Hoffman (1865–1946) was born in Varel, Germany.
He immigrated to the United States in 1884 and began a career in the
insurance industry in 1887. He worked for companies in both the North
and the South until taking a position with Prudential as an expert on
statistics. In 1902 Prudential rewarded him by making him a company
officer. Not a professionally trained social scientist himself, Hoffman based
most of his statistical analyses on the data produced by social science
research. These statistics determined company rates and profit margins.
Hoffman was so respected that he received a gold medal for the Prudential
exhibit Insurance Methods and Results at the 1904 St. Louis International Exposition. He also lectured at various universities, including the
Wharton School of Finance at the University of Pennsylvania. His published essays include titles such as "Suicide and Modern Civilization,"
"Tornadoes and Tornado Insurance," "Medical and Social Aspects of
Child Labor," "Life Insurance as a Science," "The Jews as a Life Risk,"
and "The Portuguese Population in the United States."*

The selection included here is chapter 4 from his book Race Traits and
Tendencies of the American Negro, *published for the American Economic
Association. Appearing in August 1896, it could not have influenced the*
Plessy *decision. Nonetheless, it is an excellent summary of existing studies
conducted on African Americans. The late nineteenth century saw the rise
of the professional social sciences, such as sociology, economics, political
science, and anthropology, all of which established their credentials by
relying on detailed measurement and seemingly objective statistical data.*

Frederick L. Hoffman, *Race Traits and Tendencies of the American Negro* (New York:
Macmillan, 1896), 177–207.

Fascinated by perceived racial differences, many social scientists hoped to serve the nation by using their methods to provide a scientific basis for policy decisions aimed at solving the country's "race problem." But almost all of their research was guided by a set of assumptions that today is called "scientific racism."

Within this paradigm, different races occupied different levels on an evolutionary scale. Whites occupied the highest scale and set the standard by which all others were measured. (Not surprisingly, almost all members of these supposedly objective scientific communities were white.) Many scientists, however, used their statistics to make a further point. Africans, they argued, were a special case because they not only occupied a lower evolutionary scale than whites but also were "outcasts from evolution," incapable of ever reaching full human development. If, indeed, races were so naturally different, it seemed naive to pass laws and establish social policy aimed at racial equality.

For instance, in the preface to his book Hoffman faults the "great attempts at world bettering" that ignored studies of "racial traits and tendencies." A "vast sum of evil consequences," he warns, is the "natural result of misapplied energy and misdirected human effort." Claiming that his German origins freed him from "a personal bias" that might have influenced a native-born American on the issue of race in the United States, Hoffman offers data "free from the taint of prejudice or sentimentality." Prejudice, he implies, comes from the sectional loyalty of southerners; sentimentality from well-meaning but naive champions of black equality. Indeed, to his editors he wrote that his statistics would provide a firmer foundation for making judgments about racial relations than the "many foolish utterances" made by optimists "like Tourgée," Plessy's lawyer.

Today Hoffman's statistics themselves look foolish to most scientists. But the scientific community did not start to move from the paradigm of scientific racism until 1911, with the publication of The Mind of Primitive Man *by the German-born, Jewish American anthropologist Franz Boas. Scientific racism was further discredited by the uses put to it by Nazi Germany in its genocidal treatment of Jews during World War II. As W. E. B. Du Bois pointed out, scientific racism in the United States provided the Nazis with a powerful model. In fact, because Boas was Jewish, his books that scientifically refuted scientific racism were burned by the Nazis. But even before this racist act in Germany, Boas's work met resistance from people in the United States who believed in white superiority. For instance, when Boas's early work appeared in an*

1894 article, it was regarded as daring but "speculative" and even "unscientific."[1]

The following selection is Hoffman's statistical analysis of the consequences of "race amalgamation" or racial interbreeding. Since one of the arguments for the reasonableness of laws mandating segregation was that they would reduce possibilities of harmful interracial sexual contact, the conclusions that he draws are helpful in understanding the majority opinion of the scientific community on racial issues at the time of the Plessy decision.

In this work, the terms "colored" and "negro" have been used indiscriminately, but I have made the more extended use of the former, since the type of the pure negro is rarely met with. The race is so hopelessly mixed that it is difficult to arrive at a clear definition, and the term "colored" will probably serve as well as the awkward phrase, "persons of African descent."

Of the original African type few traces remain, and the race is largely a cross between the African and the white male; for no considerable crossing of negroes with white females has ever taken place. The instances where white women have married colored men are very rare and the few cases that occur cannot possibly have affected the traits and tendencies of the race. On the other hand, the infusion of white blood, through white males, has been widespread, and the original type of the African has almost completely disappeared. A small settlement near Mobile, Ala., a few years ago was asserted to have preserved the purity of the race: but I am informed by Dr. D. T. Rogers, the health officer of Mobile, that this is no longer true.[2] It is therefore a question of great

[1] See Melville J. Herkovits, *Franz Boas* (New York: Scribner's, 1953), 4, and William Benjamin Smith, *The Color Line* (New York: McClure, Phillips, 1905), 131. [Editor's note. All notes are Hoffman's unless identified otherwise.]

[2] This settlement consisted originally of thirty full blooded Dahomeyans, brought over in the "Clothilde" in 1859, the last cargo of slaves brought to this country. They were exceedingly fine specimens of the native African and in the course of a few years became an industrious, peaceable community. For a considerable period no intercourse with the native colored population took place, but of late years they have mixed and intermarried with the latter. The result of this inter-marriage is given fully in the following extracts from a letter of Dr. Rogers, written from Mobile, Ala., Dec. 18, 1895, who kindly investigated the matter for me. "The settlement is located about three miles from Mobile. Some years ago they all lived together on their own land, which was given to them, but in the course of time, as they married, they have moved away from the old place and now are scattered over a section of about two square miles. The old original Africans were fine specimens of the African race, all being tattoo marked and speaking their own language. They are large, well developed and healthy, and in this respect superior to the other colored people. They have largely married among themselves but also among other

importance to know what influence, favorable or otherwise, the infusion of white blood has had on the physical, moral and mental characteristics of the race. It is of further importance to ascertain, if possible, whether there is a decided tendency towards a mixture of the two races, and if so, whether this tendency is in the direction of lawful marriage or of concubinage and prostitution.

It is an open question whether crossing leads to the improvement or deterioration of races. There is no agreement amongst high authorities. Gobineau maintains that intermixture of different races leads to final extinction of civilization. Serres and others maintain that crossing of races is the essential lever of all progress.[3] Topinard holds that crossing of races anthropologically remote does not increase fecundity; while M. Quatrefages holds the contrary opinion. Nott, Knox and Perrier hold that intermixture of races would lead to decay, while M. Bodichon declares that the era of universal peace and fraternity will be realized by crossing. The latter opinion is shared by Waitz, Deschamps, and many others.

But it would seem that the majority of the writers draw their conclusions from insufficient evidence and isolated cases of fecundity or sterility, which had little or no bearing upon the future progress of the races. I have failed to find in any of the works on Anthropology a statement of facts which would warrant definite conclusions one way or the other.

The imperfect state of vital statistics, even at the present time, makes it difficult if not impossible to settle scientifically the question of increase or decrease in fecundity. This question would seem to have been the main object of the many inquiries in regard to the effect of crossing, and the physiological effects seem to have been generally ignored. Not one of the many writers on the subject deals in a satisfactory way at all with the comparative vitality of mixed races, and although many statements as to comparative mortality are made, they are usually based on insufficient evidence. Finally, it would seem that past inquiries have been directed rather to establishing one theory or another as to the unity or plurality of the human race, than to the far more important end of proving in a scientific way whether a race has actually been benefitted intellectually, morally, or physically by crossing. Again, the distinction pointed

---

colored people in this section. The increase in the population has not been greater than that of the native colored people. *The offspring of those who have married native born colored persons exhibit characteristics of an inferior physique to those of the original Africans and they do not enjoy good health.*"

3 Waitz, "Anthropology," p. 347

out by Topinard has not been sufficiently drawn, that there is or may be a wide difference in the effects of crossing of races anthropologically remote from each other, as compared with races which have arrived at about the same stage of development.

That races of similar culture and physical and psychical development can intermarry to mutual advantage is too patent a fact to need instances in its support. That the children of mixed parentage of Indo-Germanic stock, irrespective of nationality, are superior to the parents, is a fact which we observe in every day life. But it is an entirely different matter when Germans and Italians, English and Spaniards, Swedes and Turks intermarry and have children.[4] And it may be said, only with emphasis, that the cross-breed of white men and colored women is, as a rule, a product inferior to both parents, physically and morally. Waitz himself expresses the opinion that "with regard to sexual intercourse and the quality of the offspring there exists both in individuals, as well as between different nations, not exactly antipathy, but incompatibility which though not explicable as to its origin, is sufficiently established."[5]

That such antipathy does exist is sufficiently proven by the fact that white women of this country do not and never have shown a decided inclination to marry negroes, and the most careful inquiry fails to show that there has been developed any tendency towards a change in their attitude. The underlying cause for this antipathy is what Westermark calls "the law of similarity," which, according to this eminent writer "does more than anything else to maintain the separation of the different classes." "A civilized race," he writes, "does not readily intermingle with one less advanced in civilization, for the same reasons which prevent a lord from marrying a peasant girl. And, more than anything else, . . . the enmity, or at least the want of sympathy, due to differences of interests, ideas and habits, which so often exists between different peoples or tribes, helps to keep the races separate."[6]

Again, "Affection depends in a very high degree upon sympathy. Though distinct aptitudes, these two classes of emotions are most intimately connected: affection is strengthened by sympathy and sympathy is strengthened by affection. Community of interest, opinions, sentiments of culture and mode of life, as being essential to close sympathy, is therefore favorable to close affection. The contrast must not be so

---

[4] *Journal of the Royal Statistical Society,* 1865, pp. 274–75.
[5] "Introduction to Anthropology," by Dr. Theodore Waitz, (London, 1863,) Vol. I, p. 185.
[6] "Human Marriage," p. 282.

great as to exclude sympathy."[7] Finally, "want of sympathy prevents great divisions of human beings, such as different races or nations, hereditary castes, classes and adherents of different religions . . . from intermarrying, even where personal affection plays no part in the choice."[8]

There would seem therefore to be in operation a most powerful cause, which for ages to come will make amalgamation of the white and colored races, in this country at least, an impossibility. "Between him (the negro) and the white, the race antipathy seems too strong for any great degree of amalgamation ever to take place while the mulatto has the infertility of a hybrid."[9] But we have to face the fact that the races do mix in spite of the effect of the law of similarity which makes intermarriage of such rare occurrence. The crossing of the white and colored races in this country is, therefore, not within the lawful bounds of marriage, but outside of the pale of the moral law. That an immense amount of concubinage and prostitution prevails among the colored women of the United States is a fact fully admitted by the negroes themselves. It is most prevalent, as is natural, in the large cities, but exists also to a large extent in the rural portions of the country. Of the two evils, prostitution for gain prevails the more widely, and it is but natural that we should find on investigation that the inevitable consequences of a life of sexual immorality have very seriously affected the physical and moral characteristics of the colored race.

These consequences fall most heavily on the offspring. The children of colored women and white men, of whatever shade of color, are morally and physically the inferiors of the pure black. It has been stated by Nott and proved by subsequent experience, that the mulatto is in every way the inferior of the black, and of all races the one possessed of the least vital force. I cannot do better than give in full the opinions of the examining surgeons of the army during the war, as to the vitality and general physical condition of the mulatto. The following are excerpts from the report of the Provost-Marshal General.

There are few if any pure Africans [in Vermont], but a mixed race only. They probably lose in vitality what they gain in symmetry of form by admixture; they die early of scrofula[10] or tuberculosis.[11]

[7] "Human Marriage," p. 362.
[8] Ibid, p. 544.
[9] Charles Morris, "The Aryan Race," p. 316.
[10] Tuberculosis of the lymph nodes. [Editor's note.]
[11] Page 192, B. F. Morgan, M. D., Rutland, Vt.

Although I have known some muscular and healthy mulattoes, I am convinced that, as a general rule, any considerable admixture of white blood deteriorates the physique and impairs the powers of endurance, and almost always introduces a scrofulous taint.[12]

I believe a genuine black far superior in physical endurance to the mulatto or yellow negro; the last named are with few exceptions, scrofulous or consumptive.[13]

The colored men, as far as my observation goes, make excellent soldiers, . . . The mulatto, however, is comparatively worthless, subject to scrofula and tuberculosis.[14]

The chief disability being, ... among those of mixed blood, a tendency to scrofula.[15]

The majority of those rejected were of northern birth and generally mulattoes.[16]

In this country the mixture [of the colored] with the whites contributes greatly to lower their health and stamina and we find comparatively few of mixed breeds who are free from scrofula.[17]

The pure Africans, that is, with no admixture of white blood, as a class were the most muscularly developed of any men examined. The mulattoes have more intelligence . . . but they were scrofulous and consumptive.[18]

The African race, when pure and not mixed with white blood, is more capable of enduring hardships . . . than the white race.[19]

The pure blooded African is in every way physically the equal to the European. . . . Their mixture with the white race deteriorates very much from their physical development.[20]

The conviction arising from an examination of a few hundred of various shades of color is that the negro proper is well adapted for military service, but that the mulatto and all varieties of mixture of black and white blood have degenerated physically, being very often found with tuberculosis and other manifestations of imperfect organism.[21]

In contrast with the foregoing opinions, in only one instance was an opinion given, which was favorable to the mixed type and that was based on only two cases, which make it of no determining value.

[12] Page 199, H. B. Hubbard, M. D., Taunton, Mass.
[13] Page 225, C. G. McKnight, M. D., Providence, R. I. [Hoffman's note.] *Consumptive* means "tubercular"; *consumption* was a common term for tuberculosis. [Editor's note.]
[14] Page 261, C. L. Hubbell, M. D., Troy, N. Y.
[15] Page 302, J. Rallston Wells, M. D., Philadelphia, Pa.
[16] Page 304, J. H. Mears, M. D., Frankfort, Pa.
[17] Page 311, R. H. Smith, M. D., West Chester, Pa.
[18] Page 353, Thos. F. Murdoch, M. D., Baltimore, Md.
[19] Page 394, J. R. Veeter, M. D., Jefferson City, Mo.
[20] Page 403, David Noble, M. D., Hillsborough, Ohio.
[21] Page 418, L. M. Whiting, M. D., Alliance, Ohio.

These emphatic opinions of qualified medical men, with abundant opportunity for observation, is fully supported by the results of the investigations of Dr. Gould. Some of the data collected by Dr. Gould have already been referred to in the previous chapter, but the following summary of comparative physical measurements of the pure and mixed races may not be out of place at this time. As regards weight, there is very little difference. The average was 141.4 lbs. for the white, 144.6 for the full black, and 144.8 for the mulatto. As I have stated before, I attach less value to this test, as applied to the colored race than to the white race, since the increase in weight is one of quantity only instead of quantity and quality combined. The average circumference of the chest was 35.8 inches for the white, 35.1 for the full black, and 34.96 for the mulatto. The difference is in favor of the full black, but too slight to be of any importance.

The capacity of the lungs, the most important of all determining factors among physical measurements, was 184.7 cubic inches for the white, 163.5 for the full black and only 158.9 for the mulatto. This low vital capacity is without question the most serious fact affecting the longevity of the mixed races, and one which explains the lower vitality and less resistance to disease than is found in the negro of pure blood. The rate of respiration is also unfavorable for the mixed race, and according to Gould is 16.4 per minute for the white, 17.7 for the pure black and 19.0 for the mulatto in usual vigor.

On the basis of these observations, the conclusion is warranted, that the mixed race is physically the inferior of the white and pure black, and as a result of this inferior degree of vital power we meet with a lesser degree of resistance to disease and death among the mixed population, in contrast with the more favorable condition prevailing among the whites and pure blacks. Morally, the mulatto cannot be said to be the superior of the pure black. In the absence of comparative statistics it is next to impossible to prove this assertion, based largely on individual observation, which may and may not be accurate.This much, however, is probably true, that most of the illicit intercourse between whites and colored is with mulatto women and seldom with those of the pure type. From such instances as have come to my notice, the few white men who have married colored females usually prefer the mulatto, and the same selection no doubt prevails among those who disregard the law of sexual morality.

Intellectually, the mulatto is undoubtedly the superior of the pure black. Of this there is much evidence sufficiently well known not to need presentation in detail. It may, however, be of value to give a few data showing the physiological changes that have taken place in the mixed races as a consequence of the infusion of white blood. In the work of Gould information is given showing the comparative cranial measurements of the pure black and the mixed type, and it is shown that as regards circumference of the head and the facial angle, the mulatto approximates the white race more nearly than the pure black. As regards the former, the average circumference of the head was 22.1 inches for the white, 22.0 for the mulatto, and 21.9 for the full black. The facial angle measured 72.0° for the white, 69.2° for the mulatto, and 68.8° for the full black. These facts are fully supported by the observations of Dr. Sanford B. Hunt, who carefully investigated the weight of the brain as affected by crossing. According to Dr. Hunt, the average weight of the brain increases according to the extent of crossing, so that the type presenting the largest admixture with the white, presents also the heaviest weight of the brain. The table of Dr. Hunt is given in full on account of its great value.

The table clearly proves that there is an increase in brain weight with an increase in the proportion of white blood, and this fact agrees with what we should expect from the greater circumference of the head and the larger facial angle of the mulatto as compared with the pure negro. We have, therefore, the contrast of the mulatto being physically and possibly morally the inferior of the pure blooded negro, while intellectually he is the superior.

This statistical fact could easily be supported by numerous instances of exceptional individual progress, which as a rule has been made by those who had a large proportion of white blood in their veins. But important as these exceptional instances may be, they must not be compared, as they too often are, with the intellectual progress of the

Weight of the Brain of White and Colored Soldiers[22]

NO. OF CASES	DEGREE OF COLOR	WEIGHT OF BRAIN	
24	whites	1424	grammes
25	three parts white	1390	
47	half white	1334	
51	one-fourth white	1319	
95	one-eighth white	1308	
22	one-sixteenth white	1280	
141	pure negroes	1331	

[22] *Anthropological Review,* VII, "The Negro as a Soldier."

whites. I cannot do better in illustration of this point than to quote Vogt's remarks on the well known case of Lille Geoffroy, who was the offspring of a Frenchman and a negro woman of Martinique: "As a proof in favor of the scientific and artistic capacity of the negro, we find cited in nearly all works the instance of Mr. Lille Geoffroy, of Martinique, an engineer and mathematician and correspondent member of the French Academy. The fact is that the mathematical performances of the above gentleman were of such a nature that, had he been born in Germany of white parents, he might, perhaps, have been qualified to be a mathematical teacher in a middle class school or engineer of a railway; but having been born in Martinique, of colored parents, he shone like a one-eyed man among the totally blind. M. Lille besides, was not a pure black but a mulatto."[23]

This distinction, so ably pointed out, is almost always lost sight of in discussions on the intellectual progress, not only of the mulatto, but also of the negro. Yet it is the most important, since it alone will separate the real from the unreal.[24]

I may state here that together with an increase in so-called education there has not been as much progress in morality as would take place if the education were genuine and not, as it is in fact, a mere varnish of questionable value. And for this reason the mere fact that there has been an increase in brain weight, in cranial capacity, is of very little importance as compared with the fact that there has been a decrease in vital force by reason of the infusion of white blood. It is only another illustration of the fact that when a race of a lower degree of civilization comes in contact with a superior race it will first imitate the superior race in the external, I might say the ornamental, characteristics, rather than in the useful and permanent. Thus the long heel of the negro has decreased from 0.82 inches in the black to 0.57 inches in the mulatto, compared with 0.48 inches in the white. The same has been shown to be true as

[23] Vogt, "Lectures on Man," pp. 192–3.
[24] The remarks of Vogt are applicable to the numerous recent instances where degrees from colleges and universities, and honors as class orators, have been conferred upon negroes who, had they been white men, would never had been for an instant considered deserving of such exceptional appreciation of their intellectual efforts. Honors thus easily gained by members of the colored race, must in the end prove more of a hinderance than a help to real intellectual progress, since the distinction thus conferred is out of proportion to the efforts or achievements by the person thus distinguished. The consequences of such utterly unjustifiable action on the part of great institutions of learning are met in the excessive laudations of their own intellectual or other efforts on the part of the negro writers themselves, and a want of genuine respect for great learning and hard and unremitting mental labor. And as a result the more subtle and important effects of education and the higher life are lost, and only vanity and foolish pride of race are fostered.

regards the facial angle, which is of no possible value as a vital factor. Other points could be given to show that in the least important physical characteristics the mixed race has a tendency to resemble the white, while in the more important, that is in vital and moral characteristics, it is inferior even to the pure black.

On the strength of the foregoing facts and observations, the conclusions would seem warranted that the crossing of the negro race with the white has been detrimental to its true progress, and has contributed more than anything else to the excessive and increasing rate of mortality from the most fatal diseases, as well as to its consequent inferior social efficiency and diminishing power as a force in American national life.

If the above conclusion is accepted, it is of no small importance to ascertain whether the tendency of the race is towards amalgamation or isolation. It was brought out in the first part of this work that there is a positive tendency on the part of the colored population in the rural sections of the South to congregate in counties where the race is most numerous. For the large cities the same tendency was shown in the congregation of the colored population in a few wards, usually the worst sections of the city from a sanitary or moral standpoint. It was also shown, for Chicago at least, that this congregation was towards the section containing large numbers of houses of ill-fame, and the conclusion is inevitable that the majority of the colored living in this section were directly or indirectly connected with this lowest phase of city life. Hence, as regards the large cities, it is doubtful whether the congregation of the negroes into a few wards indicates a tendency towards race isolation and race purity. If in this connection we take into consideration the further fact that in the colored race the females outnumber the males more greatly than is true for the white race, the conclusion seems fairly warranted that large numbers of colored women who drift from the country into the cities, from whatever cause, adopt a life of prostitution for gain. And for this unfortunate social fact, the lower classes of white men are almost entirely responsible. For while irregular sexual relations between the two sexes of the colored race prevail all over the South, it is more in the nature of concubinage than prostitution for gain. That lawful marriage between the two races is rare and of even less frequent occurrence now than thirty years ago, will presently be shown by such statistics as I have been able to collect. Before I consider the available data, I wish to deal briefly with the theory of race amalgamation as it has been advocated with more or less persistency during the present century.

One of the earliest discussions on the subject of the gradual absorption of the colored race of this country by the whites, I have met with in the *Edinburg[h] Review* for 1827, which contains the following state-ment: "We entertain little doubt that when the laws which create a distinction between the races shall be completely abolished, a very few generations will mitigate the prejudices which those laws have created and which they still maintain. . . . At that time, the black girl who, as a slave would have attracted a white lover, will, when her father gives her a good education and can leave her a hundred thousand dollars, find no difficulty in procuring a white husband."

The laws which made a distinction between the races have been abolished, and at least one generation has passed since then, but the two races are to-day more than ever removed from amalgamation by means of lawful marriage. Even the wealth of a colored girl would not procure for her a *good* white husband. A marriage for a consideration would, of course, be a return to marriage by purchase, which, fortu-nately, is gradually passing away. A "lover" who would be attracted by a $100,000 girl would be such in name only.

Lyell,[25] in 1849, expressed a similar opinion in the following words: "This incident [the runaway match of a white man with a mulatto seam-stress] is important from many points of view, and especially as proving to what an extent the amalgamation of the two races would take place, if it were not checked by artificial prejudices and the most jealous and severe enactments of law."[26]

But the most determined attempt to create a national sentiment in favor of race assimilation on a large scale was made during the period of the war by a Mr. Croly and others, who brought together in a pamphlet their views on the subject, views which were fully shared by the more zealous advocates of the abolition of slavery. Thus Mr. Wendell Phillips[27] in his Fourth of July oration of 1863, advocated "amalgamation to the fullest extent." Mr. Theodore Tilton,[28] editor of the *Independent,* in a

---

[25] Sir Charles Lyell (1797–1875), the author of *Principles of Geology,* was the leading geologist of Victorian Britain. [Editor's note.]

[26] "Second Visit to the United States," (New York, 1849), Vol. II, p. 216.

[27] Wendell Phillips (1811–1884), from Massachusetts, was a major figure in the antislavery movement. After the Civil War he devoted himself to prohibition, penal reform, women's suffrage, better treatment of Native Americans, and the labor movement. [Editor's note.]

[28] Theodore Tilton (1835–1907), from New York, was the managing editor of the Congregationalist journal the *Independent.* He took a radical stand on Reconstruction and supported women's suffrage. His career was ruined by the national publicity about the trial resulting from his suit against his friend Henry Ward Beecher, the famous minister, for committing adultery with his wife, Elizabeth Tilton. In 1883, Tilton left the United States for Europe, never to return. [Editor's note.]

speech expressed himself as follows: "I am not advocating the union of whites and blacks. This is taking place without advocacy. It neither waits for the permission of an argument in favor of it nor stays at the barrier of an argument against it. I am often asked, 'would you marry a black woman?' I reply . . . I have a wife already and, therefore, will not. I am asked, 'do you think a white man ought ever to marry a black woman?' I reply, when a man and a woman want to get married, it is their business, not mine or anybody else's." And again by the same writer: "The history of the world's civilization is written in one word — which many are afraid to speak — many afraid to hear — and that is amalgamation."

But neither Mr. Phillips nor Mr. Tilton went as far as the authors of "Miscegenation," who advocated complete amalgamation not only of whites and blacks but also of whites and Chinese and all other races of whatever state of culture.

> All that is needed to make us the finest race on earth is to engraft upon our stock the negro element, which Providence has placed by our side on this continent. Of all the rich treasures of blood vouchsafed to us, that of the negro is most precious because it is the most unlike any other that enters into the composition of national life.
>
> The white people of America are dying for want of fresh blood. They have bone and sinew, but they are dry and shriveled for lack of the healthful juices of life.
>
> The fact may be startling, but the student of ethnology will be willing to admit that in course of time the dark races must absorb the white.
>
> Let the war go on, until church and state and society recognize not only the propriety but the necessity of the marriage of white and black . . . in short, until the great truth shall be declared in our public documents and announced in the messages of our Presidents, that it is desirable that the white man shall marry the black woman and the white woman the black man. . . . It is only by the infusion into the very system of the vital forces of a tropical race, that the white race may regain health and strength.[29]

It is not necessary to comment on any of the foregoing utterances. They are reproduced for the purpose of showing, that, for a time at least, the complete absorption of the negro by the white race, or of the white by the negro race, was seriously discussed and advocated by some of the foremost men of the day.

The fundamental error, which underlies the argument in favor of race assimilation or absorption, has been pointed out in the beginning. To

---

[29] "Miscegenation," by D. G. Croly and others. New York, 1864.

ignore the law of similarity would, in itself, lead to disastrous consequences. It is, for instance, a well known fact that a lower fecundity prevails in the case of marriages between Jews and Christians than for marriages among persons of the same creed. This is at[t]ributed by Walcker [30] to the dissimilarity of the two contracting parties, the disappointment which follows such unions on account of the inability of the Christian to adopt the mode of living or sympathize with the inner life of the Jew and *vice versa*. That is to say, the barriers which make marriages of Jews and Christians less fruitful are psychological rather than physiological. It has been found that the number of children to a marriage was 4.35 where both persons were of the same religion (Christian), but only 1.58 where the father was Christian and the mother a Jewess. When both were Jews the number of births to a marriage was 4.21, but only 1.78 where the father was evangelical, and 1.66 where the father was a Catholic.[31]

After all the centuries of contact of the Jews with Christians only about five per cent of them marry persons of any other religion than their own. In Algeria, intermarriages of Jews with Christians are not on the increase and the same has been said of the Jews in other countries.[32] Yet the differences that separate the Jew from the Gentile are as nothing compared with the gulf that separates the white from the colored race. Frequently as races have intermixed with one another they have been usually of types of similar degree of culture and mental development.

Among more recent writers, Dr. Leffingwell has advanced the opinion that "before half a dozen centuries have expired, the African will have as completely merged his race in the three hundred millions of people on the American continent as Phenician and Greek, Saracen, Roman and Norman have blended into the Neapolitan who basks in the sunshine of San Lucia."[33]

The few generations of the editor of the *Edinburgh Review* have been expanded by Dr. Leffingwell into a few centuries. The former have passed and no amalgamation has taken place, nor are there any indications whatever that a few centuries will accomplish what has not been

---

[30] Dr. Karl Walcker, "Grundriss der Statistik" (Berlin, 1889), p. 138.

[31] *Journal of the American Statistical Association,* vol. III, p. 245.

[32] Marriages of Jewish women to European men, 1888–90, 26 cases; 1891–3, 20 cases. Marriages of Jewish men to European women, 19 cases during the first three years; 15 cases during the last three years. Only one marriage of a Jewish woman to a Mussulman [Muslim] is recorded during the six year period and none between a native woman and a Jewish man. For further details see "Statistique Générale de l' Algérie," Alger, 1891 and 1894.

[33] "Illegitimacy," p. 75.

accomplished thus far. The opinion of Dr. Leffingwell, that as a matter of course "the greater part of this change (from pure to mixed races) will be effected by lawful marriage" is not supported by a single statistical fact. Evidence of this will be produced farther on, when it will be shown that intermarriage between the two races is less frequent now than ever before, although it has been at all times of rare occurrence.

Mr. T. T. Fortune, the editor of the New York *Age,* (a paper devoted to the interest of the colored race), at the Africa Congress of the Atlanta Exposition, expressed his view in the following words: "The minority race alongside a majority race is destined to be absorbed by the majority race. If the white race did not want to absorb the black it ought to have left it in Africa. If the white man did not want to be absorbed by the black race it ought to have staid out of Africa."

In contrast with the view of Dr. Leffingwell and Mr. Fortune, we have the opinion of Dr. Alexander, the author of a history of African colonization, who wrote fifty years ago: "Two races of men, nearly equal in numbers, but differing as much as the whites and blacks, cannot form one harmonious society in any other way than by amalgamation; but the whites and blacks in this country by no human efforts, could be amalgamated into one homogeous [sic] mass in a thousand years."[34] Mr. Bruce, in his work, "The Plantation Negro as a Freeman," asserts, that illicit sexual intercourse between the two races has diminished since the war.

> A far more remarkable evidence of social antipathy of the white people to the negro is the fact that illicit sexual intercourse between the races has diminished so far as to have almost ceased outside the cities and towns, where the association being more casual, is more frequent. This is due to the attitude of the whites, for the negresses are less modest as a class than they were before the abolition of slavery, since they are now under no restriction at all. In consequence of this reserve on the part of the white men, the mulattoes are rapidly decreasing in numbers with the progress of time, and the negroes as a mass are gradually but surely reverting to the African type. . . . As his skin darkens in its return to that of his remote ancestors, the prospects of blacks and whites lawfully mixing their blood fades to the thinnest shadow of probability. . . . The few white women who have given birth to mulattoes have always been regarded as monsters; and without exception they have belonged to the most impoverished and degraded caste of whites, by whom they are scrupulously avoided as creatures who have sunk to the level of the beasts of the field.[35]

---

[34] "A History of Colonization on the West Coast of Africa," (Philadelphia, 1846), p. 17.
[35] Bruce, "The Plantation Negro as a Freeman," pages 53–55.

The opinion of Mr. Bruce is accepted by Mr. Bryce,[36] who also holds that there is less intercourse between the white male and the colored female under conditions of freedom than there was under slavery. In the *Scottish Geographical Magazine,* he expresses his opinion, which is in marked contrast with the view of those who believe in the possibility of an extensive race amalgamation.

> Nothing better illustrates the assimilative power of a vigorous community than the way in which the immigrants into the United States melt like sugar in a cup of tea, and see their children grow up no longer Germans or Norwegians or even Irish or Italians or Czechs, but Anglo-Americans. With the negroes, on the other hand, there is practically no admixture; and so far as can be foreseen they will remain, at least in the sub-tropical part of the South, distinctly African in their physical and mental characteristics for centuries to come. The same remark holds true of the white and black races of South Africa, where the process of blood mixture, which went on to some extent between the Dutch and the Hottentots, has all but stopped.[37]

According to Mr. Bryce there is therefore to be observed not only a decrease in the tendency towards mixture of the white and colored races in this country, but also as between the whites and blacks of South Africa. Hence, neither do the whites absorb the negroes of this country, nor the negroes of Africa the whites who have settled there.

Instances where two or more races have dwelt together for ages without amalgamation are frequent and need not be dwelt upon at length here. According to Mr. Westermark, "marriages between Lapps and Swedes rarely occur, being looked upon as dishonorable by both peoples. They are equally uncommon between Lapps and Norwegians and it rarely ever happens that a Lapp marries a Russian." Count de Gobineau, according to Westermark remarks that "not even a common religion and country can extinguish the herditary aversion of the Arab to the Turk, of the Kurd to the Nestorian of Syria, of the Magyar to the Slav."[38]

[36] James Bryce (1838–1922) was a British politician and diplomat. He was Regius Professor of Civil Law at Oxford from 1870 to 1893, during which time he wrote his well-known analysis of American society *The American Commonwealth* (1888), which includes a section on race relations. In 1891 he was asked by the *North American Review* to contribute an essay, which he titled "Thoughts on the Negro Problem." In 1897 he wrote *Impressions of South Africa,* which included a comparison of South Africa's "race problem" with that of the United States. He was the British ambassador to Washington from 1907 to 1913. [Editor's note.]

[37] "Assimilation of Races in the United States," etc., Professor James Bryce in *Scottish Geographical Magazine,* 1892. Reprinted in Smithsonian Report, 1893, page 586, *et seq.*

[38] "Human Marriage."

An interesting instance is presented in the case of the Ainos of Japan, who are a distinct race from the Japanese, and who, after centuries of close association, are as distinct in their character and habits of life as if they had never come in contact with the superior race of Japanese. It is said that the Ainos, being unable to affiliate more closely with the Japanese, are doomed to extinction. The half castes die out with the third or fourth generation and the children of Japanese and Ainos are never vigorous and healthy.[39]

The Eurasian race of India present almost identically the same problem as the negroes of this country. According to Sara J. Duncan there is no remote chance of its ever being re-absorbed by either of its original elements, the prejudices of both Europeans and natives being far too vigorous to permit intermarriage with a race of people who are neither one nor the other. I may be permitted to give here the consequences of such intermixture of Europeans with Indians in Calcutta, where some 20,000 of Eurasians live.

> It is a hard saying, but it suffers little contradiction, that morally the Eurasians inherit defects more conspicuously than virtues from both races from which they spring. Drunkenness is not common among them, nor is brutality. . . . But their indolence and unthrift are proverbial, as are their cupidity and instability of character. . . . The social evil among the lower classes is very hideous. They seem to have a code of their own, which is capable of infinite infraction, and they touch a level of degradation which is far lower than any reached by the pure heathen about them. This is apparently an ineradicable thing, for it has its root in physical inheritance and its reason is racial.[40]

In the West Indies the coolies of Trinidad do not mix with the negro or the mulatto. According to Froude they are proud and will not intermarry with the African.[41] According to the registrar-general of Trinidad "very few East Indian women have intermarried with the native colored population in which the gradations from white to black are so fine that no census enumeration by complexions has been attempted."[42]

Intermarriage of the negro with the Indian of this country has also been infrequent, although there has at all times been a considerable intermixture of the Indian with the white race. Of the evil effect of such marriages the agent in charge of the Crow agency of Montana wrote as follows:

[39] "The Ainos of Yezo, Japan," by Romyn Hitchcock, report of the National Museum, Smithsonian Institute, 1890.
[40] *Popular Science Monthly,* Nov., 1892.
[41] "The English in the West Indies," p. 74.
[42] Census of Trinidad, 1891, p. 18.

One great drawback to the advancement of these people [Crow agency, Montana] is the intermarriage of white men among them. As a rule, any white man who will marry an Indian woman is unfit to associate with the Indian. The presence of such men is a great detriment to the Indians. The average Indian is far superior to the majority of whites who marry Indian women. . . . As a rule, the full blooded Indian stands a much better chance to become a man than the half-breed. The presence of these men causes more trouble in the management of the Indian than all other causes combined.[43]

This severe condemnation of intermarriage of whites with Indians is fully confirmed by the investigations of Dr. Holden, who lived for a good many years among the Indians as Agency physician: "Tribes who have been isolated, or who have held aloof from the whites, retained their tribal relations and declared for non-intercourse with the whites, are chaste and free from taint. The tribes who have opened their arms to receive the white man have been subdued by him, have been debauched and inoculated with venereal poison." [44]

There is therefore abundant proof that there is a natural aversion between some races and that attempts to cross this natural barrier, determined by the "law of similarity" have invariably lead to the most disastrous consequences. It is largely to the frequency of illicit intercourse between white males and colored females that we must attribute the wide prevalence of syphilis and scrofula among the mixed population, as well as the excessive mortality, the lower fecundity, the increasing tendency to consumption and other tubercular diseases, the smaller chest expansion and vital capacity. All are the consequences of a union of two races in violation of a natural law — a law which superficial writers have hoped to see overcome by legislative enactment.

The following facts will prove that such marriages are becoming more and more infrequent in this country as well as in the West Indies. The table below [p. 94] will show for the state of Michigan the marriages that have taken place between whites and colored of both types, that is, pure black and mixed. The table covers a period of 20 years and is of exceptional value as indicating the tendency of the race in the direction of amalgamation by lawful marriage.[45]

According to the table before us, during a period of twenty years only 18 white men married colored females, while 93 white females were

[43] Report of the Commissioner of Indian Affairs, 1874, page 261.
[44] *American Journal of Obstetrics,* 1892, p. 58.
[45] For this table I am under obligations to the Hon. Washington Gardner, secretary of state of Michigan.

Inter-Marriages of White and Colored in Michigan —1874–1893

| | | WHITE MALES MARRIED TO | | WHITE FEMALES MARRIED TO | | |
	PERIODS	BLACK FEMALES	MULATTO FEMALES	BLACK MALES	MULATTO MALES	TOTAL
	1874–78	2	5	8	7	22
	79–83	1	2	8	12	23
	84–88	1	4	21	14	40
	89–93	2	1	10	13	26
20 years	74–93	6	12	47	46	111

married to colored men. On the basis of the number of persons married during the first ten years, there was one mixed marriage to every 6,220 persons married, as compared with a rate of one to every 7,931 during the next ten years. It is a matter of some surprise to find that the numbers of blacks and mulattoes who married white women were almost equal, indicating no decided preference on the part of the white woman for colored persons of mixed parentage; but among the white men who married colored women, the larger number selected mulattoes. This fact supports my observation that for purposes of prostitution and concubinage women of mixed blood are preferred to those of the African type.

The next two tables give the same information for the state of Rhode Island, the city of Providence and the state of Connecticut.

Inter-Marriages of Whites and Colored in Rhode Island 1881–1893

		RHODE ISLAND	PROVIDENCE
1881		No return	5
1882		No return	5
1883		6	1
1884		2	3[a]
1885		7	6
1886		7	4
1887		7	7
1888		4	4
1889		5	4
1890		3	2
1891		10	5
1892		4	3
1893		3	3
	13 years	58	52

[a] In 1884 more mixed marriages were reported in Providence than in the state of Rhode Island. I have not been able to ascertain the cause of this error, which is probably a clerical one in favor of Providence.
[b] Eleven years, 51 white females, 7 white males.

Inter-Marriages in Connecticut — 1883–1893

YEAR	NO. OF CASES	YEAR	NO. OF CASES
1883	7	1889	6
1884	4	1890	8
1885	6	1891	7
1886	6	1892	6
1887	3	1893	4
1888	8		
11 years, 1883–93, 65 cases.[a]			

[a] Mixed marriages, 1894, 10.

In the table for Rhode Island, which has been combined with the data for Providence, a numerical as well as relative decrease is shown. The rate of intermarriages was one to every 1,012 persons married, for the period 1884–88, and one to every 1,327 for the period 1889–93.[46]

For the city of Providence, in which the large majority of such marriages in the state of Rhode Island are shown to occur, the rate of mixed marriages to total of persons married was one in every 579 persons married during 1881–85, one in every 612 during the five years, 1886–90, and one in every 1,030 during the period 1891–94. For Connecticut the

[46] For Boston, I have not been able to obtain a complete record, but the table below, compiled from the reports of the city registrar of Boston, 1855–1890, will show that while mixed marriages increased to the period 1873–77, they have since remained almost stationary in numbers, and in proportion to the increase in the population they have materially declined. The registration reports for very recent years no longer contain information on this point, for, in the words of the registrar, "it cannot possibly interest anyone to know how many white persons marry colored individuals." It is a fact, not generally known, that a few years ago a bill was introduced in the Massachusetts legislature by the only colored member of that body, by which the use of the word "colored" was to be prohibited in all public documents. Considerable opposition was necessary to prevent the passage of this uncalled for measure.

Mixed Marriages in Boston, Mass., 1855–1890

	TOTAL	AVERAGE PER ANNUM
1855–1859	50	10.
1862–1866	45	9.
1867–1871	88	17.6
1873–1877	172	34.4
1878–1882	121	24.2
1883–1887	124	24.8
1890	24	24.

It is not at all improbable, however, that in some of these cases the woman were octoroons [persons having one-eighth black ancestry], passing as white when obtaining their marriage certificate.

ratio was one to every 1,951 persons married during 1883–88, and one to every 2,036 in 1889–93. On the basis of these figures, therefore, the conclusion seems fully warranted that in this country lawful marriage between whites and blacks is on the decrease.

As will be seen from the table below for Bermuda, the same holds true for the West Indies.

Mixed-Marriages in Bermuda, W. I., 1872–1895[a]

YEAR	NO. OF CASES	YEAR	NO. OF CASES
1872	5	1884	2
1873	10	1885	1
1874	11	1886	6
1875	11	1887	3
1876	21	1888	8
1877	6	1889	4
1878	10	1890	4
1879	11	1891	4
1880	10	1892	8
1881	5	1893	9
1882	1	1894	2
1883	8	1895	7
12 years	109	12 years	58

[a]Compiled from the reports of the registrar general of Bermuda, W. I., 1872–1895.

In Bermuda mixed marriages have decreased from 107 (*sic*) during the twelve years 1872–83, to 58 during the twelve years 1883–95. The rarity of such marriages in the West Indies is referred to by Mr. Froude, who cites the case of a Scotchman, the keeper of the reservoir of the water works of Port-of-Spain, who had married a colored woman, as "a remarkable exception to an almost universal rule."

That the whites of the West Indies are leaving the islands and that the proportion of whites to colored is gradually decreasing is a well known fact. It is, therefore, no surprise that in some of the islands the mixed element should gradually decrease and revert to the original type, if we accept the theory that the mixed type of the negro can only maintain itself by constant infusion of new blood. In Barbadoes the proportion of those of mixed blood has decreased from 24.5 per cent. in 1871, to 24.1 per cent. in 1891, while at the same time the proportion of pure blacks has increased from 65.5 per cent. in 1871, to 67.3 per cent. in 1891. The whites decreased during the same period from 10.0 per cent. in 1871, to 8.6 per cent. in 1891.[47] That is to say, the loss in

[47]Census of Barbadoes, 1891.

white population was made good by the pure blooded negro and not by the mulatto. Hence, neither in this country nor in the West Indies is there any decided tendency towards the amalgamation of the two races by lawful marriage.

It is an open question whether there is a decrease in sexual intercourse outside of matrimony between the males of the white and the females of the colored race. Mr. Bruce maintains, and Mr. Bryce seems to accept the conclusion, that there is less intercourse between whites and blacks now than formerly. It will always be difficult to prove this point. My own investigations indicate that there is an immense amount of prostitution for gain prevailing among the colored women in large cities. Mr. Bruce dealt entirely with the country negro as he knows him in Southside, Virginia. In such large cities of Virginia, as Richmond, and Norfolk, the conditions in the past cannot have been worse than they are at the present time. Even in the Capitol City the number of illegitimate births is more than ten times as large for the colored as for the whites. The comparative percentages of illegitimates in the total number of births were as follows:

Illegitimate Births in Washington, D.C.

	PERCENTAGE OF ILLEGITIMATE AMONG TOTAL BIRTHS	
	WHITE	COLORED
1879	2.3	17.6
1883	3.6	19.0
1889	3.6	23.5
1894	2.6	26.5
Average for 16 years	2.9	22.5

Making an allowance for an improvement in the registration of births, it is nevertheless clear that there is no tendency towards a decrease in the illegitimacy, but very probably the reverse tendency. As I have stated before, the larger amount of illicit intercourse prevails between mulattoes and whites, and hence the figures as regards the rate of illegitimacy are of some value. They are fully supported by similar information from Knoxville, Tenn., and Mobile, Ala., but want of space forbids my giving the figures here. Statistics for the West India Islands prove that there, too, immorality, as shown by the rate of illegitimate births, is on the increase, and the hopeful view of those who expected that emancipation would speedily change the former condition of excessive immorality and vice into one of virtue and chastity has not been fulfilled.[48] On the contrary, we are reliably informed that never at any time in the past was vice so flagrant and marriage treated with such indifference as at the present time.

The fact that lawful marriage between the races is not on the increase, so rare, indeed, as to have no influence whatever on the destiny of the race, does not, therefore, prove that intermixture through prostitution is less frequent now than formerly. It is my firm conviction that unlawful intercourse between the two races is excessively prevalent at the present time in the large cities as well as in the rural sections of the country.

The question may be asked, among what class of white women is marriage with colored men most frequent, and what class of white men marry colored women? It is not easy to reply to this question in a satisfactory manner. So far as I know, no one has taken the trouble to investigate this point in a scientific way, but perhaps my own investigation, based unfortunately on a very limited number of cases, may prove a stimulus towards a more elaborate inquiry.

I have been able during a number of years to collect information of a fairly reliable character in regard to 37 mixed relations of which 8 were those of white men who lived with colored women and 29 those of white women who lived with colored men.

Of the eight white men, four were lawfully married while the other four were living openly in concubinage. Three of the men were criminals or under suspicion of being such; one man had killed another for insulting remarks concerning his negro wife, one killed his mistress in a fit of jealousy, one was stabbed and horribly burned by vitrol by his colored mistress, one killed his colored mistress by slow poison to obtain possession of her property, the ill gotten gains from a house of ill-fame. The others were more or less outcasts. One was a saloon keeper, one had deserted his family for his negro mistress, two were men of good family but themselves of bad reputation.

Of the twenty-nine women, only nineteen were lawfully married to the colored men with whom they were living, while ten lived in open concubinage. So far as my information goes only five of the nine were of foreign birth, one English, one German and three Irish. Of the nineteen that were married, four were known prostitutes, two were guilty of bigamy, four either sued for divorce or had deserted their husbands. Five were apparently of respectable parentage and living in content with their husbands; while for four the information is wanting. Of the ten who

[48] "The Negro in the West Indies," *Publications of the American Statistical Association,* Vol. IV, p. 195, *et seq.*

were not married, eight were known prostitutes, one was insane and only one was known to be the daughter of respectable parents.

Of the twenty-nine colored men who married or lived with white women, only one, an industrious barber, was known to be of good character. Five were of fair repute; nine were idlers, loafers or drunkards; eleven were of proven criminal and anti-social tendencies; while for three the character could not be ascertained. Of the eleven criminals, two were murderers, three were thieves, three were guilty of bigamy, one was the keeper of a house of ill-fame, while the last two were arrested for inhuman cruelty to their own or foster children. The result of the twenty-nine cases of race mixture prove that of the women, twelve were known prostitutes, three were of ill repute, charged in addition with cruelty and abuse of children, two were murdered by their colored husbands, one committed suicide, one became insane, two sued for divorce, two deserted their husbands,[49] five were apparently satisfied with their choice, while for four the information could not be obtained. Thus out of twenty-nine instances only five gave any indications of not having been absolute failures and of the five in only one instance is the proof clear that the marriage was a fair success.

Comment on these cases is hardly necessary. They tend to prove that as a rule neither good white men nor good white women marry colored persons, and that good colored men and women do not marry white persons. The number of cases is so small, however, that a definite conclusion as to the character of persons intermarrying is hardly warranted. However, it would seem that if such marriages were a success, even to a limited extent, some evidence would be found in a collection of thirty-six cases. It is my own opinion, based on personal observation in the cities of the South, that the individuals of both races who intermarry or live in concubinage are vastly inferior to the average types of the white and colored races in the United States; also, that the class of white men who have intercourse with colored women are, as a rule, of an inferior type.

Hence the conclusion is unavoidable that the amalgamation of the two races through the channels of prostitution or concubinage, as well as through the intermarrying of the lower types of both races, is contrary

---

[49] In the first of these two cases the woman when leaving her colored husband wrote him a letter from which I give the following excerpt: "It is just two years and five months since we were united to love and obey each other, but time has changed us and I have not the least love for you any more. I have learned to love another man who wants to marry me and I hope you will give me my freedom in black and white. The love I had for you was only a childish fancy. . . . I am tired of knocking about this hard world and want to get a home, as I want to travel up the ladder and not fall down as I did. I am going on twenty years old and want to make a true and upright woman for this man that wishes to make me his wife and give me a home." (New York *Sun,* March 24, 1896.)

to the interest of the colored race, a positive hinderance to its social, mental and moral development. But aside from these considerations, important as they are, the physiological consequences alone demand race purity and a stern reprobation of any infusion of white blood. Whatever the race may have gained in an intellectual way, which is a matter of speculation, it has been losing its greatest resources in the struggle for life, a sound physical organism and power of rapid reproduction. According to Herbert Spencer[50] "sexual relations unfavorable to the rearing of offspring, in respect either of number or quality, must tend to degradation or extinction."[51] All the facts thus far brought out in this work prove the truth of this assertion. All the facts obtainable which depict truthfully the present physical and moral condition of the colored race, prove that the underlying cause of the excessive mortality and diminishing rate of increase in population is a low state of sexual morality, wholly unaffected by education.

This condition can be improved only by the development of a higher morality. Amalgamation with whites by means of lawful marriage is a remote contingency, which needs no consideration on the part of those who concern themselves with the amelioration of the condition of the colored race. The conclusion of Mr. Tucker that, "Seventeen years since the war have brought great changes to the colored race, great improvements in many things to some of them, but no change in morals,"[52] is fully applicable to the race of the present day, thirty years after the war. The fact that more than one-fourth of their children, are admitted to have been born out of wedlock, in the Capitol City of the country, where opportunities for moral advancement have been better than elsewhere, fully justifies the application of Mr. Spencer's condemnation of unchastity as "tending towards the production of inferior individuals and, if, prevailing widely, as a cause of decay of society." Unchastity, "conflicting as it does with the establishment of normal monogamic relations . . . is adverse to those higher sentiments which prompt such relations. In societies characterized by inferior forms of marriage, or by irregular connections there cannot develop to any great extent that powerful combination of feelings . . . affection, admiration, sympathy, . . . which in so marvelous a manner has grown out of the sexual instinct. And in

---

[50] Herbert Spencer (1820–1903) was the British author of *The Principles of Sociology*. A social Darwinist, he viewed all of life as a continuing development from lower to higher stages and coined the phrase "survival of the fittest" in 1864. He believed that human progress was not an accident but a necessity. [Editor's note.]

[51] "Principles of Ethics," Part II, page 448.

[52] "The Relations of the Church to the Colored Race," (Jackson, Miss., 1882,) p. 18.

the absence of this complex passion, which manifestly pre-supposes a
relation between one man and one woman, the supreme interest in life
(the raising up of members of a new generation) disappears, and leaves
behind relatively subordinate interests. Evidently, a prevalent unchastity
severs the higher from the lower components of the sexual relation: the
root may produce a few leaves, but no true flower."[53]

[53] "Inductions of Ethics," p. 463.

HENRY M. FIELD

Capacity of the Negro —
His Position in the North.
The Color Line in New England

1890

*The younger brother of Supreme Court Justice Stephen J. Field, Henry Martyn
Field (1822–1907) was born in Stockbridge, Massachusetts. His father was
a Congregationalist minister whose ancestors had immigrated to Boston in
1629. Henry attended Williams College and theology school. In 1842 he was
appointed pastor of a Presbyterian church in St. Louis. Resigning five years
later, he traveled to Europe, where he saw the worst year of the Irish potato
famine and the 1848 revolution in Paris. He returned in 1851 as pastor of
the Congregationalist church in West Springfield, Massachusetts. Resigning
in 1854, he went to New York City and bought an interest in the journal the
Evangelist, which he later controlled as owner and editor.*

*Field was a liberal and progressive influence within the Presbyterian
church, and his journal provided him with a large audience that was
increased by a series of books describing his journeys around the world
(in 1875–1876), to Asia (in 1882), and to the Mediterranean (in 1886–
1887). After these foreign journeys, Field undertook a tour of the South,
which resulted in the 1890 publication of* Bright Skies and Dark Shadows. *Under the bright skies of the South, Field declares, shadows creep,
as the palms and orange groves are disturbed by the "ghost of something
gone, that, though dead and buried, sleeps in an unquiet grave, and*

Henry M. Field, *Bright Skies and Dark Shadows* (New York: Scribner's, 1890), 131–53.

*comes forth at midnight to haunt us in our dreams": the "Race Problem."
Boasting "no superior wisdom," claiming only "a few grains of common-
sense, an earnest desire for the good of both races, and a boundless char-
ity," Field offers his observations on the problems of race and then turns
to a description of a famous battlefield, the home of Andrew Jackson,
and the graves of Confederate heroes Robert E. Lee and Stonewall Jackson. The selection here comes from this book, which draws a double lesson
from history: "to honor all the heroic dead, and to think kindly and
generously on the living."*

    *Field's views on the "Race Problem" are important for an under-
standing of the climate in which the Plessy decision was rendered because
they are those of a liberal northerner with strong religious convictions.
Attempting to be fair to both white and black southerners, Field admits
the existence of a color line in the North. He also opposes the solution
advocated by some white supremacists, like John Tyler Morgan (see `p.
62), and some blacks, like the Reverend H. M. Turner, for blacks to
return to Africa. For Field, like Plessy's lawyer Albion W. Tourgée, the
black is here to stay. "He has as good a right to be here as we have. He
was born on this side of the Atlantic. He knows no more of Africa than
we do, nor half as much. The only country he knows under the broad
canopy of heaven, is America." The only question, therefore, is "Whether
the two races, white and black, can live side by side without constant
collision?" But, as this selection reveals, Field's answer to how harmony
between the races can be achieved is much closer to the Supreme Court's
than to Tourgée's. Toward the end of the chapter, for instance, he confronts the fact that frequently on railroads "decent and well-behaved"
blacks and "even ministers of the Gospel" have been roughly removed
from cars for which they have paid full fare. "There is a plain rule of
justice," he reasons, "which ought to be recognized and enforced, viz: that
every man is entitled to what he pays for. If there be on the part of the
whites an unwillingness to occupy the same cars and to sit in the same
seats with the blacks, let them be separate; only let equally good cars be
provided for both, if both pay for them." Anticipating the logic of the
Court six years later, he concludes that the racial separation is the result
of instinct. "We cannot fight against instinct, nor legislate against it; if
we do, we shall find it stronger than our resolutions and our laws."
Racial instinct, Field laments elsewhere in his book, "hangs over the
future a veil through which no human eye can see. The final solution
must be left to God and to time."*

I should have more hope of the progress of the African in the future, if he had made more progress in the past. But his history is not encouraging. What he has done on his native continent is all a blank; but what has he done since he was transplanted to America? — for he has been here as long as the white man. The first slaves were brought to Jamestown, Va., in 1619, the year before the Pilgrims landed on Plymouth Rock. Thus the two races began their career together on the Western Continent, and yet who can for an instant compare the achievements of the one with those of the other! During the long lapse of two hundred and seventy years, the negro race has not produced a single great leader. It will not do to say that this has been because they were kept down. A great race, numbering millions, cannot be kept down. Besides, in half the country there was no effort to keep them down: for slavery in the North was abolished a century ago, and yet the same inferiority exists. I do not mention this with any feeling of pride in the superiority of the white race; on the contrary it is with extreme regret that I recognize the backwardness of my colored brethren. But I cannot draw pictures of fancy that are not borne out by facts. I must see things as they are: or at least as they appear to my eyes; and so seeing, it seems to me that the few colored people that are scattered here and there in the villages of New England, do not compare well with some splendid old types of the race whom I knew in my childhood. If the reader will indulge me in the episode, I should like to give him a picture or two of pure African genius half a century ago.

Although we of the North know much less of the colored people than those who live at the South (as they are so much fewer in numbers here than there), yet we know something of them, and I for one have personal reasons to remember them with a very strong feeling, as to one of that race I owe a debt which I can never repay, since she took me almost from the moment that I was born. When I opened my eyes on this world, almost the first human face into which I looked wore a dark skin. As my mother was very ill, and it was feared nigh unto death, I was taken away from her to the little cabin of a poor negro woman, who watched over me with a mother's tenderness; and when a few weeks later I was carried to the old meeting-house to be baptized, it was in her black arms that I was held, while my sainted father sprinkled the water on my little head, and gave me the name of an English missionary, whose fame was then in all the Christian world.

As this black woman, who was known by the name of Mumbet (a

contraction, I suppose, for Mammy Betty), was no ordinary person, I may briefly tell her history. She was born a slave, not far from the Hudson River — in what year she never knew — but was bought by Col. Ashley of Sheffield, Mass., when she was still such a child that she was carried on the straw in the bottom of a sleigh over the mountains to her home in the valley of the Housatonic. As she grew up she was noted for her activity and courage, and her high spirit, as if the blood of old African kings was flowing in her veins. She was ready to do any amount of hard work, but would not submit to cruelty, and on one occasion, when her mistress in a fury of passion struck at her sister with a hot shovel, she threw herself between them, and received the blow on her arm, that left a scar which she carried with her to her grave. From that moment she left the house; neither commands nor entreaties could induce her to return, till her master resorted to the law to gain possession of his slave. Judge Sedgwick of Stockbridge defended her, on the ground that the Constitution of Massachusetts, then recently adopted, had declared that "all men were born free and equal." The court sustained him, and declared that she was free. Thus slavery was abolished in Massachusetts, not by a direct act of legislation, but by the decision of the courts. In gratitude to her defender and liberator, she attached herself to his family, in which she remained for many years. Devoting herself to the care of his children and his property, she became his defender as he had been hers. On one occasion, in Shays' Rebellion[1] (which caused so much trouble after the close of the Revolutionary War), a party of insurgents came to the house to search for the Judge, and went into every room, running their bayonets under the beds to find him. But this old black servant, who had the heart of a lioness, confronted them at every step, following them up-stairs and down-stairs, into garret and cellar, armed with a huge shovel with which she could have dealt a tremendous blow. Hearing them speak of a favorite horse which they would take with them, she flew to the stable, and led it to the road, and then with a blow sent it flying till it was out of sight. Thus she outwitted them, and sent them away with scorn, remaining "solitary and alone," proud mistress of the scene.

But the greatest proof of gratitude to her benefactor was her devotion to his children, who, owing to the prolonged illness of their mother, were left almost wholly to the care of this old family servant.

---

[1] An insurrection of western Massachusetts farmers (1786–1787), led by Revolutionary War captain Daniel Shays to protest heavy taxation that affected many who had risked their lives to secure national independence.

Better care they could not have had. So attached to her did they become, that it is safe to say that, next to their mother, they loved this faithful creature.

It was long after the youngest of that family had been reared to manhood and womanhood, that I fell into the same loving hands, and what she did for them she did for me. Thus my acquaintance with the colored race began very early, indeed with my very existence. And though so long ago, it would be ungrateful even at this distance of years to disown the obligation.

In the village burial ground, where are gathered in one enclosure the members of that distinguished family, this old negro woman is laid by the side of Miss Catherine Sedgwick, the celebrated authoress — I presume at her request, from a natural feeling that even in death she would nestle in her old nurse's arms. On the plain stone that marks her grave is the following inscription:

ELIZABETH FREEMAN
known by the name of
MUMBET
died Dec. 28, 1829.
Her supposed age was 85 years.

She was born a slave and remained a slave nearly thirty years. She could neither read nor write, yet in her own sphere she had no superior nor equal. She neither wasted time nor property. She never violated a trust, nor failed to perform a duty. In every situation of domestic trial she was the most efficient helper and the tenderest friend. Good mother, farewell!

Was ever a more beautiful tribute paid to womanly fidelity and devotion? As I stand by that grave I think what I too owe to that fidelity which "never violated a trust, nor failed to perform a duty." As after her death, one of the Sedgwicks, paying a tribute to her memory, said, "But for her care I should not now probably be living to give this testimony," so it may have been in my case. When I think of this: that I may have owed my life to the care that watched over my helpless infancy, I cannot recall the name of that faithful woman without a feeling of love and of gratitude, that predisposes me to a kindly interest in all her unhappy race.

But the genius of those old Africans did not run wholly to the woman side. There was a man in the town who was an equally noted character. This was "Agrippa Hull," whose life began towards the middle of the last century, and who had been in the Revolutionary Army from near the beginning to the very end of the war, though not for the most part as a soldier, but a servant, in which capacity he was for four years attached to Kosciusko, whom he accompanied in his Southern campaigns. He used to tell of bloody scenes that he witnessed, especially at the hard-fought battle of Eutaw Springs, where his part was to hold the wounded as they were laid upon the operating board to have their limbs amputated — "the hardest day's work," he said, "that he ever did in his life."

These trying scenes were sometimes varied by those of a different character. He used to tell a story that reflected on himself, but showed in a pleasant light the good nature of Kosciusko. On one occasion the General had been invited by a neighboring planter to go with him on a hunting excursion, and rode off, expecting not to return till the next day. Having the field all to himself, Agrippa set out to make the most of it; and arrayed himself in his master's uniform, with the military cap on his woolly head and sword in hand, wherewith he figured as a foreign officer, even to imitating the broken English of the distinguished Pole — a performance that was greatly to the amusement of the soldiers and camp-followers; until suddenly the General, having been overtaken and driven back by a thunderstorm, rode up! Poor Agrippa was ready to sink into the earth, expecting severe punishment. But to his surprise, the General entered into the humor of the thing, and burst into a hearty laugh, adding "This is too good to keep," and immediately had his black imitator mounted on a horse, and sent through the camp, to the unbounded merriment of the soldiers. This was worse than being flogged or put in irons, and Agrippa used to say that he would rather have been drummed out of camp to the tune of the Rogue's March, than be made such a laughing-stock. However, the joke answered one good purpose, as this mirthful scene was a relief to grim-visaged war, and made a welcome diversion to the monotonous life of soldiers far from home, in the gloom of the Southern forests.

Of course Agrippa had many stories to tell of the great men whom he met at the headquarters of Kosciusko. He was very proud when now and then he had the honor of holding the bridle for Washington, as he mounted to ride to the field. It was one of the delights of my boyish days to go to the little house of this old African, and hear him tell of those times of war, with all their scenes so strange and stirring.

He had a great deal of mother wit, which shone out most at weddings and other festive occasions, when he passed round the cake and wine — for sixty years ago there could be no wedding without wine: the parties would hardly have thought themselves legally married. As he made the circuit of the company, he had some joke for every one; he even noticed poor little me, for I was then a very minute specimen of humanity, and I counted it a mark of distinction, when he patted me on the head, and bestowed his approbation in the highly musical lines —

"Henry Martyn
Is a gentleman for sartin,"

which I cherish to this day, as the first and only instance in which my name has been embalmed in poetry!

Though he knew his place perfectly, yet he could hold his own with the best of white folks; and if anybody snubbed him for his color, he would not be offended, but answer pleasantly that "many a good book was bound in black, and that the cover did not matter so much as the contents," ending the brief passage of words by asking, "Which is the worse: the white black man or the black white man — to be black outside or to be black inside?"

Agrippa and Mumbet! what a couple they make! When I think of these dear old souls, how can I help loving them? Both ripened with age, as religion came to give the crowning grace to their characters. Agrippa was not, when young, at all religiously inclined. The army was not a good school of religion or of morals, and many of those who came back from the wars were more given to drinking and cursing than to prayer. But a more quiet and peaceful life, with the influences of his New England surroundings, made him a new man; and in the prayer-meetings no one was more fervent than Agrippa. The memory of his past life seemed to be a constant source of humiliation, and his penitence showed itself in his confessions and prayers for forgiveness. Sometimes his language was a little too strong, as when he thanked God that "white folks were so kind to a poor old black nigger"; and again he used homely phrases, as when he besought the Lord "that every tub might stand on its own bottom"; which, however, was not so grotesque as the prayer of a noted Baptist preacher of the county — a white man at that — Elder Leland, who (if we may believe the rustic chroniclers of the time, and who would doubt them?) once prayed "that we might all hitch our horses together in God's everlasting stable"! But words are little where the heart is found, and quaint as might be the words of poor Agrippa, none who heard him could doubt that his prayers went up like sweet incense to the throne; and as for Mumbet, though her skin was black, her heart was white, and she too, like so many of her race, is now without fault before the throne of God.

Of course there were not many such characters anywhere. But here and there the like of this old nurse might be found in the early days of New England. Generally they were the retainers of rich families, in which they had lived for years, till they became an important, and almost necessary, part of the establishment. As I have taken one instance from my own very limited experience, I will venture to add another from fiction, inasmuch as the character is drawn from real life. Many of my readers are familiar with "The Minister's Wooing," by Mrs. Stowe,[2] the scene of which is laid in Newport: that, before the Revolution and some years after, was the chief Northern port for the importation of slaves from Africa; and here were found in the godly families of Puritan New England, servants that had been born on the other side of the ocean, on the dark slave coast; some of whom, in disproof of the common idea that native Africans are all of a low type of humanity, possessed great natural intelligence; and though, like Mumbet, they "could neither read nor write," showed such strength of character that they became the stay and staff of their households, and were "in every situation of domestic trial the most efficient helpers and the tenderest friends." Such an one was "Candace,"[3] who proved herself in her new sphere a true "Queen of Ethiopia." The first picture we have of her, presents her as "a powerfully built, majestic black woman, corpulent, heavy, with a swinging majesty of motion, like that of a ship in a ground swell. Her shining black skin and glistening white teeth were indications of perfect physical vigor which had never known a day's sickness: and her turban, of broad red and yellow bandanna stripes, had a warm tropical glow."

This robust exterior was the fit embodiment of a mind of great native independence, which did not hesitate even to wrestle with the hard theological problems of the day. As she was under the ministry of old Dr. Samuel Hopkins, the great theologian, she was put duly through the Catechism, or "Catechize," as she called it, in which there were some things hard to be understood, and some which she flatly rejected, as, for instance, being held responsible for Adam's sin, to which she said:

> "I didn't do dat ar', for one, I knows. I's got good mem'ry — allers knows what I does — nebber did eat dat ar' apple — nebber eat a bit ob him. Don't tell me!"

---

[2] Harriet Beecher Stowe (1811–1896), daughter of minister Lyman Beecher and author of *Uncle Tom's Cabin.*

[3] The original of this remarkable character, I am told, was an old servant in the family of Dr. Lyman Beecher, when he lived in Litchfield, Conn. [Field's note.] In the Bible, Candace is the queen of Ethiopia (Acts 8:27); the name may have been a generic title for all Ethiopian queens (like "pharaoh" for king). [Editor's note.]

It was of no use to tell her of all the explanations of this redoubtable passage — of potential presence, and representative presence, and representative identity, and federal headship. She met all with the dogged
"Nebber did it, I knows; should 'ave 'membered, if I had. Don't tell me!"
And even in the catechizing class of the Doctor himself, if this answer came to her, she sat black and frowning in stony silence even in his reverend presence.

From this error she was reclaimed by a personal influence which has been known to change other than dark-skinned unbelievers. It was a mysterious conversion, which came in this way:

Candace was often reminded that the Doctor believed the Catechism, and that she was differing from a great and good man; but the argument made no manner of impression on her, till one day, a far-off cousin of hers, whose condition under a hard master had often moved her compassion, came in overjoyed to recount to her how, owing to Dr. Hopkins's exertions, he had gained his freedom. The Doctor himself had in person gone from house to house, raising the sum for his redemption; and when more yet was wanting, supplied it by paying half his last quarter's limited salary.
"He do dat ar'?" said Candace, dropping the fork wherewith she was spearing doughnuts. "Den I'm gwine to b'liebe ebery word *he* does!"
And accordingly, at the next catechizing, the Doctor's astonishment was great when Candace pressed up to him, exclaiming,
"De Lord bress you, Doctor, for opening the prison for dem dat is bound! I b'liebes in you now, Doctor. I's gwine to b'liebe ebery word you say. I'll say de Catechize now — fix it any way you like. I *did* eat dat ar' apple — I eat de whole tree, an' swallowed ebery bit ob it, if you say so."

If those who read this with a smile infer from it that the faith of such a woman was a mere assent to whatever she was told, they would be greatly mistaken. Religion was the very core of her being, but it was a religion which had an African type. It did not come through the intellect, by any form of reasoning, but through the heart, and was hence far more powerful than any conversion worked out through a process of the understanding, as it enabled this poor black woman to be a minister of consolation, when the great divine, to whom she looked up with awe, would have driven a poor, unhappy soul to despair.
The crisis came in the family of Squire Marvin, in which Candace lived, when the report came that a son who had run away and gone to sea, had been lost. Far away on the other side of the world, the ship had gone down with all on board. The terrible tidings threw the poor mother into an agony of despair, which was not relieved at all,

but rather intensified, by her religious belief, for it compelled her to think that her son had not only lost his life, but his soul! The cold, hard creed of the day made light of human suffering. Human beings were but "worms of the dust," mere animalculae, cast into the great crushing machine of the Almighty decrees, to be ground to powder and blown to the winds. What mattered it? Though this "machine" crushed man to atoms; though it broke every bone in his body; though his flesh was torn and bleeding, and his very soul doomed and damned; yet the mild-eyed preacher looked on with serene complacency, believing that it was all for the glory of God, in comparison with which the happiness of the whole human race was not of the slightest consequence.

This might be orthodox divinity, but it was terrible for a mother in agony for her son. What comfort could she find in a great machine, rolling on piteously, crushing human hearts and hopes? Under this strain the poor woman was driven almost to insanity. Her husband, well meaning (but awkward and clumsy, as men are apt to be in such circumstances), came into the room, and tried to take her in his arms; but she pushed him away, with the piercing shriek, "Leave me alone! I am a lost spirit!" What followed can only be told by the writer, whose powerful pen alone is adequate to describe the scene:

> At this moment, Candace, who had been anxiously listening at the door for an hour past, suddenly burst into the room.
> "Lor' bress ye, Squire Marvyn, we won't hab her goin' on dis yer way," she said. "Do talk *gospel* to her, can't ye? — ef you can't, I will.
> "Come, ye poor little lamb," she said, walking straight up to Mrs. Marvyn, "come to old Candace!" — and with that she gathered the pale form to her bosom, and sat down and began rocking her, as if she had been a babe. "Honey, darlin', ye a'n't right — dar's a dreffül mistake somewhar," she said. "Why, de Lord a'n't like what ye tink — He *loves* ye, honey! Why, jes' feel how *I* loves ye — poor ole black Candace — an' I a'n't better'n Him as made me! Who was it wore de crown o' thorns, lamb? — who was it sweat great drops o' blood? — who was it said 'Father, forgive dem'? Say, honey! — wasn't it de Lord dat made ye? — Dar, dar, now ye'r' cryin'! — cry away and ease yer poor little heart! He died for Mass'r Jim — loved him and *died* for him — jes' give up His sweet, precious body and soul for him on de Cross! Laws, jes' *leave* him in Jesus' hands! Why, honey, dar's de very print o' de nails in His hands now!"
> The flood-gates were rent; and healing sobs and tears shook the frail form, as a faded lily shakes under the soft rains of Summer. All in the room wept together.

"Now, honey," said Candace, after a pause of some minutes, "I knows our Doctor's a mighty good man, an' larned — an' in fair weather I ha'n't no 'bjection to yer hearin' all about dese yer great an' mighty tings he's got to say. But, honey, dey won't do for you now; sick folks mus'n't hab strong meat; an' times like dese, dar jes' a'n't but one ting to come to, an' dat ar's *Jesus.* Jes' come right down to whar poor ole black Candace has to stay allers — it's a good place, darlin'! *Look right at Jesus.* Tell ye, honey, ye can't live no other way now. Don't ye 'member how He looked on His mother, when she stood faintin' an' tremblin' under de Cross, jes' like you? He knows all about mothers' hearts; He won't break yours. It was jes' 'cause He know'd we'd come into straits like dis yer, dat He went through all dese tings — Him, de Lord o' Glory! Is dis Him you was a-talkin' about? — Him you can't love? Look at Him, an' see ef you can't. Look an' see what He is! — don't ask no questions, an' don't go to no reasonin's — jes' look at *Him,* hangin' dar, so sweet an' patient, on de Cross! All dey could do couldn't stop His lovin' 'em; He prayed for 'em wid all de breath He had. Dar's a God you can love, a'n't dar? Candace loves Him — poor, ole, foolish, black, wicked Candace — an' she knows He loves her" — and here Candace broke down into torrents of weeping.

They laid the mother, faint and weary, on her bed, and beneath the shadow of that suffering Cross came down a healing sleep on those weary eyelids.

"Honey," said Candace, mysteriously, after she had drawn Mary out of the room, "don't ye go for to troublin' yer mind wid dis yer. I'm clar Mass'r James is one o' de 'lect; and I'm clar dar's consid'able more o' de 'lect dan people tink. Why, Jesus didn't die for nothin' — all dat love a'n't gwine to be wasted. De 'lect is more'n you or I knows, honey! Dar's de *Spirit* — He'll give it to 'em; an' ef Mass'r James *is* called an' took, depend upon it de Lord has got him ready — course He has — so don't ye go to layin' on your poor heart what no mortal cretur can live under, 'cause, as we's got to live in dis yer world, it's quite clar de Lord must ha' fixed it so we *can,* and ef tings was as some folks suppose, why, we *couldn't* live, and dar wouldn't be no sense in anyting dat goes on."

This was the very oil of consolation poured on the wounds and bruises of that great agony. The poor black woman had done what the learned theologian could not do. To the mother in her anguish, this simple Gospel was better than the whole Hopkinsian theology. What does one care for any "system" when the heart is breaking? It needs only to be brought into the immediate presence of Christ the Consoler. It is one great gift of the African nature, that it takes hold of the Living Person, rather than of the abstract idea. It does not come to its perfect trust by any logical process, but by the instinct of love and gratitude, clinging to the Master as a shipwrecked sailor clings to the life-boat in a stormy sea. There are times when the tropical fervor of the African "fuses" the Gospel so as to take in its vital glow and heat when the larger brain of the Anglo-Saxon would remain cold and insensible.

These are pleasant pictures to dwell upon of the colored race in the early days of New England, recalling as they do the sweet Arcadian simplicity of that olden time which has passed away. Who of my readers has not known such dear old saints in black, who have long since "gone to glory," and who that remembers them can help feeling the warmest regard for this simple and affectionate race?

From the past we turn to the present, and ask for the children of these fathers and mothers. With such grand characters as examples, they would seem to need only to have their limbs unbound by the abolition of slavery, to start forward in a career of progress that should furnish the decisive proof of the capacity of the African race. And yet here we are doomed to a great disappointment. The black man has had every right that belongs to his white neighbor: not only the natural rights which, according to the Declaration of Independence, belong to every human being — the right to life, liberty, and the pursuit of happiness — but the right to vote, and to have a part in making the laws. He could own his little home, and there sit under his own vine and fig-tree, with none to molest or make him afraid. His children could go to the same common schools, and sit on the same benches, and learn the same lessons, as white children.

With such advantages, a race that had natural genius ought to have made great progress in a hundred years. But where are the men that it should have produced to be the leaders of their people? We find not one who has taken rank as a man of action or a man of thought: as a thinker or a writer; as artist or poet; discoverer or inventor. The whole race has remained on one dead level of mediocrity.

If any man ever proved himself a friend of the African race it was Theodore Parker,[4] who endured all sorts of persecution and social ostracism, who faced mobs, and was hissed and hooted in public meetings, for his bold championship of the rights of the negro race. But rights are one thing, and capacity is another. And while he was ready to fight for them, he was very despondent as to their capacity for rising in the scale of civilization. Indeed he said in so many words: "In respect to the power of civilization, the African is at the bottom, the American Indian next." In 1857 he wrote to a friend: "There are inferior races which have always

---

[4] Theodore Parker (1810–1860) was a Unitarian minister from Massachusetts. In 1848 he published *A Letter to the People of the United States Touching the Matter of Slavery*. He campaigned vigorously against the fugitive slave law.

borne the same ignoble relation to the rest of men, and always will. In two generations what a change there will be in the condition and character of the Irish in New England! But in twenty generations the negroes will stand just where they are now; that is, if they have not disappeared. In Massachusetts there are no laws now to keep the black man from any pursuit, any office that he will; but there has never been a rich negro in New England; not a man with ten thousand dollars, perhaps none with five thousand dollars; none eminent in anything, except the calling of a waiter."

That was more than thirty years ago. But to-day I look about me here in Massachusetts, and I see a few colored men; but what are they doing? They work in the fields; they hoe corn; they dig potatoes; the women take in washing. I find colored barbers and white-washers, shoe-blacks and chimney-sweeps; but I do not know a single man who has grown to be a merchant or a banker; a judge, or a lawyer; a member of the legislature, or a justice of the peace, or even a selectman of the town. In all these respects they remain where they were in the days of our fathers. The best friends of the colored race — of whom I am one — must confess that it is disappointing and discouraging to find that, with all these opportunities, they are little removed from where they were a hundred years ago.

In the above I have spoken only from my own observation, and am therefore equally surprised and gratified to find that others, with wider opportunities, find more that is hopeful and encouraging. Thus Mr. A. H. Grimké, a colored man, who is a lawyer in Hyde Park, near Boston, reports as follows:

"There are about a dozen colored lawyers in Massachusetts, a majority of whom are justices of the peace. There has been a colored man in the Legislature every year since 1882. Prior to that period, there was a colored member of the Legislature every second or third year since the close of the war. Twice during these periods, two colored men were members at the same time. Every year there are three or four colored members of the Republican State Convention, and this year there was a colored member of the Democratic State Convention as well. Mr. J. C. Chappelle is at present a member of the Republican State Central Committee. In my own town of Hyde Park, a colored man is Scaler of Weights and Measures. If you will allow a personal reference, I am one of the trustees of a public institution (the Westborough Insane Hospital), recognized as one of the most important in the State, and I am, in addition, Secretary of the Board. The expenditures of this hospital are about $100,000 a year. Judge Ruffin was appointed Judge of the Charlestown Municipal Court in 1883, and filled the position with credit to himself and the community until his death about three years afterwards. Dr. Grant is one of the best dentists in Boston, and has a large practice among both races. He is a man of inventive skill in his profession. His invention in relation to cleft plates[5] is well known here and elsewhere. Besides, he has been for years an instructor in the Dental College connected with Harvard University — mechanical dentistry being his department. John H. Lewis has a merchant tailoring establishment in Washington street, Boston, and does the second largest business in New England. His transactions annually exceed $100,000; he has just started a branch store in Providence, R. I. Mr. Joseph Lee is owner and proprietor of one of the first-class hotels of the East. The richest people of the State are guests at the Woodland Park Hotel, at Auburndale. His business is rapidly increasing, he has already enlarged the original building, and is about to enlarge a second time to meet the increasing demands of the public. The property is valued at about $120,000. Beside Mr. Lewis above mentioned, there are three colored merchant tailors doing a handsome business in Boston.

"In New Bedford, one of the largest and finest drug stores is owned and conducted by a young colored man. In that city the colored people are butchers, fruiterers, grocers, master ship-builders, etc. Colored young women have taught in the public schools of Boston within the past few years, and one, Miss Baldwin, has been for some years one of the most popular teachers in the public schools of Cambridge."

This is very gratifying: and it is from no wish to belittle its significance, that I suggest, that if it be made a test of the capacity of a race, it would be necessary to press the inquiry a little farther. Dr. Blyden,[6] who has himself no tinge of whiteness, and is very proud of his pure African blood, says: "You talk of *two* races, but there are *three!*" Such is the division in Jamaica, where they are distinguished as the whites and the blacks and *the browns;* and it is said that the browns are much more particular than the whites in standing aloof from the blacks. It is to the credit of the mulattoes of this country, that they cast in their lot with the weaker race, but in distinguishing what is due to native genius, we must recognize that it is not commonly the pure African

---

[5] Cleft palate.
[6] Edward Wilmont Blyden (1832–1912) was born in the Danish West Indies to Togo slave parents. Refused the opportunity to study at Rutgers Theological College because of his race, he went to Liberia and studied with Presbyterian missionaries. He eventually rejected Christianity as a white man's religion and converted to Islam. Known as the intellectual father of black nationalism, he urged a return to Africa. As a celebrant of "negritude," which stressed the positive aspects of being black, he concluded that mulattoes had no important role to play in black nationalism.

who comes to the front. Of this Mr. Grimké is himself a proof: for the colored men in the North who bear that honored name, have the best white blood of South Carolina in their veins. But putting every one of these to the account, how far could a dozen or two of isolated individuals, go to prove the capacity of a whole race, the mass of whom are still far, far behind?

With this experience of slow progress here in our own New England, it might be in better taste to be a little more guarded and careful in judging our brethren of the South, where the failure of the blacks to improve their condition is ascribed to "unjust laws," to "race-prejudice," to the "color-line," and to every other cause except natural incapacity or want of application. But can we truly say that they impose hardships upon the negro from which he is free at the North; that he has here rights and opportunities that are denied to him there? Do a few degrees of latitude make so great a difference in his position?

The first charge in the indictment against the South, is "unjust laws"! But what laws? Are not the laws affecting human rights the same in all parts of the country?

I am now writing in New England, where the very air that blows over the hills is an inspiration of liberty. This grand old State of Massachusetts, in which I was born, is my model of a free commonwealth, a genuine democracy of the highest kind, in which there is an absolute equality of civil rights, and the nearest approach to an equality of conditions. This is a reflection very gratifying to our State pride, all the more as it is in such contrast with what we are accustomed to think of the South, but just emerged from the barbarism of slavery.

But as I am indulging in this comparison, so flattering to ourselves and so disparaging to others, I begin to reflect that perhaps I have forgotten the changes wrought by the war: the great Act of Emancipation, and the amendments to the Constitution, which guarantee to all the same civil rights, "without distinction of race, color, or previous condition of servitude." This is broad enough to cover "all sorts and conditions of men." It is the law, not for one State alone, but for all; and hence it follows that the status of the negro at the South is precisely the same — so far as the law is concerned — as at the North; he has exactly the same rights in South Carolina, that he has here in good old Massachusetts!

The statement put in this frank, blunt way, is somewhat startling: it is what Dick Swiveller would call "an unmitigated staggerer," and we do not quite like to admit it, and would not, if the words were not so plain that there can be but one interpretation.

But here a friend, seeing my perplexity, comes to my relief by saying "Oh, well! it is not *the law* of which we complain — that is all right enough; but it is the color line that runs through everything at the South — the bitter prejudice against the black race — which is so unjust and so cruel."

This gives a new turn to my thoughts, and as I sit brooding over it, I am happy to see another friend appear, who can enlighten me on the subject. It is General Armstrong,[7] the head of the famous Hampton School in Virginia. He is a typical American; born in the Sandwich Islands, the son of a missionary; educated at Williams College in Massachusetts, which he left to enter the army, and fought bravely at Gettysburg; and at the end of the war was placed in charge of the "contrabands" who were gathered in great numbers at Fortress Monroe, out of which grew in time an institution for teaching them both to read and to work. To this he has given more than twenty years of the hardest labor, till under his care it has grown to great proportions; sending out from year to year hundreds of young men, with an education sufficient to be able to teach others; and who, at the same time, while supporting themselves by manual labor, have learned some useful industry, by which they can afterwards take care of themselves. In carrying out this grand design, General Armstrong has been a public benefactor. No man in this country has done more for the education and elevation of the colored race. No man understands better all the conditions of the Race Problem, as it is now being worked out in the Southern States. To him therefore I turn eagerly, enlarging with virtuous indignation on the "color line" that is kept up at the South and the race-hatred, when I am taken aback at hearing him say that "There is a great deal more antagonism between the two races here at the North than at the South!" "What?" I ask with surprise, almost doubting if I heard him correctly, when he repeats the remark as positively as before: "I find much more mutual repulsion between the whites and blacks here in Massachusetts than down in Old Virginia." This was another "staggerer," which set me thinking, and has kept me thinking ever since.

Is this statement true? Can it be that there is a color line in Massachusetts? Alas! I am afraid there is even here, in dear old Stockbridge, which is so near heaven that I have heard some of my neighbors say they were not impatient to make the change. It does not show itself much, because

---

[7] Samuel Chapman Armstrong (1839–1893) established the Hampton Normal and Agricultural Institute in 1868 for freedmen and, later, Native Americans. Students paid boarding expenses by working at and mastering manual arts while learning basic academic skills.

we have but few colored people; if there were more, the feeling would be more pronounced. True, they have the same rights of person and property as white folks. I never heard of their being subject to any injustice because of their color. On the contrary, if anybody were to attempt to do them wrong, it would be the impulse of many, as it would be mine, to befriend them just because they are fewer and weaker. Here then is absolute equality before the law; but that does not imply social equality, of which (in the sense of social intercourse) there is none.

In making these comparisons, we are able to strike a balance between the North and the South as a field for the negro; and now I ask my colored brother if, looking about him at the whole situation, he does not agree that, with all its drawbacks and disadvantages, he has just as good a chance to make a man of himself in Georgia and South Carolina, as in Massachusetts or Connecticut?

True, there are some things which grate harshly, such as the exclusion of negroes, even though they may be men of education, from places of entertainment — from hotels and theatres, and seats in drawing-room cars — a grievance so great that it has been thought deserving of a special enactment for its punishment. The Civil Rights bill, of which Charles Sumner was the father, and which he left on his death-bed as a sacred charge to his party to carry through Congress, made it a law that the blacks should have the same rights in hotels and on railroads as whites, disregard of which was to be punished by fine and imprisonment! As the law was soon declared unconstitutional by the Supreme Court of the United States, it fell to the ground; but if it had not, it would have been difficult or impossible to enforce it. Nor can we of the North blame the South for this: for whether the exclusion of colored people from hotels be right or wrong, just or unjust, we cannot reproach others for doing what we do ourselves. So long as negroes are not received at the principal hotels in the North, it would be a piece of pharisaical hypocrisy to require that they should be at the South. We must not try to enforce in the St. Charles Hotel in New Orleans, what cannot be enforced in the Fifth-avenue Hotel in New York!

Why, even here in New England, we find the same race-prejudice. Take our own happy valley. If a colored man were to come from the city to spend a few weeks in the country, and should apply for rooms at the Stockbridge House, would he be received? There might be no objection to him personally, but the landlord, though he is one of the most obliging of men, would say that the admission of a colored man to the same rooms and the same table, would give offence to his white guests; and that, however he might wish to do it, he could not.

As to equality on railways, there is more ground for complaint, as cases are frequently reported in which colored men, who are as decent and well-behaved as the common run of white passengers, and even ministers of the Gospel, are turned out of cars, for which they have paid full fare, with a degree of roughness and violence which has excited indignation, not only at the North, but among the best men at the South. There is a plain rule of justice, which ought to be recognized and enforced, viz: that every man is entitled to what he pays for. If there be on the part of the whites an unwillingness to occupy the same cars and to sit in the same seats with the blacks, let them be separate; only let equally good cars be provided for both, if both pay for them. In Georgia I am told that this is now required by law; but the law, it would seem, does not always suffice to protect the blacks from the violence of ruffians who invade the cars, and drive them out from seats for which they have paid, and to which they are legally entitled. Here is a case for those who have framed a righteous law, to see that it is enforced. A black man's money is just as good as a white man's, and if he pays the same fare, he is entitled to the same accommodation.

Whatever inequality there may be of rights and privileges at the South, I certainly do not mean to apologize for any wrong or injustice to the colored man. I wish simply to show that the color line, of which we hear so much, is not peculiar to one section of the country; that it exists at the North as well as at the South; and that, if we would be just, we must recognize the fact, and not ascribe what we call race-prejudice to the peculiar perversity of our Southern brethren. I ask that we judge them by the same rule that we adopt for ourselves, and that we do not condemn them for the very things of which we are guilty.

As a basis of comparison, I have taken the highest standard. New England is my mother, and my model of all that is good. I am proud not only of the freedom, but of the equality, that exists among these hills, where it matters not if a man be rich or poor, white or black. I am willing to give to the black man every right which I ask for myself; but I cannot compel my neighbor to invite him to his house; nor indeed do I feel at liberty myself to invite him to a company, in which there are those who would be offended by his presence. This would be rude to them, and would make all uncomfortable. A gentleman must be governed by a scrupulous delicacy, and that would dictate that he should not give pain on one side or on the other. Social intercourse cannot be regulated by law; it must be left to those natural attractions and affinities which the

Almighty has planted in our breasts. That the whites should desire to keep to themselves, is not to be ascribed to arrogance; it does not even imply an assumption of superiority. It is not that one race is above the other, but that the two races are different, and that, while they may live together in the most friendly relations, each will consult its own happiness best by working along its own lines. This is a matter of instinct, which is often wiser than reason. We cannot fight against instinct, nor legislate against it; if we do, we shall find it stronger than our resolutions and our laws.

BOOKER T. WASHINGTON

Atlanta Exposition Address
September 18, 1895

The most compelling account of the life of Booker Taliafero Washington (1856–1915) is his autobiography, Up from Slavery *(1901), which was translated into at least eighteen languages. Washington was born a slave on a Virginia plantation. His mother was Jane Ferguson, a cook for her owners; his father was rumored to be a white man from a neighboring farm. After emancipation his mother moved with her children to West Virginia. In most states under slavery it was illegal to teach blacks to read and write. Fascinated by this symbol of freedom, the young Washington, according to his autobiography, felt an "intense longing to learn to read" that motivated him "to walk several miles at night" after a long day working at a salt furnace "in order to recite my night-school lessons." His drive to learn and improve himself led him to the Hampton Institute, a school founded for blacks and Native Americans during Reconstruction. In addition to academic lessons at Hampton he learned the skilled trade of a brick mason.*

In 1881 Washington was recommended to become head of a new institute for blacks established in Tuskegee, Alabama, by the joint efforts of a former slave owner and an ex-slave. Under his leadership the Tuskegee Institute became the most famous school for blacks in the country. With the death of Frederick Douglass in 1895, Washington became the acknow-

Booker T. Washington, *Up from Slavery* (New York: Doubleday, Page, 1901), 218–25.

are how inferior both blacks and whites
see blacks

But why should they have to? By having to do so justimbles

ledged spokesperson for blacks. *The event that brought him national fame was a speech at the Cotton States and International Exposition at Atlanta, Georgia, on September 18, 1895. His speech is reprinted here.*

The mere fact that a black had been invited by the white organizers to speak at this prestigious affair was a newsworthy item for the national press. Washington's invitation was seen as a sign of progress in race relations. The reception of his speech signaled that whites across the country recognized him as an important figure. The speech reveals Washington's strategy for blacks to advance, as he had, toward respectful recognition by whites. Rather than pose a threat by demanding immediate political and social equality, blacks should, according to Washington, first prove themselves worthy of respect and self-government by demonstrating discipline through hard work and mastery of skilled trades. Political and social recognition would come once blacks established a firm basis in moral respectability and economic independence.

Condemned by some black leaders, Washington's accommodationist strategy was praised by moderate whites in both the North and the South, as it gave hope that blacks and whites could live in harmony. Washington received even more notice when President Theodore Roosevelt invited him to dine at the White House in 1901. But even before that highly publicized event, Washington had received a letter from President Grover Cleveland congratulating him on his Atlanta Exposition speech. Cleveland enthusiastically remarked, "Your words cannot fail to delight and encourage all who wish well for your race; and if our coloured fellow-citizens do not from your utterances gather new hope and form new determination to gain every valuable advantage offered them by their citizenship, it will be strange indeed."

This praise from a Democratic president whom Plessy's attorney Tourgée had vilified as an opponent of black rights indicates some of the political effect that Washington's speech might have had. Its style is influenced by the Bible, which Washington read every day. In its most famous passage, however, Washington uses a secular metaphor: "In all things that are purely social we can be as separate as the fingers, yet one as the hand in all things essential to mutual progress." Although Washington would speak out against the Plessy decision (see his response in chapter 3), this metaphor could be read as supporting segregation. Indeed, in 1890 Washington had protested the practice of forcing blacks to ride in separate cars, adding that "it is not the separation that we complain of, but the unequality of accommodations." As written, the Louisiana law mandated equal accommodations.

Mr. President[1] and Gentlemen of the Board of Directors and Citizens.

One-third of the population of the South is of the Negro race. No enterprise seeking the material, civil, or moral welfare of this section can disregard this element of our population and reach the highest success. I but convey to you, Mr. President and Directors, the sentiment of the masses of my race when I say that in no way have the value and manhood of the American Negro been more fittingly and generously recognized than by the managers of this magnificent Exposition at every stage of its progress. It is a recognition that will do more to cement the friendship of the two races than any occurrence since the dawn of our freedom. *, blacks will a part of*

Not only this, but the opportunity here afforded will awaken among us a new era of industrial progress. Ignorant and inexperienced, it is not strange that in the first years of our new life we began at the top instead of at the bottom; that a seat in Congress or the state legislature was more sought than real estate or industrial skill; that the political convention or stump speaking had more attractions than starting a dairy farm or truck garden.

A ship lost at sea for many days suddenly sighted a friendly vessel. From the mast of the unfortunate vessel was seen a signal, "Water, water; we die of thirst!" The answer from the friendly vessel at once came back, "Cast down your bucket where you are." A second time the signal, "Water, water; send us water!" ran up from the distressed vessel, and was answered, "Cast down your bucket where you are." And a third and fourth signal for water was answered, "Cast down your bucket where you are." The captain of the distressed vessel, at last heeding the injunction, cast down his bucket, and it came up full of fresh, sparkling water from the mouth of the Amazon River. To those of my race who depend on bettering their condition in a foreign land or who underestimate the importance of cultivating friendly relations with the Southern white man, who is their next-door neighbour, I would say: "Cast down your bucket where you are" — cast it down in making friends in every manly way of the people of all races by whom we are surrounded.

Cast it down in agriculture, mechanics, in commerce, in domestic service, and in the professions. And in this connection it is well to bear in mind that whatever other sins the South may be called to bear, when it comes to business, pure and simple, it is in the South that the Negro is

[1] The president of the Atlanta Exposition, not of the United States.

direct address to backs

given a man's chance in the commercial world, and in nothing is this Exposition more eloquent than in emphasizing this chance. Our greatest danger is that in the great leap from slavery to freedom we may overlook the fact that the masses of us are to live by the productions of our hands, and fail to keep in mind that we shall prosper in proportion as we learn to dignify and glorify common labour and put brains and skill into the common occupations of life; shall prosper in proportion as we learn to draw the line between the superficial and the substantial, the ornamental gewgaws of life and the useful. No race can prosper till it learns that there is as much dignity in tilling a field as in writing a poem. It is at the bottom of life we must begin, and not at the top. Nor should we permit our grievances to overshadow our opportunities.

To those of the white race who look to the incoming of those of foreign birth and strange tongue and habits for the prosperity of the South, were I permitted I would repeat what I say to my own race, "Cast down your bucket where you are." Cast it down among the eight millions of Negroes whose habits you know, whose fidelity and love you have tested in days when to have proved treacherous meant the ruin of your firesides. Cast down your bucket among these people who have, without strikes and labour wars, tilled your fields, cleared your forests, builded your railroads and cities, and brought forth treasures from the bowels of the earth, and helped make possible this magnificent representation of the progress of the South. Casting down your bucket among my people, helping and encouraging them as you are doing on these grounds, and to education of head, hand, and heart, you will find that they will buy your surplus land, make blossom the waste places in your fields, and run your factories. While doing this, you can be sure in the future, as in the past, that you and your families will be surrounded by the most patient, faithful, law-abiding, and unresentful people that the world has seen. As we have proved our loyalty to you in the past, in nursing your children, watching by the sick-bed of your mothers and fathers, and often following them with tear-dimmed eyes to their graves, so in the future, in our humble way, we shall stand by you with a devotion that no foreigner can approach, ready to lay down our lives, if need be, in defence of yours, interlacing our industrial, commercial, civil, and religious life with yours in a way that shall make the interests of both races one. In all things that are purely social we can be as separate as the fingers, yet one as the hand in all things essential to mutual progress.[2]

---

[2]Washington's metaphor of separate fingers and united hand may have been inspired by a speech made by former President Rutherford B. Hayes on May 20, 1880, at Hampton

There is no defence or security for any of us except in the highest intelligence and development of all. If anywhere there are efforts tending to curtail the fullest growth of the Negro, let these efforts be turned into stimulating, encouraging, and making him the most useful and intelligent citizen. Effort or means so invested will pay a thousand per cent interest. These efforts will be twice blessed — "blessing him that gives and him that takes."

There is no escape through law of man or God from the inevitable: —

> The laws of changeless justice bind
> Oppressor with oppressed;
> And close as sin and suffering joined
> We march to fate abreast.

Nearly sixteen millions of hands will aid you in pulling the load upward, or they will pull against you the load downward. We shall constitute one-third and more of the ignorance and crime of the South, or one-third its intelligence and progress; we shall contribute one-third to the business and industrial prosperity of the South, or we shall prove a veritable body of death, stagnating, depressing, retarding every effort to advance the body politic.

Gentlemen of the Exposition, as we present to you our humble effort at an exhibition of our progress, you must not expect overmuch. Starting thirty years ago with ownership here and there in a few quilts and pumpkins and chickens (gathered from miscellaneous sources), remember the path that has led from these to the inventions and production of agricultural implements, buggies, steam-engines, newspapers, books, statuary, carving, paintings, the management of drug-stores and banks, has not been trodden without contact with thorns and thistles. While we take pride in what we exhibit as a result of our independent efforts, we do not for a moment forget that our part in this exhibition would fall far short of your expectations but for the constant help that has come to our educational life, not only from the Southern states, but especially from Northern philanthropists, who have made their gifts a constant stream of blessing and encouragement.

Institute where Washington was teaching at the time. Washington used the metaphor earlier than the Atlanta speech: In an April 30, 1885, letter to the Montgomery *Advertiser* asking for equal railroad accommodations for equal pay, Washington concludes, "We can be as separate as the fingers, yet one as the hand for maintaining the right." Edward Wilmont Blyden, the intellectual father of black nationalism, praised Washington's Atlanta speech and found the metaphor "apt and expressive" and a "common one among the aboriginies of Africa." (For more on Blyden, see p. 114 n. 6.)

The wisest among my race understand that the agitation of questions of social equality is the extremest folly, and that progress in the enjoyment of all the privileges that will come to us must be the result of severe and constant struggle rather than of artificial forcing. No race that has anything to contribute to the markets of the world is long in any degree ostracized. It is important and right that all privileges of the law be ours, but it is vastly more important that we be prepared for the exercises of these privileges. The opportunity to earn a dollar in a factory just now is worth infinitely more than the opportunity to spend a dollar in an opera-house.

In conclusion, may I repeat that nothing in thirty years has given us more hope and encouragement, and drawn us so near to you of the white race, as this opportunity offered by the Exposition; and here bending, as it were, over the altar that represents the results of the struggles of your race and mine, both starting practically empty-handed three decades ago, I pledge that in your effort to work out the great and intricate problem which God has laid at the doors of the South, you shall have at all times the patient, sympathetic help of my race; only let this be constantly in mind, that, while from representations in these buildings of the product of field, of forest, of mine, of factory, letters, and art, much good will come, yet far above and beyond material benefits will be that higher good, that, let us pray God, will come, in a blotting out of sectional differences and racial animosities and suspicions, in a determination to administer absolute justice, in a willing obedience among all classes to the mandates of law. This, this, coupled with our material prosperity, will bring into our beloved South a new heaven and a new earth.

CENTRAL LAW REVIEW

January 17, 1896

This following short commentary from a St. Louis, Missouri, law journal provides insight into legal attitudes at the time of the Plessy decision. Legal mandates for separate cars, the commentary asserts, are a protective measure for blacks, providing legal remedies if unruly whites enter their cars to insult or abuse them. The implication is that "separate-coach laws" are a valuable police action guaranteeing the public peace.

In many of the Southern States the legislature has wisely provided for the separation of white and colored passengers on railroad trains, by the passage of what is known as "separate coach laws." In the transportation of passengers, prior to the enactment of these laws, the frequent disturbances arising between the two races, resulting often in serious injuries being inflicted by the one on the other, and the danger to other passengers, led to their enactment as a police regulation, in order to prevent, as far as possible, these altercations upon railroad trains, and to check the disposition of those of the dominant race to offend and humiliate those who were entitled to the protection of the law. No discrimination is made by the law in favor of the one race or the other. Each have the same facilities as to transportation, as to conveniences and accommodations, in the coach to which they are assigned. In order to make this law the more effectual, heavy penalties are imposed on the railroad companies for not having separate coaches, and upon the conductors, or those in charge of trains, for not assigning to each white or colored passenger their respective compartment.

An interesting phase of this law came up in the recent Kentucky case of Quinn v. Louisville & N. R. Co., 32 S. W. Rep. 742. There it appeared that a conductor of one of defendant's trains, whereon were separate coaches for white and colored persons, as provided by the Kentucky statute, allowed an intoxicated white passenger to enter and remain in a coach reserved for colored persons, where he created a disturbance, was guilty of obscene language and otherwise maltreated a colored passenger. It was held that the railroad company was responsible for his conduct while there and liable in damages to the passenger. The court stated that while the mere presence of the intruder into the coach for colored persons, with the knowledge of the conductor, would not give to the occupants a cause of action against the corporation, they could not concur with counsel or the court below that the separate coach law has no application to the facts of this case. If, they say, each one of the passengers had been assigned the coach required by the statute, and the white passenger had left his coach, and gone into the coach with these colored people, without the knowledge of the conductor, while he was attending to his duties in the other cars, and had there abused and insulted the appellant, it is plain no action could be maintained against the company; but when the white passenger is assigned to the cars set apart for those of another race, the company will be held responsible for his bad conduct, affecting the rights of other passengers, although the conductor may be ignorant of what is transpiring; and where the conductor, or those managing the train, knows that one is in the wrong car, it is his duty to expel him, and, by consenting to his remaining, the company becomes responsible for his conduct so long as he does remain. If a contrary rule is applied, and no liability exists on the part of the corporation to the passenger, the separate coach law becomes a dead letter, and those who are entitled to its protection have no means of enforcing its provisions but by an indictment, where a penalty may be adjudged in favor of the State.

3

Responses to *Plessy*

THE PRESS

The *Civil Rights Cases* provoked a national response. But the *Plessy* case was, for the most part, treated with neglect or apathy. A number of papers listed it without comment along with the Supreme Court's other decisions announced on May 18, 1896. Some ignored it altogether, highlighting instead decisions involving a millionaire and a well-known playwright. During oral argument the *Washington Post* noted in "Capital Chat" that Plessy's attorney was Albion W. Tourgée and, comparing Tourgée's task to the title of his most famous novel, added, "One of the visitors to the court expressed the opinion that it was another fool's errand," since the outcome was sure to be against Plessy. The black press, represented in the following selections by the *Weekly Blade,* the *A.M.E. Church Review,* and *Our Day,* did give more coverage to the case.

Surprisingly, a few pro-Democratic papers praised the soundness of Justice Harlan's reasoning in his dissent, noting, as the New Haven *Register* did, that the Court's rationale could be used to separate Catholics and Protestants. This argument is repeated in the Rochester, New York, *Democrat and Chronicle.* A reason for Democratic support of Harlan is suggested in the May 21, 1896, St. Louis *Globe-Democrat,* which remarked: "For the first time in a Presidential year since the Republican party was founded there is an utter absence in Republican gatherings" of any reference to the problem of race in the South.[1]

---

[1] Many selections in this chapter are cited or reprinted in Rayford W. Logan, *The Betrayal of the Negro* (New York: Collier, 1965), and Otto H. Olsen, ed., *The Thin Disguise: "Plessy v. Ferguson"* (New York: Humanities Press, 1967).

TIMES-PICAYUNE (NEW ORLEANS)

Equality, but Not Socialism

May 19, 1896

The Louisiana Law which requires that the railways operating trains within the limits of the State shall furnish separate but equal facilities for white and negro passengers was passed upon by the Supreme Court of the United States, and was yesterday declared to be constitutional. . . .

As there are similar laws in all the States which abut on Louisiana, and, indeed, in most of the Southern States, this regulation for the separation of the races will operate continuously on all lines of Southern railway. Equality of rights does not mean community of rights. The laws must recognize and uphold this distinction; otherwise, if all rights were common as well as equal, there would be practically no such thing as private property, private life, or social distinctions, but all would belong to everybody who might choose to use it.

This would be absolute socialism, in which the individual would be extinguished in the vast mass of human beings, a condition repugnant to every principle of enlightened democracy.

TRIBUNE (NEW YORK)

The Unfortunate Law of the Land

May 19, 1896

The Supreme Court of the United States has decided that the Louisiana law requiring separate cars for white and colored passengers on the railroads of that State is not in contravention of the Federal Constitution, and this ruling must be accepted as the law of the land. There will, however, be widespread sympathy with the strong dissenting opinion of Justice Harlan, who says there is no more reason for separate cars for whites and negroes than for Catholics and Protestants. It is unfortunate, to say the least, that our highest court has declared itself in opposition to the effort to expunge race lines in State legislation.

UNION ADVERTISER (ROCHESTER, NEW YORK)

State Sovereignty

May 19, 1896

The Supreme Court of the United States yesterday made two important decisions in affirmance of State Sovereignty "within the powers not delegated to the United States by the constitution, nor prohibited by it to the States."

The first declares constitutional the state law of Louisiana, involved in what is popularly known as the "Jim Crow" case at the South, which requires railroad companies to provide separate coaches for whites and blacks. Of the nine Justices but one dissented — Harlan.

The second declares constitutional the state law of Georgia which prohibits railroads from running freight cars in that state on Sunday.

With the expediency of these the Court had nothing to do. The question was purely one of state power. Of course, in each case, the jurisdiction of the state is over railroads operated within its own territory alone.

DEMOCRAT AND CHRONICLE (ROCHESTER, NEW YORK)

A Strange Decision

May 20, 1896

The supreme court of the United States has decided that the law of Louisiana requiring the railroads of that state to provide separate cars for white and colored passengers is constitutional. The majority of the court seems to have reasoned by analogy, assuming that if the laws of congress requiring separate schools for the two races is constitutional, therefore the laws requiring separate cars likewise comes under the protection of the fundamental national law.

Justice Harlan's vigorous dissent denouncing these laws as mischievous comes very much nearer the sentiment of the American people upon that question than the decision of the majority does. Justice Harlan says with entire truth that it would be just as reasonable for the states to pass laws requiring separate cars for Protestants and Catholics or for descendants of those of the Teutonic race and those of the Latin race.

The announcement of this decision will be received by thoughtful and fair-minded people with disapproval and regret. It is not in harmony with the principles of this republic or with the spirit of our time. It is a concession to one of the lowest and meanest prejudices to which the human mind is liable, the prejudice which draws a line between citizens and discriminates against people of a specified race and color. It puts the official stamp of the highest court in the country upon the miserable doctrine that several millions of American citizens are of an inferior race and unfit to mingle with citizens of other races.

The certain consequences of this decision will be to encourage Southern legislatures in passing other laws detrimental to the interests of the colored people of those states. Florida has a law which makes the teaching of white and colored children together in schools a crime. Under that law recently several Northern gentlemen and ladies constituting the faculty of an admirable Congregational school at Orange Park, an institution supported by the National Congregational Association, were arrested and held for trial. If there is any ground for the supreme court decision in the railroad cases there seems to be no doubt that these black laws of the Southern states regarding schools would also be sustained by that tribunal. In that case the large educational interests of the religious denominations, chiefly supported by Northern contributions and unselfish services, would be seriously affected.

This question came before the Methodist General Conference on May 9th and strong resolutions condemning the Florida law were unanimously adopted without reference to a committee. In Georgia a short time ago an attempt was made to enact a similar law, but fortunately the public sentiment of that state appeared to be too enlightened to support the movement and the bill failed.

REPUBLICAN (SPRINGFIELD, MASSACHUSETTS)

May 20, 1896

The South ought to be happy now that the United States supreme court has affirmed the constitutionality of the Louisiana law providing separate coaches for negro passengers on the railroads. The law may now be expected to spread like the measles in those commonwealths where white supremacy is thought to be in peril. Did the southerners ever pause to indict the Almighty for allowing negroes to be born on the same earth with white men? We fear it was the one great mistake in creation not to provide every race and every class with its own earth.

EVENING JOURNAL (NEW YORK)

May 20, 1896

State laws providing for separate cars for colored persons have been declared constitutional by the United States Supreme Court. The case was one which came from Louisiana on appeal against the decision of the State courts in favor of the East Louisiana Railway for compelling colored persons to ride in "jim crow" cars provided especially for their use. The road lies wholly within Louisiana, hence there was no question involving the Interstate Commerce law broached in the case. The court decided simply that the local road can regulate its local traffic, in the matter of separating the two races, according to the custom which prevails in the South. The judgment of the court is that the practice of separate cars is analogous to the laws of Congress and of many States in maintaining separate schools for the two races.

In justification of this law it is urged that while many colored people are less objectionable than many of the white race to first-class passengers, the majority of them are not only objectionable, but their presence in the same cars with the whites is a source of constant disorder. Hence it is simply a police regulation which any State has a perfect right to sanction. Of course, this decision does not interfere with the colored passengers' right to demand safe and comfortable accommodations, nor prevent them from suing for damages in the event of injury of person or loss of property.

Colored persons are entitled to all the common rights which pertain to any other persons, but they frequently exaggerate a denial of special privileges, not necessary to them, though hurtful to others, into rights. They are getting their rights; soon they will have their own privileges. They ought to deserve both, then there will be no need to appeal to the courts. In this State colored persons have the same rights in public conveyances, halls and hotels that others have, but they find it produces less friction and promotes their welfare not to use them offensively.

JOURNAL (PROVIDENCE, RHODE ISLAND)

May 20, 1896

The constitutionality of the Louisiana law for separate railroad carriages for whites and blacks has been settled. The Supreme Court of the United States declares that the principle on which the law is based is one which the State Legislatures may adopt at any time, since Congress itself has already passed such discriminative legislation in other forms. One may understand from that, inferentially, that there is no equal rights legislation to force whites to grant equality of social usage to the colored. Everybody, of course, knows that such is the fact, and yet in spite of the absence from the statute books of laws of that character, people do not cease sending inquiries to the Supreme Court regarding the constitutionality of State laws like this lately passed by the Louisiana Legislature. As was to be expected, Justice Harlan dissented from the view of his colleagues. He took the ground that it was as improper for a State to compel the colored people to separate from the white in cars as it would be for a law to be executed requiring separate coaches for Protestants and Roman Catholics. It must be admitted that that is a suggestive argument. Think of having trains on our railroads made up of some coaches for the members of the A. P. A. [American Protestant Association] and others for the religious body which they profess to fear and would like to persecute!

DISPATCH (RICHMOND, VIRGINIA)

Separate Coaches

May 21, 1896

The Supreme Court of the United States has affirmed the constitutionality of the Louisiana statute providing the separate coaches for white and colored passengers on the railroads in that State. This decision was hardly expected. It is none the less a law of the land. We quote an exchange as follows:

> The necessity for such a law exists only in the South, and the statute would never have been enacted but for conditions which made the separation of the races in railroad travel apparently unavoidable, in order to secure the comfort of all concerned. The railroads are required to supply colored passengers with accommodations substantially equal to those with which the whites are furnished, and there is thus no unfair discrimination. The matter of separate coaches has been agitated for several years in the Southern States, and it has been feared that a law to this effect would not stand the test of the courts. Now that the Supreme Court has declared the Louisiana statute constitutional, it is probable that the Legislatures of other Southern states will enact similar laws.

Some colored people make themselves so disagreeable on the cars that their conduct leads white men to ponder the question whether such a law as that of Louisiana is not needed in all the Southern States.

WEEKLY BLADE (PARSONS, KANSAS)

May 30, 1896

The Democratic majority of the Supreme Court of the United States has wantonly disgraced . . . the highest tribunal of this the land that has proclaimed it the world over that "all men are created equal" by declaring . . . the "Jim Crow" car laws of the South to [be] constitutional. When such an august body stoops so low, then it is time to put an end to the existence of infernal, infamous bodies. If such an act as the Louisiana "Jim Crow" car law can be declared constitutional then it is time to make null and void all that tail end of the constitution; for it is certain that under such circumstances it is of no earthly use. Justice Harlan was the only one on that bench with grit enough in him to utter a protest against this damnable outrage upon a race that for more than 275 years labored the yoke of bondage, but in 30 years of partial freedom has reached the very gate of the nation's most noble.

A.M.E. CHURCH REVIEW (PHILADELPHIA)
June 1896

We have here attempted to give the essential parts of each of the three arguments, that of plaintiff, that of Court, and that of the dissenting Justice. We believe such a parallel statement, in epitome, of the sides furnishes the strongest argument that can be made against the soundness of the decision.

Briefly stated, the Court virtually takes the position that any law not involving the rights of the Negro to sit upon juries and to vote, is constitutional, on the ground that race conflicts will arise, if the prejudices of large numbers of the white race are thwarted.

Justice Harlan takes the ground that the intent and purpose of the constitution was to wipe out all official knowledge of race among citizens, by both State and nation, and that greater evils are in store by validating laws made in hate than can result from standing upon the broad grounds of right and humanity.

Which is the right position? Let the great American people answer as it answered once before when plausible sophistry had well-nigh obscured the plain teachings of Him who inspired the saying, "God is no respecter of persons;" "Of one blood hath God created all the nations of the earth;" for in Christ Jesus there is neither Jew nor Greek, bond nor free, Scythian nor Barbarian.

BOOKER T. WASHINGTON

Who Is Permanently Hurt?

June 1896

The United States Supreme Court has recently handed down a decision declaring the separate coach law, or "Jim Crow" car law constitutional. What does this mean? Simply that the separation of colored and white passengers as now practiced in certain Southern States, is lawful and constitutional.

This separation may be good law, but it is not good common sense. The difference in the color of the skin is a matter for which nature is responsible. If the Supreme Court can say that it is lawful to compel all persons with black skins to ride in one car, and all with white skins to ride in another, why may it not say that it is lawful to put all yellow people in one car and all white people, whose skin is sun burnt, in another car. Nature has given both their color; or why cannot the courts go further and decide that all men with bald heads must ride in one car and all with red hair still in another. Nature is responsible for all these conditions.

But the colored people do not complain so much of the separation, as of the fact that the accommodations, with almost no exceptions, are not equal, still the same price is charged the colored passengers as is charged the white people.

Now the point of all this article is not to make a complaint against the white man or the "Jim Crow Car" law, but it is simply to say that such an unjust law injures the white man, and inconveniences the negro. No race can wrong another race simply because it has the power to do so, without being permanently injured in morals, and its ideas of justice. The negro can endure the temporary inconvenience, but the injury to the white man is permanent. It is the one who inflicts the wrong that is hurt, rather than the one on whom the wrong is inflicted. It is for the white man to save himself from this degradation that I plead.

If a white man steals a negro's ballot, it is the white man who is permanently injured. Physical death comes to the negro lynched — death of the morals — death of the soul — comes to the white man who perpetrates the lynching.

Booker T. Washington, "Who Is Permanently Hurt?" *Boston Our Day,* June 1896.

LEGAL PERIODICALS

The *Plessy* case received little attention in legal periodicals. The *Harvard Law Review* and the *Yale Law Journal* virtually ignored it. Extensive space was given in the *Virginia Law Register,* which reprinted the entire decision and added the short editorial comment reprinted here. Of the following four responses, only that of the *American Law Review* expressed sympathy for Harlan's dissent, although the *Central Law Review* did call it "vigorous." The *Michigan Law Journal* might have been interested because Justice Henry B. Brown, who wrote the majority opinion, developed his legal and judicial career in Michigan.

CENTRAL LAW JOURNAL

August 14, 1896

The case of Plessy v. Ferguson was on writ of error to the Supreme Court of Louisiana. The decision was that an act requiring white and colored persons to be furnished with separate accommodations on railway trains does not violate Const. Amend. 13, abolishing slavery and involuntary servitude; that a State statute requiring railway companies to provide separate accommodations for white and colored persons, and making a passenger insisting on occupying a coach or compartment other than the one set apart for his race liable to fine or imprisonment, does not violate Const. Amend. 14, by abridging the privileges or immunities of United States citizens, or depriving persons of liberty or property without due process of law, or by denying them the equal protection of the laws. The opinion of the court by Mr. Justice Brown shows very clearly that the distinction between laws interfering with the political equality of the negro and those requiring the separation of the two races in schools, theaters, and railway carriages has been frequently drawn by that court. Strander [Strauder] v. West Virginia, 100 U. S. 303; Virginia v. Rives, 100 U. S. 313; Neal v. Delaware, 103 U. S. 370; Hall v. De Cuir, 95 U. S. 485; Civil Rights Cases, 109 U. S. 3; Louisville, N. O. & T. Ry. Co. v. State, 133 U. S. 587. Similar statutes for the separation of the two races upon public conveyances were held to be constitutional in Railroad v. Miles, 55 Pa. St. 209; Day v. Owen, 5 Mich. 520; Railway Co. v. Williams, 55 Ill. 185; Railroad

Co. v. Wells, 85 Tenn. 613, 4 S. W. Rep. 5; Railroad Co. v. Benson, 85 Tenn. 627, 4 S. W. Rep. 5; The Sue, 22 Fed. Rep. 843; Logwood v. Railroad Co., 23 Fed. Rep. 318; McGuinn v. Forbes, 37 Fed. Rep. 639; People v. King (N. Y. App.), 18 N. E. Rep. 245; Houck v. Railway Co., 38 Fed. Rep. 226; State v. Judge, 44 La. Ann. 770; Louisville, N. O. & T. Ry. Co. v. State, 66 Miss. 662.

It will be observed that in the present case there was no question of interference with or regulation of interstate commerce. Mr. Justice Harlan dissented from the conclusion of the court presenting his views in a vigorous manner.

MICHIGAN LAW JOURNAL

1896

In the Supreme Court of the United States was decided lately the case of *Plessy* v. *Ferguson*. In this case the question at issue was whether or not an act was constitutional which directed separate coaches and accommodations to be provided on railway trains for white people and colored people and which made a passenger liable to fine or imprisonment who insisted on occupying a coach or compartment other than the one set apart for his race. The act has been held constitutional and not contrary to the Constitution Amendment 14. The opinion is by Justice Brown and a distinction is made between laws interfering with the political equality of the two races and those requiring their separation in schools, theatres, etc. The opinion shows that acts under the second class have been in many cases held constitutional.

Michigan Law Journal 5 (1896): 298.

Constitutional Law: Thirteenth and Fourteenth Amendments — Separate Railway Coaches for White and Colored Persons. — In *Plessy* v. *Ferguson,*[1] the question before the Supreme Court of the United States was whether one of those statutes which have been generally enacted throughout the Southern States since the Supreme Court of the United States declared the Civil Rights Law unconstitutional,[2] providing separate railway coaches for colored persons, and requiring the company to transport them in such coaches separately from white persons, was in contravention of the Thirteenth or the Fourteenth Amendment to the constitution of the United States. The court, affirming the Supreme Court of Louisiana,[3] held that no such constitutional right was violated, although the person complaining was a citizen of the United States of mixed descent, seven-eighths Caucasian and one-eighth African blood, and although the mixture of colored blood was not discernible in him. The opinion of the court was written by Mr. Justice Brown, and he clearly shows that the conclusion of the court is in accordance with the analogies of other decisions both in the Federal and in the State tribunals. Mr. Justice Harlan delivered a strong dissenting opinion, which, whatever may be thought of it now, will do him honor in the estimation of future generations, who will study with curiosity these statutes, which will have become dead letters.

---

[1] 163 U. S. 537.
[2] United States *v.* Stanley, 109 U. S. 3.
[3] Ex parte Plessy, 45 La. Ann. 80; *s. c.* 18 South Rep. 639.

American Law Review 30 (1896): 784–85.

VIRGINIA LAW REGISTER

1896

After printing the opinion in full, the Register's *editor adds the following comment.*

We take it that the decision of the Supreme Court in this case settles the question of the validity of a State law requiring, as a police regulation, the separation of the white and colored races, in transportation on railroads, steamboats and the like. A like separation exists in churches, schools, theatres, hotels, etc. It will continue until the leopard changes his spots and the Ethiopian his skin. Nature has ordained it, and it is in vain that human legislation attempts to contravene the ordinance. The legislature may enact that the sun shall rise in the West and set in the East, but the sun will continue, all the same, to rise and set as *nature* has ordered.

Virginia Law Register 2 (1896): 347.

AFRICAN AMERICAN INTELLECTUALS

This section includes substantial contributions by two of the foremost African American intellectuals of the time, W. E. B. Du Bois and Charles W. Chesnutt. While the Du Bois essay does not explicitly mention *Plessy v. Ferguson,* it does provide a valuable perspective on the majority's logic. The Chesnutt selection, which has never been previously published, demonstrates the detailed legal knowledge of this African American lawyer best known today for his literary accomplishments. Both selections should be compared with Booker T. Washington's "Atlanta Exposition Address" (p. 119). These three selections reveal differences within the African American community on how to respond to the conditions addressed in the *Plessy* case.

W. E. B. DU BOIS

Strivings of the Negro People

1897

*In the ninety-five years that he lived, William Edward Burghardt Du
Bois (1868–1963) established himself as the foremost African American
intellectual of the twentieth century. He wrote important works of history,
sociology, prose fiction, and essays. He was also an important political leader,
one of the founders in 1909 of the National Association for the Advancement
of Colored People (NAACP), which had as a primary goal overturning
the* Plessy *decision. Born in Great Barrington, Massachusetts, he attended Fisk University in Nashville, Tennessee, a black school founded
during Reconstruction. He then moved to Harvard University, where he
received his Ph.D. in 1895. His Harvard education included work with
the philosopher William James, two years studying abroad at the University of Berlin, and contact with the famous German social thinker
Max Weber.*

*Du Bois began his teaching career at Wilberforce University in Ohio
and the University of Pennsylvania, but his chances for advancement at
an elite northern school were precluded by the color line. In 1897 he took
a position at the all-black University of Atlanta. Du Bois's first book,* The
Suppression of the African Slave Trade *(1896), initiated the Harvard
Historical Studies series. In it and subsequent works his rigorous and
original scholarship corrected the inaccuracy of widespread white beliefs
about the inferiority of African culture.*

*On September 24, 1895, Du Bois sent Booker T. Washington a
letter congratulating him on his "phenomenal success at Atlanta," calling
Washington's speech at the Atlanta Exposition (see p. 119) "a word fitly
spoken." He also wrote to the New York* Age *that Washington's Atlanta
speech "might be the basis of a real settlement between whites and blacks
in the South." If whites would open economic opportunities to blacks,
blacks might cooperate politically with southern white Democrats. But
for Du Bois this possible compromise was undermined by the successful
movement, begun at this time, to disfranchise blacks, and he increasingly
distanced himself from Washington's accommodationist thought. Stressing
the need to demand the right to vote and the importance of higher learn-*

W. E. B. Du Bois, "Strivings of the Negro People," *Atlantic Monthly*, August 1897,
194–98.

ing, Du Bois became a spokesperson for a more assertive stance from blacks.

The selection printed here is an 1897 essay, which, with significant modifications (some of which are noted), became the first chapter of his remarkable The Souls of Black Folk *(1903). Marking his break with Washington,* Souls *is a poignant account of the spiritual strivings of a group of people denied possibilities for advancement in American society. In the essay printed here, Du Bois describes "double-consciousness," the sense of identity thrust upon black Americans living in a world in which white political and economic leaders assumed that to be American was to be white. In such a world black citizens were not simply Americans but African Americans. This doubleness gave them "two unreconciled strivings," one generated by their American citizenship, the other by their African descent. On the one hand, the possession of "two souls" was a gift that gave blacks a "second sight," the vision of both an insider and an outsider that made for a critical perspective on the strengths and weaknesses of American society. On the other, it deprived blacks of a secure sense of identity. Forced to see through the eyes of the dominant white culture, an African American had a tendency to judge himself by white standards, to measure "one's soul by the tape of a world that looks on in amused contempt and pity." In a world in which whites assumed that blacks were inferior, double-consciousness could, therefore, lead to the internalization of a sense of inferiority.*

Decided a year before the appearance of Du Bois's essay, Plessy v. Ferguson *gave legal sanction to a form of second-class citizenship that fed the negative aspect of double-consciousness. Indeed, although Du Bois did not explicitly mention the case, his essay can be read as a response to the Court's logic. In the majority opinion, Justice Henry B. Brown claimed that Plessy's argument was flawed because it assumed that the "enforced separation of the two races stamps the colored race with a badge of inferiority. If this be so, it is not by reason of anything found in the act, but solely because the colored race chooses to put that construction upon it." Du Bois's description of double-consciousness explains why, given the unequal power relations between blacks and whites in American society, blacks had little choice but to construe it that way.*

Between me and the other world there is ever an unasked question: unasked by some through feelings of delicacy; by others through the difficulty of rightly framing it. All, nevertheless, flutter round it. They approach me in a half-hesitant sort of way, eye me curiously or compassionately, and then, instead of saying directly, How does it feel to be a problem? they say, I know an excellent colored man in my town; or, I fought at Mechanicsville;[1] or, Do not these Southern outrages make your blood boil? At these I smile, or am interested, or reduce the boiling to a simmer, as the occasion may require. To the real question, How does it feel to be a problem? I answer seldom a word.

And yet, being a problem is a strange experience, — peculiar even for one who has never been anything else, save perhaps in babyhood and in Europe. It is in the early days of rollicking boyhood that the revelation first bursts upon one, all in a day, as it were. I remember well when the shadow swept across me. I was a little thing, away up in the hills of New England, where the dark Housatonic[2] winds between Hoosac and Taghanic to the sea. In a wee wooden schoolhouse, something put it into the boys' and girls' heads to buy gorgeous visiting-cards — ten cents a package — and exchange. The exchange was merry, till one girl, a tall newcomer, refused my card, — refused it peremptorily, with a glance. Then it dawned upon me with a certain suddenness that I was different from the others; or like, mayhap, in heart and life and longing, but shut out from their world by a vast veil.[3] I had thereafter no desire to tear down that veil, to creep through; I held all beyond it in common contempt, and lived above it in a region of blue sky and great wandering shadows. That sky was bluest when I could beat my mates at examination-time, or beat them at a foot-race, or even beat their stringy heads. Alas, with the years all this fine contempt began to fade; for the world I longed for, and all its dazzling opportunities, were theirs, not mine. But they should not keep these prizes, I said; some, all, I would wrest from them. Just how I would do it I could never decide: by reading law, by healing the sick, by telling the wonderful tales that swam in my head, — some way. With

for whites, not blacks this world

[1] A Civil War battle was waged at Mechanicsville, Virginia, on June 26, 1862.

[2] A river near Du Bois's birthplace in western Massachusetts.

[3] The metaphor of the veil is one of Du Bois's most famous, and there is much speculation on its source. It may be a self-conscious echo of the situation in Nathaniel Hawthorne's short story "The Minister's Black Veil." It could also be an allusion to a passage from Henry M. Field's *Bright Skies and Dark Shadows* (see p. 101). Calling for softening "the bitterness, and slowly removing obstacles out of the way" so as to "'turn the hearts' of the two races toward each other," Field nonetheless concludes, "But when we have done all, we have still to confess that there hangs over the future a veil through which no human eye can see. The final solution must be left to God and to time." In his essay Du Bois might be suggesting to Field, a minister who also hailed from western Massachusetts, that, since this veil has been created by human beings, they have a responsibility to do something about it.

other black boys the strife was not so fiercely sunny: their youth shrunk into tasteless sycophancy, or into silent hatred of the pale world about them and mocking distrust of everything white; or wasted itself in a bitter cry, Why did God make me an outcast and a stranger in mine own house? The "shades of the prison-house"[4] closed round about us all: walls strait and stubborn to the whitest, but relentlessly narrow, tall, and unscalable to sons of night who must plod darkly on in resignation, or beat unavailing palms against the stone, or steadily, half hopelessly watch the streak of blue above.

After the Egyptian and Indian, the Greek and Roman, the Teuton and Mongolian, the Negro is a sort of seventh son, born with a veil, and gifted with second-sight in this American world, — a world which yields him no self-consciousness,[5] but only lets him see himself through the revelation of the other world. It is a peculiar sensation, this double-consciousness, this sense of always looking at one's self through the eyes of others, of measuring one's soul by the tape of a world that looks on in amused contempt and pity. One ever feels his two-ness, — an American, a Negro; two souls, two thoughts, two unreconciled strivings; two warring ideals in one dark body, whose dogged strength alone keeps it from being torn asunder. The history of the American Negro is the history of this strife, — this longing to attain self-conscious manhood, to merge his double self into a better and truer self. In this merging he wishes neither of the older selves to be lost. He does not wish to Africanize America, for America has too much to teach the world and Africa; he does not wish to bleach his Negro blood in a flood of white Americanism, for he believes — foolishly, perhaps, but fervently[6] — that Negro blood has yet a message for the world. He simply wishes to make it possible for a man to be both Negro and an American without being

[4] This phrase comes from the fifth stanza of William Wordsworth's 1807 poem "Ode: Intimations of Immortality from Recollections of Early Childhood": "The Soul that rises with us, our life's Star, / Hath had elsewhere its setting, / And cometh from afar: / Not in entire forgetfulness, / And not in utter nakedness, / But trailing clouds of glory do we come / From God, who is our home: / Heaven lies about us in our infancy! / Shades of the prison-house begin to close / Upon the growing Boy." In *The Souls of Black Folk,* Du Bois removed the quotation marks around the phrase.

[5] In *Souls* Du Bois added the word *true* before *self-consciousness*. This addition might signal Du Bois's growing awareness of the positive possibilities of double-consciousness. In the 1897 essay he denies African Americans any self-consciousness whatsoever. In the revision, he states that they have a self-consciousness, but not as true a one as desired.

[6] In *Souls* the phrase "for he believes — foolishly, perhaps, but fervently — " was replaced by the much more assertive "for he knows."

cursed and spit upon by his fellows, without losing the opportunity of self-development.[7]

This is the end of his striving: to be a co-worker in the kingdom of culture, to escape both death and isolation, and to husband and use his best powers.[8] These powers, of body and of mind, have in the past been so wasted and dispersed as to lose all effectiveness, and to seem like absence of all power, like weakness.[9] The double-aimed struggle of the black artisan, on the one hand to escape white contempt for a nation of mere hewers of wood and drawers of water, and on the other hand to plough and nail and dig for a poverty-stricken horde, could only result in making him a poor craftsman, for he had but half a heart in either cause. By the poverty and ignorance of his people the Negro lawyer or doctor was pushed toward quackery and demagogism, and by the criticism of the other world toward an elaborate preparation that overfitted him for his lowly tasks. The would-be black savant was confronted by the paradox that the knowledge his people needed was a twice-told tale[10] to his white neighbors, while the knowledge which would teach the white world was Greek to his own flesh and blood. The innate love of harmony and beauty that set the ruder souls of his people a-dancing, a-singing, and a-laughing raised but confusion and doubt in the soul of the black artist; for the beauty revealed to him was the soul-beauty of a race which his larger audience despised, and he could not articulate the message of another people.

This waste of double aims, this seeking to satisfy two unreconciled ideals, has wrought sad havoc with the courage and faith and deeds of eight thousand thousand people,[11] has sent them often wooing false gods

[7] In *Souls* Du Bois ended this sentence, "without having the doors of Opportunity closed roughly in his face."

[8] In *Souls* Du Bois added "and his latent genius."

[9] In *Souls* Du Bois added a passage after *dispersed* to counter the impression of apparent weakness: "The shadow of a mighty Negro past flits through the tale of Ethiopia the Shadowy and of Egypt the Sphinx. Throughout history, the powers of single black men flash here and there like falling stars, and die sometimes before the world has rightly gauged their brightness. Here in America, in the few days since Emancipation, the black man's turning hither and thither in hesitant and doubtful striving has often made his very strength to lose effectiveness, to seem like absence of power, like weakness. And yet it is not weakness, — it is the contradiction of double aims."

[10] "Twice-told tale" could allude to Hawthorne's collection of short stories *Twice-Told Tales*. If so, such an allusion, just as Du Bois is about to discuss the "confusion and doubt in the soul of the black artist," dramatizes Du Bois's own double-consciousness as an artist. Of black descent, he worked within a tradition established by white writers like Hawthorne.

[11] Using the new 1900 census, Du Bois in *Souls* changed "eight thousand thousand people" to "ten thousand thousand." This revision is significant because some had used the 1890 census to argue that the population of blacks was decreasing, a sign that, as members of a weaker race, blacks were dying out. The increase in black population between 1890 and 1900 countered such arguments.

and invoking false means of salvation, and has even at times seemed destined to make them ashamed of themselves. In the days of bondage they thought to see in one divine event the end of all doubt and disappointment; eighteenth-century Rousseauism[12] never worshiped freedom with half the unquestioning faith that the American Negro did for two centuries. To him slavery was, indeed, the sum of all villainies, the cause of all sorrow, the root of all prejudice; emancipation was the key to a promised land of sweeter beauty than ever stretched before the eyes of wearied Israelites. In his songs and exhortations swelled one refrain, liberty; in his tears and curses the god he implored had freedom in his right hand. At last it came, — suddenly, fearfully, like a dream. With one wild carnival of blood and passion came the message in his own plaintive cadences: —

"Shout, O children!
    Shout, you're free!
The Lord has bought your liberty!"[13]

Years have passed away, ten, twenty, thirty. Thirty years[14] of national life, thirty years of renewal and development, and yet the swarthy ghost of Banquo[15] sits in its old place at the national feast. In vain does the nation cry to its vastest problem, —

"Take any shape but that, and my firm nerves
Shall never tremble!"[16]

The freedman has not yet found in freedom his promised land.[17] Whatever of lesser good may have come in these years of change, the shadow of a deep disappointment rests upon the Negro people, — a

[12] Jean-Jacques Rousseau (1712–1778), a French philosopher, was a strong advocate of political freedom. In *Souls* Du Bois dropped the allusion to "eighteenth-century Rousseauism."

[13] A black freedom spiritual. In *Souls* Du Bois changed the last line to "For God has bought your liberty."

[14] In *Souls* Du Bois substituted *forty* for *thirty*.

[15] In Shakespeare's *Macbeth* the ghost of Banquo comes back at a dinner feast to haunt his murderer. Allusions to this scene were common in the period. In *Souls* Du Bois dropped Banquo's name and wrote, "and yet the swarthy spectre sits in its accustomed seat at the Nation's feast." But the allusion to Banquo remains because of the lines from Shakespeare that follow. By evoking the image of a ghost haunting the national feast, Du Bois could once again be posing a challenge to Field's account of the color line. Recall that Field referred to the shadows and specters of the "Race Problem" haunting the "bright skies" of the South.

[16] *Macbeth* 3.4.102–3.

[17] In *Souls* Du Bois preceded this sentence with "The Nation has not yet found peace from its sins."

[handwritten marginalia: "personification" "a lot of personification" "it's so dramatic"]

disappointment all the more bitter because the unattained ideal was unbounded save by the simple ignorance of a lowly folk.

The first decade was merely a prolongation of the vain search for freedom, the boon that seemed ever barely to elude their grasp, — like a tantalizing will-o'-the-wisp, maddening and misleading the headless host. The holocaust of war, the terrors of the Kuklux Klan, the lies of carpet-baggers, the disorganization of industry, and the contradictory advice of friends and foes left the bewildered serf with no new watchword beyond the old cry for freedom. As the decade closed, however, he began to grasp a new idea. The ideal of liberty demanded for its attainment powerful means, and these the Fifteenth Amendment gave him. The ballot, which before he had looked upon as a visible sign of freedom, he now regarded as the chief means of gaining and perfecting the liberty with which war had partially endowed him. And why not? Had not votes made war and emancipted millions? Had not votes enfranchised the freedmen? Was anything impossible to a power that had done all this? A million black men started with renewed zeal to vote themselves into the kingdom. The decade fled away, — a decade containing, to the freedman's mind, nothing but suppressed votes, stuffed ballot-boxes, and election outrages that nullified his vaunted right of suffrage. And yet that decade from 1875 to 1885 held another powerful movement, the rise of another ideal to guide the unguided, another pillar of fire by night after a clouded day. It was the ideal of "book-learning;" the curiosity, born of compulsory ignorance, to know and test the power of the cabalistic letters of the white man, the longing to know. Mission and night schools began in the smoke of battle, ran the gauntlet of reconstruction, and at last developed into permanent foundations. Here at last seemed to have been discovered the mountain path to Canaan;[18] longer than the highway of emancipation and law, steep and rugged, but straight, leading to heights high enough to overlook life.[19]

Up the new path the advance guard toiled, slowly, heavily, doggedly; only those who have watched and guided the faltering feet, the misty minds, the dull understandings, of the dark pupils of these schools know how faithfully, how piteously, this people strove to learn. It was weary work. The cold statistician wrote down the inches of progress here and there, noted also where here and there a foot had slipped or some one

[18] The land promised by God to Abraham in the Old Testament (Genesis 12:7, 15:18).
[19] In *Souls* Du Bois left out some details of this paragraph having to do with election abuses and the establishment of mission and night schools, perhaps because he treated these matters in more detail in later chapters.

had fallen. To the tired climbers, the horizon was ever dark, the mists were often cold, the Canaan was always dim and far away. If, however, the vistas disclosed as yet no goal, no resting-place, little but flattery and criticism, the journey at least gave leisure for reflection and self-examination; it changed the child of emancipation to the youth with dawning self-consciousness, self-realization, self-respect. In those sombre forests of his striving his own soul rose before him, and he saw himself, — darkly as through a veil; and yet he saw in himself some faint revelation of his power, of his mission. He began to have a dim feeling that, to attain his place in the world, he must be himself, and not another. For the first time he sought to analyze the burden he bore upon his back, that dead-weight of social degradation partially masked behind a half-named Negro problem. He felt his poverty; without a cent, without a home, without land, tools, or savings, he had entered into competition with rich, landed, skilled neighbors. To be a poor man is hard, but to be a poor race in a land of dollars is the very bottom of hardships. He felt the weight of his ignorance, — not simply of letters, but of life, of business, of the humanities; the accumulated sloth and shirking and awkwardness of decades and centuries shackled his hands and feet. Nor was his burden all poverty and ignorance. The red stain of bastardy, which two centuries of systematic legal defilement of Negro women had stamped upon his race, meant not only the loss of ancient African chastity, but also the hereditary weight of a mass of filth from white whore-mongers and adulterers, threatening almost the obliteration of the Negro home.

A people thus handicapped ought not to be asked to race with the world, but rather allowed to give all its time and thought to its own social problems. But alas! while sociologists gleefully count his bastards and his prostitutes, the very soul of the toiling, sweating black man is darkened by the shadow of a vast despair. Men call the shadow prejudice, and learnedly explain it as the natural defense of culture against barbarism, learning against ignorance, purity against crime, the "higher" against the "lower" races. To which the Negro cries Amen! and swears that to so much of this strange prejudice as is founded on just homage to civilization, culture, righteousness, and progress he humbly bows and meekly does obeisance. But before that nameless prejudice that leaps beyond all this he stands helpless, dismayed, and well-nigh speechless; before that personal disrespect and mockery, the ridicule and systematic humiliation, the distortion of fact and wanton license of fancy, the cynical ignoring of the better and boisterous welcoming of the worse, the all-pervading desire to inculcate disdain for everything black, from Toussaint[20] to the devil, — before this there rises a sickening despair that would disarm and discourage any nation save that black host to whom "discouragement" is an unwritten word.

They still press on, they still nurse the dogged hope, — not a hope of nauseating patronage, not a hope of reception into charmed social circles of stock-jobbers, pork-packers, and earl-hunters, but the hope of a higher synthesis of civilization and humanity, a true progress, with which the chorus "Peace, good will to men,"

"May make one music as before,
But vaster."[21]

Thus the second decade of the American Negro's freedom was a period of conflict, of inspiration and doubt, of faith and vain questionings, of *Sturm und Drang.*[22] The ideals of physical freedom, of political power, of school training, as separate all-sufficient panaceas for social ills, became in the third decade dim and overcast. They were the vain dreams of credulous race childhood; not wrong, but incomplete and over-simple. The training of the schools we need to-day more than ever, — the training of deft hands, quick eyes and ears, and the broader, deeper, higher culture of gifted minds. The power of the ballot we need in sheer self-defense, and as a guarantee of good faith. We may misuse it, but we can scarce do worse in this respect than our whilom masters. Freedom, too, the long-sought, we still seek, — the freedom of life and limb, the freedom to work and think. Work, culture, and liberty, — all these we need, not singly, but together; for to-day these ideals among the Negro people are gradually coalescing, and finding a higher meaning in the unifying ideal of race, — the ideal of fostering the traits and talents of the Negro, not in opposition to, but in conformity with, the greater ideals of the American republic, in order that some day, on American soil, two world races may give each to each those characteristics which both so sadly lack. Already we come not altogether empty-handed: there is to-day no true American music but the sweet wild melodies of the Negro slave;

---

[20] Inspired by the French Revolution, Toussaint L'Ouverture led a revolt of blacks against the white French government of Haiti in August 1791.

[21] These two lines come from the prologue to Alfred Lord Tennyson's "In Memoriam" (lines 28–29). The poem's Christmas setting inspires the line "Peace and goodwill, to all mankind" (28, line 12). In *Souls* Du Bois dropped the two lines from the first chapter and used them to end the ninth chapter. He also added a line to produce "That mind and soul according well, / May make one music as before, / But vaster."

[22] Literally, "storm and stress" in German. In the latter half of the eighteenth century, *Sturm und Drang* German literature portrayed emotional individuals revolting against societal pressures.

the American fairy tales are Indian and African; we are the sole oasis of simple faith and reverence in a dusty desert of dollars and smartness. Will America be poorer if she replace her brutal, dyspeptic blundering with the light-hearted but determined Negro humility; or her coarse, cruel wit with loving, jovial good humor; or her Annie Rooney with Steal Away?[23] //Ooh~ French

Merely a stern concrete test of the underlying principles of the great republic is the Negro problem, and the spiritual striving of the freedmen's sons is the travail of souls whose burden is almost beyond the measure of their strength, but who bear it in the name of an historic race, in the name of this the land of their fathers' fathers, and in the name of human opportunity.

[23] "Annie Rooney" is the title of a popular tune of the time. "Steal Away" is the title of a black spiritual. In *Souls* Du Bois changed these references to the more general "her vulgar music" and "the soul of the Sorrow Songs."

CHARLES W. CHESNUTT

The Courts and the Negro

ca. 1911

Charles Waddell Chesnutt (1858–1932) is acknowledged as the first important African American writer of fiction, although he pointed out that he was preceded by other important writers with African blood, including the Russian Alexander Pushkin and the French Alexander Dumas, the author of The Three Musketeers. *Chesnutt's parents were from North Carolina where, in the age of slavery, they were "free people of color" with substantial amounts of European blood. In 1856 they moved north, married, and occupied a small home in a German neighborhood in Cleveland, where Charles was born. Charles's father served in the Union Army as a teamster and after the Civil War returned to Fayetteville, North Carolina, as the owner of a grocery store. Living in North Carolina, Charles experienced both Reconstruction and its end.*

The Charles W. Chesnutt collection at the Fisk University library has two undated copies of this speech. The version reprinted here is copy 2; it has Chesnutt's signature and is clearly a later version, with a number of handwritten revisions. Internal evidence indicates that it was written between 1908 and 1911, most likely 1911. As it was not intended for publication, its few mechanical errors are not corrected here.

Chesnutt was an excellent student, learning European languages from a newly arrived German-Jewish immigrant. At twenty-two he was appointed principal of the State Normal Colored School. But he had already begun to contemplate a career as a writer. In 1883 he moved to New York and then to Cleveland, where he established himself as a professional stenographer and a lawyer. He also published stories in prestigious journals such as the Atlantic Monthly. *By 1905, when he abandoned his literary career, he had published three novels, two books of short stories, and a biography of Frederick Douglass, all of which appeared after the* Plessy *decision.*

In his first novel he unfavorably echoes Justice Henry B. Brown's majority argument in Plessy *that in determining reasonableness a legislature can rely on "the established usages, customs and traditions of the people." Counseling a person of color who can pass as white and wants to do so, a lawyer in the novel declares that in South Carolina, if not North Carolina, the law was in the person's favor. "But custom," he adds, "is stronger than law — in these matters it is law." Such counsel would have been extremely poignant for Chesnutt, who himself could have passed as white but chose not to. In his second novel he describes the experience of a black physician named Miller forced to ride in a Jim Crow car. He includes the following passage:*

> *At the next station a Chinaman, of the ordinary laundry type, boarded the train, and took his seat in the white car without objection. At another point a colored nurse found a place with her mistress.*
>
> *"White people," said Miller to himself, who had seen these passengers from the window, "do not object to the negro as a servant. As the traditional negro, — the servant, — he is welcomed; as an equal, he is repudiated."*

Miller's musings repeat the argument about the Louisiana law's exemption for nurses made by Plessy's attorney Albion W. Tourgée. The detail about the Chinese recalls Justice John Marshall Harlan's dissent.

Chesnutt had close contact with Tourgée. Ten years before the publication of Chesnutt's first book of stories, Tourgée offered to write a preface for such a collection. In 1893 Tourgée hoped to pressure the Supreme Court to decide in Plessy's favor by establishing a journal designed to sway public opinion, and he asked Chesnutt to serve as an editor. But Tourgée could not raise enough money to support the journal, and Chesnutt continued for twelve more years with his career as an author, although in his second novel he has a character comment, "The man who would govern a nation by writing its songs was a blethering idiot beside the fellow who can edit

*its news dispatches." In "The Disfranchisement of the Negro," his contri-
bution to the 1903 book* The Negro Problem *(edited by W. E. B. Du Bois,
Booker T. Washington, and others), he drew on his legal training.*

*The selection that follows is a previously unpublished speech Chesnutt
gave after he abandoned his literary career. It offers a concise history of
the Supreme Court's rulings affecting blacks. It also makes clear the importance* Plessy *has in that history.*

The function of courts in the organization of modern society is to protect
rights, — to pass upon disputes between man and man or between the
individual and the State; and then, by their mandate, to set in motion
the arm of the executive to prevent or punish a wrong or to enforce a
right. Obviously if this great power be not rightly exercised, if it be
swayed by prejudice or class interest, justice will not be done.

The rights of citizens of the United States are embodied in constitutions and statutes. But these, at best, are mere declarations of principles,
which, in the complex and shifting nature of society, it is left for courts
to apply to the particular instance. And in so doing courts often give to
constitutions and statutes constrictions which have the effect of greatly
enlarging or narrowing their scope and sometimes, as I shall show, of
even altering the whole course of government on matters of the most
vital consequence. If public opinion acquiesce in these interpretations,
they remain the law; if not, the legislature assumes to correct them by
new statutes, and the process is thus begun all over again. Nowhere, in
the history of our jurisprudence, has this power of courts been more
strongly exerted than in the matter of Negro rights, and nowhere has
it been more swayed by prejudice and class interest. We are taught, and
properly taught, to hold our courts in high respect. As a rule this is not
difficult. But courts are made up of human beings. Under wigs and
gowns and titles and deferential formulas, judges are simply men, and
subject, as other men, to every human frailty. I shall endeavor to trace,
of course in an inadequate and sketchy way the history of Negro rights
as affected by the decisions of the Supreme Court of the United States.
This can be done most effectively by reference to a few leading cases.
For the Court rarely reverses itself, and has followed the prevailing
public opinion so closely, in its interpretation of the Constitution and
laws applying to the Negro, that its decisions have seldom been disturbed by legislative enactment.

The historic antebellum case was, of course, the Dred Scott decision.
Dred Scott was returned to slavery, and citizenship of the United States

was denied to negroes, thus repealing so far as it applied to them, Article 4 Section 2 of the Constitution: "The citizens of each State shall be entitled to all privileges and immunities of citizens of the several States." Of this decision the venerable Justice Harlan said, in his dissenting opinion in the civil rights cases (109 U. S.): "It is said that the case of Dred Scott vs. Sandford overruled the action of two generations, virtually inserted a new clause in the Constitution, changed its character, and made a new departure in the workings of the federal government." Thus vast and portentous is the power resting in the hands of nine men who hold their office for life and are directly responsible to no one. This decision was purely a political one and deserved the outburst of indignation which greeted it and did so much to bring about the ultimate abolition of slavery.

How different was the attitude of Lord Mansfield in the parallel English case.[1] A negro who had been in England was sought to be returned to a British colony as a slave. He claimed his freedom. Lord Mansfield might have made a similar ruling to that of the Supreme Court, with much better warrant, for there was no written constitution to restrain him, and by custom negro slaves had often been brought into England by their masters and returned to the colonies. But the English jurist seized his opportunity to recognize a principle which enlarged human rights. The Supreme Court chose to give a narrow and strained interpretation of the law and thereby restrict human rights.

I think it is exceedingly unfortunate for the Negro that the seat of government should be located in the South. Inevitably the administration, the courts, the whole machinery of government takes its tone from its environment. The influence of social life upon government is well known — it has always been the power behind the throne. The fate of nations has more often been settled in clubs and parlors than in courts and parliaments. The influence of southern customs and southern caste which is and always has been enthroned at Washington, has colored the attitude of Presidents and congressmen and judges toward the Negro. To men living in a community where by law all men are denied the suffrage, it does not seem such an enormity that the Negro elsewhere should be left without it. To men living in a community where service and courtesy in public places is in large measure denied the Negro, there seems no particular enormity in separate car laws and similar iniquities. Had the capital of this nation been left at Philadelphia or

---

[1] William Murray, Earl of Mansfield (1705–1793), British lord chief justice (1756–1788), ruling in *Somerset v. Stewart* (1772).

established in Boston or New York, the Negro would long since, in my opinion, have had his rights enlarged and recognized. Justice Mansfield lived in a free country. Justice Taney lived in Maryland, and the Supreme Court sat in Washington.

The Dred Scott decision, with all its implications, remained the law until it was overturned by revolution, and the effort made to fix, by the Constitution, the rights of the colored race to equal citizenship. Certainly the language of the amendments is plain enough to bear that interpretation; and certainly that was the intent of those who drew them and promoted their passage. But they were, after all, mere statements of principles, not difficult of application in the North, but involving a social revolution in the South. It was necessary to embody them in federal and state statutes, and then, in order to render them effective, to enforce their application.

The Thirteenth Amendment abolished slavery and by implication extended to the former slaves the rights as well as the status of free men. The Fourteenth Amendment extended citizenship of the United States in terms to all persons born or naturalized in the country and subject to its jurisdiction; forbade the making of enforcement of any law which abridged the privileges or immunities of citizens or which should deprive any person of life, liberty or property without due process of law or deny to any person within its jurisdiction the equal protection of the laws.

One of the earliest federal statutes intended to carry into effect the principles of the Thirteenth and Fourteenth Amendments was the civil rights bill of 1866, by which were fixed the rights of negroes in the courts, their right to contract, to sue, to be parties, to testify, and their full and equal benefit of all laws and proceedings for the security of persons and property as is enjoyed by white citizens. In general these rights have been respected, so far as statutes and Supreme Court decisions are concerned, although the right to contract in marriage, and certain other rights, have been limited under the principle of police power in the State.

In the case of Virginia vs. Reeves, 100 U. S. 313 (1879)[2] it was held by the Supreme Court:

"The Fourteenth Amendment was ordained to secure equal rights to all persons, and extends its protection to races and classes, and prohibits any state legislation which has the effect of denying to any race or class, or to any individual, the equal protection of the laws. The plain object

[2] *Virginia v. Rives,* 100 U. S. 313 (1880).

of this amendment, as well as of the statutes enacted prior thereto, was to place the negro race, with respect to its civil rights, upon the same level with the white. They made the rights and responsibilities, civil and criminal, of the two races exactly the same."

Such a statement would seem both comprehensive and conclusive. But a moment of reflection will show that it is neither. What constitutes race? When are rights equal or unequal? What is a denial of the equal protection of the laws? What are civil rights? What are civil and criminal responsibilities, and when are they the same, and exactly the same?

The answers of the Supreme Court to these questions, as they have come up, generally in cases based on the Fourteenth Amendment have fixed, for the present at least, the legal status of colored citizens.

When it became clear that in the former slave states civil rights, as Charles Sumner and the men of his school defined them, were to be denied the Negro in spite of the Fourteenth Amendment, the civil rights act of 1875 was enacted. It was not long before numerous cases involving this law were presented to the Supreme Court, and in 1883 (109 U. S.) five cases were considered together. By the opinion of the Court, sections 1 and 2 of the civil rights act were held unconstitutional, section 1 giving full and equal enjoyment to all citizens of the accommodations of inns, public conveyances and places of public amusement, and section 2 providing a penalty. It was held that these things were subject to regulation by the State only and that Congress had not power to legislate except as to State action which is subversive of the fundamental rights specified in the amendment, and that therefore the Fourteenth Amendment had no application. In this case Justices Bradley and Harlan filed dissenting opinions.[3] Justice Harlan based his argument upon Article IV., Section 2, of the Constitution, heretofore quoted, and maintained that no State could deny privileges and immunities to colored persons on the ground that they were extended only to whites, and that the majority opinion, to the effect that the nation, in the absence of State laws, adverse to such rights and privileges, might not interfere for their protection and security, is a denial to Congress of the power by appropriate legislation to enforce one of the provisions of the Fifteenth Amendment.[4] And quoting what I have already said in reference to the effect of the Dred Scott decision in changing the character of the Constitution, he expressed the fear that the decision in the civil rights cases would mark the opening of an era in which the rights to freedom and American

[3] Bradley wrote the majority opinion and Harlan dissented.
[4] Chesnutt meant the Fourteenth Amendment.

citizenship cannot receive from the nation efficient protection. These were prophetic words.

In the course of the opinion of the Court, Justice Bradley said, very truly:

"When a man has emerged from slavery and by the aid of beneficent legislation has shaken off the inseparable concomitants of that state, there must be some stage in the progress of his elevation when he takes the rank of a mere citizen; and ceases to be the special favorite of the law, and when his rights as a citizen or a man are to be protected in the ordinary modes by which other men's rights are protected."

There is nothing to indicate, except the well known facts of the situation, whether or not this perfectly correct statement was made with jocular intent. Certainly there is such a stage, but it was obvious then that the Negro had not yet reached it. And Justice Harlan further says:

"The opinion proceeds upon grounds entirely too narrow and artificial. I cannot resist the conclusion that the substance and spirit of the recent amendments to the Constitution have been sacrificed to a subtle and ingenious verbal criticism."

In the civil rights decision the Court did not hold that the things complained of were not deprivations of rights, but merely that they were not attributable to any action of the State. For it is the *State* which is prohibited by the Fourteenth Amendment from denying to any person within its jurisdiction the equal protection of the laws, and this amendment has been held not violated until the denial of the rights has some State sanction or authority. I do not recall whether this argument was made or not, but why would it not have been a good one, in that case, and in cases which are made under the civil rights laws of the northern States: Railroad companies are creatures of the State. Whatever powers they exercise are derived from the State and to that extent they are the agents of the State, and the State is responsible for their acts. Similar reasoning would apply to inns and common carriers, labor unions and other bodies, either chartered by the State or enjoying special benefits by statute or by common law.[5]

But to my mind the most important and far reaching decision of the Supreme Court upon the question of civil rights is that in the case of Plessy vs. Ferguson, a case which came up from Louisiana in 1895. (163 U. S., 537.) The opinion is a clear and definite approval of the recognition by State laws, of color distinctions, something which had theretofore been avoided in civil rights cases. It establishes racial caste in the United

---

[5] Harlan did make an argument similar to this one.

States as firmly as though it were established by act of Congress. To the opinion Mr. Justice Harlan dissented with his usual vigor, and Justice Brewer did not hear the argument or participate in the decision. The Court cited the passage quoted by me from a former decision:

"The Fourteenth Amendment was ordained to secure equal rights to all persons, and extends its protection to races and classes, and prohibits any State legislation which has the effect of denying to any race or class, or to any individual, the equal protection of the laws, and made the rights of the two races exactly the same."

And then the Court stabbed in the back, and to death, this ideal presentment of rights,[6] and threw its bleeding corpse to the Negro, — the comprehensive Negro, black, brown, yellow, and white — the plaintiff in that case, which involved the separate car law of Louisiana, was seven-eighths white and showed no sign of the darker blood — as that court's definition of his civil status:

"But in the nature of things it (the Fourteenth Amendment) could not have been intended to abolish distinctions based upon color or to enforce social, as distinguished from political, equality, or a commingling of the two races upon terms unsatisfactory to either. If the two races are to meet on terms of social equality, it must be the result of natural affinities, a mutual appreciation of each other's merits and a voluntary consent of individuals. When the government, therefore, has secured for each of its citizens equal rights before the law and equal opportunities for improvement and progress, it has accomplished the end for which it was organized, and performed all the functions respecting social advantages with which it is endowed. Legislation is powerless to eradicate racial instincts or to abolish distinctions based upon physical differences. If the civil and political rights of both races be equal, one cannot be inferior to the other civilly or politically. If one race be inferior to the other socially, the Constitution of the United States cannot put them upon the same place.

"A statute which implies merely a legal distinction between white and colored races — a distinction which is founded in the color of the two races and which must always exist so long as men are distinguished from the other race by color — has no tendency to destroy the legal equality of the two races or reestablish a state of involuntary servitude."[7]

When it was suggested in the argument that to sustain such discriminating laws might justify separate cars for people with red hair or aliens,

---

[6] Chesnutt wrote in the phrase "in the following language:" and marked the rest of the paragraph in parentheses, most likely for omission in oral presentation.

[7] Chesnutt runs together quotations taken from various parts of Brown's opinion.

or require people to walk on different sides of the street, or require colored men's houses to be in separate blocks, the Court in the opinion, said that such regulations must be reasonable. And the Court held:

"In determining the question of reasonableness, it is at liberty to act with reference to the usages, customs, and traditions of the people, with a view to the promotion of their comfort and the preservation of the public peace and good order."

It is obvious where this leaves the Negro, and it is difficult to see where the Fourteenth Amendment has any application.

The opinion in Plessy vs. Ferguson is, to my mind, as epoch-making as the Dred Scott decision. Unfortunately, it applies to a class of rights which do not make to the heart and conscience of the nation the same direct appeal as was made by slavery, and has not been nor is it likely to produce any such revulsion of feeling.

Another extract from the opinion makes one wonder whether the Court was merely playing with the subject:

"We consider the underlying failure of the plaintiff's argument to consist in the assumption that the enforced separation of the races stamps the colored race with the badge of inferiority. If this be so, it is not by reason of anything found in the act itself, but solely because the colored race chooses to put that construction upon it."

I presume that hanging might be pleasant if a man could only convince himself that it would not be painful, nor disgraceful, nor terminate his earthly career. It is perhaps true that some Negroes — I suspect very few people of mixed blood — have seemed to accept this reasoning. But I have never been able to see how a self-respecting colored man can approve of any discriminating legislation.[8]

To do so is to condone his own degradation, and accept an inferior citizenship. If discrimination must of necessity be submitted to, it should meet no better reception than silence. Protest were better still.

I need not suggest the far-reaching effect of this decision. The colored people of the South have been, it would seem, as completely segregated as the business of daily life will permit. Perhaps the lowest depths of race hatred have not been sounded, but a more humiliating, insulting, and degrading system is hardly conceivable under even a nominally free

---

[8] Chesnutt struck out the start of a paragraph that reads, "Some kinds, for instance, the separate school system, might be justified on the ground of convenience, expediency." This struck-out part of a sentence comes at the end of a manuscript page, and Chesnutt discarded the following page, so we do not know how he would have continued the paragraph. We should remember, however, that even Plessy's attorneys did not dispute the existence of segregated school systems.

government. Under Plessy v. Ferguson there is no reason why any northern State may not reproduce in its own borders the conditions in Alabama and Georgia. And it may be that the Negro and his friends will have to exert themselves to save his rights at the North.

The latest and, and since Plessy vs. Ferguson, the most serious blow delivered by the Supreme Court to Negro rights — it was in fact a restriction of the rights of white men, and involved the Negro only indirectly — is that of Berea College vs. Kentucky, (1908). A recent statute of Kentucky forbade the receiving of both the white and Negro races as pupils for instruction in any institution of learning. (Ky. Acts 1904, ch. 85, page 181.) Berea College was indicted and fined for a violation of the statute, some of which the court found unconstitutional; but it affirmed the judgment below, sustaining the constitutionality of the section upon which it was based, the principal ground of the decision being that the original charter of Berea College had been conditioned upon the right of the legislature to revoke or alter it, and that the statute of Kentucky was in effect an amendment of the charter which did not defeat or substantially impair the object of the grant being "to give instruction to all who might apply, and promote the cause of Christ." The Supreme Court of the United States accepted the decision of the Kentucky Court on the ground that the judgment being upon a non-federal ground, fairly construed, sustained the decision, and that the decision by a State court of the extent and limitation of the powers conferred by the State upon one of its own corporations is of a purely local nature. The Court did not consider the statute as a whole, but only the section above referred to.

Justice Harlan, dissenting, said: "In my judgment the Court should directly meet and decide the broad question presented by the section. It should adjudge whether the statute, as a whole, is or is not unconstitutional, in that it makes it a crime against the state to maintain or operate a private institution of learning where white and black pupils are received, at the same time, for instruction. . . . I am of the opinion that in its essential parts, the statute is an arbitrary invasion of the rights of liberty and property guaranteed by the Fourteenth Amendment against hostile state action, and is, therefore, void."

Since this decision Berea College, the attitude of which in the matter was scarcely heroic, though perhaps justified by the law of self-preservation, has set aside certain moneys and promoted the collection of a fund to establish a school which should provide for colored students the advantages formerly offered by Berea College, and since then the Jim Crow annex of that institution has been dodging injunctions and protests, seeking a place to lay its woolly head and to rest its tired feet. All honor to Justice Harlan. There is no more inspiring spectacle than this grand old man, ever steadfast to right and justice, fighting unwearingly, never yielding, and almost always defeated, for the principles which were so dearly bought by the Civil War. I know nothing with which to compare it except the staunchness of the New York *Evening Post* and the *Independent,* which, with a few individuals, amid all the ruck of concession and compromise have kept alight the torch of liberty against the day when in the language of the civil rights cases, the Negro shall "take the rank of a mere citizen . . . and when his rights as a citizen or a man are to be protected in the ordinary modes by which other men's rights are protected" — the time when the colored race shall have gained sufficient strength to protect itself, or until the democratic spirit now so nearly dead in the nation shall have become again a vivifying flame. I hope they may live to see the day.

The Right to Vote

The Fifteenth Amendment provided that "the right of citizens of the United States to vote shall not be denied or abridged by the United States, on account of race, color or previous condition of servitude," and Congress was given power in the Amendment to enforce by appropriate legislation its provisions.

The right of the colored men to vote on equal terms with white men as provided by the Fifteenth Amendment, has never been denied in terms by any state, but in effect disfranchisement is general throughout the South. A few individuals are permitted to vote, but the race is disfranchised; and the race, and not the individual, is the social unit. It was easily within the power of the government to strangle the movement for disfranchisement at its birth. It would have been as easy for the Department of Justice to work up a case involving disfranchisement, as it was to work up the recent cases against peonage, and to have them taken to the Supreme Court in the ordinary course. And the Court might have held, as it did in the cases involving the right to sit on juries, that the action of State officers charged with the execution of the law was as much a violation of the Constitution as an act of the legislature. But on the contrary, it took the narrow view, and held that so long as the State did not discriminate in terms against negroes as such, there was no violation of the constitutional provision, — though in effect it might disfranchise the race.

In the case of Giles vs. Harris (189 U. S. 475), where a negro was refused the right to register, the Court did not find that a wrong had not been done, but, assuming, for the sake of argument that the facts claimed were true and that the Constitution had been disregarded, declared itself impotent to enforce any mandate it might make in that behalf and referred the plaintiff to Congress for relief. To this decision Justices Brewer, Brown and Harlan dissented. Other cases have been before the Court, but it has steadily refused to face the main issue and has entrenched itself behind a hedge of technicalities. It will require, in all probability, some such extreme measure as that proposed, the other day, in Maryland, to force a decision; and there are those who have so little confidence in the majority of the Court as at present constituted, where similar questions are involved, as to be glad the question was not put up to them until there is some greater assurance of an effective public demand to back up a right decision.[9] There is little more that the states can do, within the limit of the Fourteenth Amendment as now construed, to further defeat Negro rights. For the Supreme Court to repeal, by judicial construction, the uniform application of the Fourteenth and Fifteenth Amendments, would be a calamity indeed.

SIXTEEN YEARS AFTER THE DECISION

Reprinted in this section are excerpts from works by two white lawyers, Charles Wallace Collins and Henry Billings Brown, the author of the majority decision in *Plessy*. Whereas Collins's selection justifies the majority opinion, Brown's, written a year before his death, shows he had second thoughts.

---

[9] The Maryland act refers either to the Straus Amendment, passed by the state legislature in 1908 but defeated by popular referendum in the 1909 general election, or, more likely, the Digges Amendment, which was defeated in the 1911 general election. Both were blatant attempts to disfranchise African Americans. The Digges Amendment, for instance, conferred the right to vote on all white males of legal age and residence but required all other male citizens — that is, African Americans — to have owned and paid taxes on at least five hundred dollars worth of real or personal property for at least two years prior to their application to register. It was such a challenge to the Fifteenth Amendment that whites in other southern states worried that it might affect their more carefully crafted evasions of the spirit of the Constitution. Indeed, in 1915 the Supreme Court struck down an Oklahoma law similar to the Straus Amendment in *Gwinn v. U. S.*, 238 U. S. 347. For more on the Maryland amendments, see Margaret Law Callcott, *The Negro in Maryland Politics, 1870–1912* (Baltimore: Johns Hopkins University Press, 1969), 126–33.

CHARLES WALLACE COLLINS

From The Fourteenth Amendment and the States

1912

Charles Wallace Collins (1879–1964) was affiliated with the University of Chicago and was a member of the Alabama bar. His 1912 book is an extensive study of the Fourteenth Amendment that grew out of a paper he read before the Government Club of Harvard University in February 1911. Parts of it were previously published in the American Law Review, *the* Yale Law Journal, *the* Columbia Law Review, *and the* South Atlantic Quarterly. *Adopting a view of history as progress, Collins argued that each generation needs to evaluate the laws that govern it: "There may not always be the necessity for a change in the organic law. There is the necessity for reëxamination and reëvaluation" (140). He claimed to examine the amendment from a perspective removed from the partisan climate in which it was passed and argued that, as an attempt to take control away from the states and give it to the federal government, the amendment had failed as a constitutional ideal. In contrast, the "ideal of local government is one of our most precious heritages from an heroic past. It is the school in which self-control, independence, and liberty are bred" (148). Surveying the vastly different local conditions from state to state, Collins claimed that "diversity makes local government essential to justice. The Supreme Court should not be required to pass upon . . . local questions" (149). When the Court goes against the wishes of the local population, he added, it breeds "disrespect and contempt among people for Federal authority" (149). The amendment's failed ideal should, according to Collins, have led to its repeal. But recognizing the difficulty of repealing an amendment, he turned his support to what he saw as a progressive bill proposed by Senator Jonathan Bourne Jr. of Oregon. That bill required a unanimous decision of the Supreme Court to declare a state law unconstitutional.*

Collins's attack on the Fourteenth Amendment was not narrowly motivated by racism. In fact, he recognized that the amendment had failed to live up to its original intention to protect the rights of freedmen and had instead become a form of protection for corporate interests: "The Amendment, though intended primarily as a protection of the negro race, has in these latter days become a constitutional guarantee to the corporations that

Charles Wallace Collins, *The Fourteenth Amendment and the States* (Boston: Little, Brown, 1912), 70–72.

no state action become effective until after years of litigation through the
State and federal courts to the Supreme Court of the United States. The
course of the Amendment is running far away from its originally intended
channel" (146). Nonetheless, Collins's comments on the Plessy *decision*
reveal a sense of white superiority in someone who saw himself as a political
progressive. Indeed, for many progressives the path forward meant facing
the difficult question of what to do with a large segment of the population
that they felt was not constitutionally suited for progress. To Collins the
Plessy *decision was based on "sound principles of political science and*
[was] justified by the logic of history and of fact" (72).

This principle of separation of African and Teuton on racial grounds is
the same whether it be the maintaining of separate schools, separate
churches, separate hotels, separate compartments in public conveyances, segregation in certain quarters — residential or business — of
towns and cities, in the park and playground systems of the larger cities,
in the theatres and other places of public amusement; in fine, the separation of the races at all times, in all places, and under all circumstances
where they would in large numbers come into physical contact the one
with the other.

In the case of Plessy v. Ferguson[1] this principle was for the first and
only time properly presented to the Supreme Court of the United States
for adjudication under the Fourteenth Amendment. As we have seen,
the Court decided that a State has the power to require the separation
of the negroes and the whites from each other on the ground of race or
color in the matter of riding on passenger trains. But in rendering the
majority opinion, Mr. Justice Brown further elaborated this principle of
race separation, using among others the following expressions: "Legislation is powerless to eradicate racial instincts or to abolish distinctions
based upon physical differences, and the attempt to do so can only result
in accentuating the difficulties of the present situation. . . . If one race
be inferior to the other socially, the Constitution of the United States
cannot put them upon the same plane."[2] The learned Justice here struck
at the root of the matter. He tacitly recognized two elements in the
problem of extreme interest — the futility of the early Congressional
ideal of the scope and of the efficiency of the Amendment; and the
"difficulties of the present situation."

[1] 163 U. S. 537 (Louisiana).
[2] 163 U. S. 544.

In the same opinion, after reviewing the decision in the Slaughter House Cases, he speaks as follows: "The object of the Amendment was undoubtedly to enforce the absolute equality of the races before the law, but in the nature of things it could not have been intended to abolish distinctions based upon color, or to enforce social, as distinguished from political, equality, or the commingling of the two races upon terms unsatisfactory to either. Laws permitting, and even requiring, their separation in places where they are liable to be brought into contact do not necessarily imply the inferiority of either race to the other, and have been generally, if not universally, recognized as within the competency of State legislatures in the exercise of their police power. The most common instance of this is connected with the establishment of separate schools for white and colored children, which has been held to be a valid exercise of the legislative power — even by courts of States where the political rights of the colored race have been longest and most earnestly enforced."[3] Here the learned Justice cites several cases from various States of the Union and quotes from one Massachusetts case *in extenso.*[4]

This decision has been quoted at some length because it is the only instance of the Supreme Court having passed upon this vital question, and settled, it seems, once for all the principle of race separation in its relationship to the Fourteenth Amendment. The opinion enunciates sound principles of political science and is justified by the logic of history and of fact.

There seems to be no limit to which a State may go in requiring the separation of the races. May it not do on a larger what it can do on a smaller scale? So long as the law operated equally on both races, could Federal intervention under the Fourteenth Amendment be invoked by either? The situation is a strange one in a government dedicated to the most exalted ideals of democracy. It is none the less inevitable, and the operation of this principle of race separation may yet prove the means of a solution of this problem with the least injustice to white or black.

[3] 163 U. S. 544.
[4] Roberts *v.* City of Boston, 5 Cush. 198. Separate schools for negroes and whites were maintained in Boston. The plaintiff, through his counsel, Mr. Charles Sumner, attacked the validity of the law. The Court decided against the plaintiff.

HENRY BILLINGS BROWN

Dissenting Opinions of Mr. Justice Harlan

1912

A year after Justice John Marshall Harlan died, retired Justice Henry Billings Brown (1836–1913), who wrote the majority opinion in Plessy, *used the pages of the* American Law Review *to reminisce on Harlan's many dissents. Printed here are Brown's comments on Harlan's dissenting opinions in the* Civil Rights Cases *and* Plessy v. Ferguson.

Mr. Justice Harlan not only believed in the loyal enforcement of the three post-bellum amendments to the Constitution, but firmly believed in the wisdom of their enactment, notwithstanding a growing sentiment in his own party that the qualification of voters had better have been left to the people of each State. The history of the Fifteenth Amendment is a forcible illustration of the futility of legislation which runs counter to a strong popular sentiment.

The Civil Rights cases[1] involved the power of Congress under the Thirteenth and Fourteenth Amendments to prohibit the denial to colored people of equal accommodation in inns, public conveyances and places of public amusement. The opinion of the Court was delivered by Mr. Justice Bradley. The Fourteenth Amendment, being only prohibitory of State action, was regarded as inapplicable to direct legislation by Congress. The case really turned upon the construction of the Thirteenth Amendment abolishing slavery and giving Congress power to enforce its provisions. He held that the action in question denying equal accommodation to all persons did not subject colored men to any form of servitude or tend to fasten upon them any badge of slavery. He also intimated that if any State denied these rights, a remedy might be found under the Fourteenth Amendment. He drew a distinction between this act and the compulsory service of slaves for the benefit of the master; restraint of his movements except by his master's will; disability to hold property, make contracts, to have a standing in court,

---

[1] 109 U. S. 3.

Henry Billings Brown, "Dissenting Opinions of Mr. Justice Harlan," *American Law Review* 46 (1912): 335–38.

to be a witness against a white person, and such like burdens and incapacities as were inseparable incidents of the institution. Mr. Justice Harlan dissented in a vigorous opinion to the soundness of which he stood to the last day of his life. Indeed, it is not too much to say that he took a special pride in it. He thought that the spirit of the amendments had been sacrificed by a subtle and ingenious verbal criticism, and that the full effect had not been given to the intent with which they were adopted. Congress, therefore, under its express provision to enforce that amendment (the Thirteenth), by appropriate legislation, may enact laws to protect the people against the deprivation, because of their race, of any civil right granted to other free men of the same State. In his opinion, the power of Congress was not necessarily restricted to legislation against slavery as an institution upheld by positive law, but may be exerted to the extent, at least, of protecting the liberated race against discrimination, in respect of legal rights belonging to free men, where such discrimination is based upon race. He thought that if any right was created by the Fourteenth Amendment, the grant of power through appropriate legislation to enforce its provisions, authorizes Congress by means of legislation operating throughout the entire Union, to guard, secure and protect that right. Disclaiming all power on the part of Congress to bring the two races into social intercourse against the wishes of either, he affirmed that no State officer or corporation, or individual wielding power under State authority for the public benefit or the public convenience, could consistently, either with the freedom established by the fundamental law or with that equality of civil rights which now belongs to every citizen, discriminate against free men or citizens in those rights because of their race or because they once labored under the disability of slavery.

Twenty-eight years have elapsed since this decision was rendered, and while it has met with the general approval of the country, there is still a lingering doubt whether the spirit of the amendments was not sacrificed to the letter, and whether the Constitution was not intended to secure the equality of the two races in all places affected with a public interest. It is somewhat remarkable that the only dissent emanated from the only Southern member of the Bench, all the others having been either born in or appointed from the North.

In Neal v. Delaware,[2] Mr. Justice Harlan, speaking for the Court, in

---

[2] 103 U. S. 370.

a criminal case, held that when the prisoner, a colored man, presented a petition to quash the indictment upon the ground that colored men had been excluded both from the grand and the petit jury upon the ground of their race and color, and the averments of the petition were not denied, the petition should have been granted and the indictment quashed.

This was but the first in a series of cases in which the deliberate exclusion of colored men from all juries because of their race or color was held to be fatal, though the fact that there were no colored men upon the particular jury which tried the case was treated as insufficient proof that such men were deliberately excluded.[3]

In line with these cases and dependent upon similar considerations is that of Plessy v. Ferguson,[4] which involved the constitutionality of a State act requiring separate but equal accommodations in different railway coaches for white and colored races. The Court had little difficulty in reaching the conclusion that the act was constitutional and analogous to the laws of several States requiring separate schools for white and colored children. It was said that separation of the two races did not involve any question of superiority or inferiority, and that the object of the Fourteenth Amendment was not to abolish the distinction based upon color or to enforce social as distinguished from political equality. The law was sustained as a reasonable exercise of the police power.

Mr. Justice Harlan dissented upon the ground that the legislation was inconsistent, not only with the equality of rights which pertain to citizenship, but with the personal liberty enjoyed by everyone within the United States. He thought that the arbitrary separation of citizens on the basis of race, while they are on a public highway, was a badge of servitude wholly inconsistent with the civil freedom and equality before the law established by the Constitution, and could not be justified upon any legal grounds. He assumed what is probably the fact, that the statute had its origin in the purpose, not so much to exclude white persons from railroad cars occupied by blacks, as to exclude colored people from coaches occupied or assigned to white persons.

---

[3] Bush v. Kentucky, 107 U. S. 110; Gibson v. Mississippi, 162 U. S. 565; Smith v. Mississippi, 162 U. S. 592; Carter v. Texas, 177 U. S. 442; Tarrance v. Florida, 188 U. S. 519; Brownfield v. South Carolina, 189 U. S. 426; Martin v. Texas, 200 U. S. 316; Rogers v. Alabama, 192 U. S. 226.
[4] 163 U. S. 537.

A similar case, applying only to intra-state commerce, was that of the Louisville &c. R. R. v. Mississippi,[5] in which Justice Harlan dissented, holding that the opinion of the Court was inconsistent with that of Hall v. De Cuir.[6] In another similar case, Chesapeake & Ohio R. Co. v. Kentucky, 179 U. S. 388, involving the separate coach law of Kentucky, he again dissented.

[5] 133 U. S. 587.
[6] 95 U. S. 485.

PART THREE

Conclusion:
In the Wake of *Plessy*

There is a danger in overemphasizing the significance of any one historical event. As important as the *Plessy* decision is, it can be argued that it was possible only within the context of a complicated network of political considerations and beliefs about the role of race in society that are more important than the decision itself.

Even in strict legal terms, there is a danger of overemphasizing the case's importance. One could certainly argue that once the *Civil Rights Cases* were decided in 1883 the decision in *Plessy* was a foregone conclusion. Indeed, prior to *Plessy* the Supreme Court had declared that railroad companies, despite their quasi-public nature, had a common-law right on their own to require separate but equal accommodations. In one of his first public comments on the 1890 Louisiana law, Tourgée noted this earlier decision, calling it "a decision that will one day rank with that in the Dred Scott case" and holding it responsible for states gaining the courage to pass Jim Crow laws.[1]

---

[1] *Daily Inter Ocean,* August 15, 1891, 4. In his column Tourgée calls attention to the irony that the Jim Crow laws had led to complaints by whites. As a result of these laws, he notes, "no matter how the white cars or compartments may be crowded, the passengers can not go into the compartments for colored people as long as there is a single colored person in them. As there are ordinarily many more white than colored travelers, the result is that one or two colored people often have half or the whole of a good car to themselves while every seat is doubly laden and men are even standing in the aisles of the white compartments, cussing the niggers for having the best end of legislation especially intended to degrade and oppress them."

But even as we guard against the danger of attributing too much importance to *Plessy,* we should not underestimate the need to understand the case. First, precisely because the case is understandable only in the context of its time, it provides an opportunity for us today to re-create the climate of thought that was so crucial in shaping the history of race relations in this country. Second, railroad companies may already have been allowed to maintain segregated facilities, but when the Supreme Court of the United States granted states the authority to require them, legal and symbolic consequences followed. Legally, the case created precedent for a comprehensive set of laws that regulated the lives of "whites" and "coloreds" in the South until 1954. Its symbolic importance is harder to determine, but clearly when the highest court in the land ruled that states could claim that legislation separating the races promoted the public good, it sent a message that African Americans would find little support from the federal judiciary. At a time when campaigns were under way to alter state constitutions to disfranchise African Americans, that message was not a comforting one. Indeed, one measure of *Plessy*'s importance is the role it played in the formation of the National Association for the Advancement of Colored People (NAACP) in 1909. One of the primary goals of the NAACP was to overturn legally mandated segregation in the United States. Doing so meant reversing the result of the *Plessy* case.

Part of the NAACP's legal strategy was to appeal to *Yick Wo v. Hopkins* (1886), which the *Plessy* majority had used as a precedent in its decision. *Yick Wo* was the case Justice Brown cited when he argued that the question facing the Court was whether the Louisiana law was a reasonable use of a state's police powers. In *Yick Wo* the Court had declared that a San Francisco ordinance regulating laundries was unreasonable and thus a violation of the equal protection clause of the Fourteenth Amendment. Even though it did not mention people of Chinese descent, in its application the city ordinance discriminated against them. In this ruling the NAACP saw a precedent for arguing that a law could on the surface seem nondiscriminatory and yet in fact be discriminatory. Its legal team planned to use this precedent to argue that, appearances to the contrary, the guarantee of equal facilities did not, even when provided, rule out discrimination.

But if their long-term strategy was to declare any law mandating racial segregation unreasonable, the NAACP's lawyers recognized that the climate for a direct attack on segregation was not good in the early years of the twentieth century. Indeed, if they made a direct attack on the "separate" clause in Jim Crow laws and lost, the Court's decision would establish yet another legal precedent that would have to be overcome.

As a result, the NAACP legal team decided to concentrate at first on winning cases in which the law was on its side. This part of the legal strategy reveals a few surprises about the ruling in *Plessy*.

As much of a defeat as *Plessy* was, it had granted two crucial legal points to African Americans, one implicit and one explicit. Never did the majority declare that African Americans were officially second-class citizens. On the contrary, the decision rested on the assumption that Jim Crow laws did not deny blacks their privileges and immunities as United States citizens. This assumption may seem contradictory since in effect segregation did perpetuate two classes of citizenship. Nonetheless, the legal implications were important, especially when we remember that in 1896 the Court had not yet ruled on whether anyone of Chinese descent could be a citizen, even if born in the country, and because a few years later the Court would rule that people brought under United States control as a result of the Spanish-American War did not have full citizenship rights (*Insular Cases,* 1901–1904).

Explicitly, in *Plessy* the majority made clear that Jim Crow laws had to have a guarantee of equal facilities. If rarely lived up to in fact, that guarantee was the basis of the first stage of the NAACP's legal strategy, which was to demand that the law deliver on its promise. Thus the first NAACP suits, in the 1930s and 1940s, demanded equality, and they generated victories and positive precedents rather than negative ones. It was not until after those victories and the end of World War II, which served in part to discredit racism, that the NAACP opted for a full-scale attack on the "separate" component of segregation laws.

This second part of the strategy was complicated legally because the NAACP's lawyers had to demonstrate that even when separate facilities had all appearance of equality they were, nonetheless, not equal. They were able to prove this paradoxical claim by focusing on what they called "intangible factors," those that could not be measured empirically. For instance, in *Sweatt v. Painter* (1950) the NAACP drew attention to the inferior facilities at the law school provided for blacks by the state of Texas. But its lawyers also successfully argued that a state might establish a segregated law school that had equality in terms of buildings, library holdings, student-to-teacher ratio, and so on, but still fail to provide equal educational opportunities because it could not duplicate the white school's reputation, its faculty, and its student body — all important factors in providing equal opportunity in the field of law. Armed with such victories, the NAACP turned its attack to segregated public schools, an attack that led to the pivotal case *Brown v. Board of Education of Topeka, Kansas* (1954).

In *Brown* Thurgood Marshall, the NAACP's leading lawyer, pre-

sented social science evidence demonstrating that black children forced
to attend separate schools, even schools with facilities equal to those of
white schools, developed "a feeling of inferiority as to their status in the
community that may affect their hearts and minds in a way unlikely ever
to be undone." Convinced, a unanimous Court ruled that "[a]ny language in *Plessy v. Ferguson* contrary to this finding is rejected." As a
result, the requirement of separate but equal facilities that the *Plessy*
majority felt was reasonable was declared unreasonable by the *Brown*
Court. As Chief Justice Earl Warren put it, "We conclude that in the field
of public education the doctrine of 'separate but equal' has no place.
Separate educational facilities are inherently unequal."[2]

Of course, as we have seen, segregated schools did not raise exactly
the same legal issues as segregated railroad cars. Nonetheless, in *Gayle
v. Browder* (1956) the Supreme Court extended its ruling to cover intrastate transportation. With that case many people felt that *Plessy* had
finally become a dead letter and that Harlan's color-blind standard had
become the law of the land. But the situation is not so simple.

Brown overturned the result of *Plessy*, but there was no language in
Brown that overturned an important legal principle on which *Plessy* was
based. The *Plessy* majority declared that racial classifications were not
inherently unconstitutional. In order to decide if they were constitutional, the Court, using the precedent of *Yick Wo*, evoked the criterion
of reasonableness. The decision as to whether a particular law is reasonable is not so much a legal question as a question of evidence. The
Court in *Brown* avoided the question of whether racial classifications
were inherently unconstitutional. Instead it ruled that evidence not available to the *Plessy* Court demonstrated that legally mandating segregated
school facilities was not a reasonable use of a state's police powers.
"Whatever may have been the extent of psychological knowledge at the
time of *Plessy v. Ferguson*," the Court declared, "this finding is amply
supported by modern authority."[3] The difference with the *Plessy* Court
was, therefore, not so much over legal principle as over evidence. On
the basis of new evidence, the Court overruled the result of *Plessy*, but
it did not adopt the principle proposed by Harlan in his *Plessy* dissent:
that the Fourteenth Amendment makes the Constitution color-blind.

The persistence of the legal principle underlying *Plessy* is demonstrated in the Supreme Court's decision in *Regents of the University of
California v. Bakke* (1978), which was instrumental in establishing
guidelines for affirmative action programs. The case involved the claim

[2] 347 U.S. 483 at 494, 494–95, and 495 (1954).
[3] 347 U.S. 483 at 494 (1954).

of Allan Bakke, a white male student, that the admissions policy of the University of California Medical School at Davis generated reverse discrimination that denied him entrance into the school. The Court divided its decision into two parts, with two different five-justice majorities. Justice Lewis F. Powell Jr. provided the fifth vote in both majorities and wrote the Court's overall decision, encompassing both majority opinions.

While not declaring racial classifications inherently unconstitutional, Powell announced that they are, nonetheless, inherently suspect and call for the most exacting judicial scrutiny.[4] When the Court applied that scrutiny to the Davis admissions policy, it concluded that the school's racial classifications were not justified under Title VI of the 1964 Civil Rights Act because they were essentially a quota system. Four justices advocated a color-blind Constitution, but, as in *Plessy,* that position remained a dissenting one.[5] Nonetheless, because these four agreed with Powell that the Davis system was inappropriate, a five-justice majority ruled that Bakke should be admitted.

Once this point had been decided, the four justices in favor of a color-blind Constitution felt that the Court had done its job and no further action was necessary. Powell, however, agreed with the other four that the issues presented by the case were so compelling that the Court should establish some guidelines for affirmative action under legislation then in effect. Recognizing that there was a compelling argument that achieving a student body representative of the diversity of the state was in the public good, Powell ruled that race can be taken into consideration as one of a number of criteria in deciding admission. In practice his ruling declared that, all other considerations being equal, a member of an underrepresented group could receive favorable treatment. Contrary to popular perceptions, these guidelines did not allow for quotas, nor did they allow admission for unqualified people. The issue was complicated, however, because gender as well as race was

---

[4] Although going along with Powell, Justices William J. Brennan Jr., Byron R. White, Thurgood Marshall (by now a Supreme Court justice), and Harry A. Blackmun claimed that racial classifications require strict, rather than exacting, judicial scrutiny. The notion that racial classifications are inherently suspect is part of *Korematsu v. United States* (1944), which grew out of the order to confine Japanese Americans to relocation camps in World War II. Writing for the Court in *Korematsu,* Justice Hugo L. Black declared, "It should be noted, to begin with, that all legal restrictions which curtail the civil rights of a single racial group are immediately suspect. That is not to say that all such restrictions are unconstitutional. It is to say that courts must subject them to the most rigid scrutiny. Pressing public necessity may sometimes justify the existence of such restrictions; racial antagonism never can" (323 U.S. 214 at 216 [1944]).

[5] Justice John Paul Stevens, joined by Chief Justice Warren E. Burger and Justices Potter Stewart and William H. Rehnquist, argued that the "proponents of Title VI assumed that the Constitution itself required a colorblind standard on the part of the government" (438 U.S. 265 at 416 [1978]).

allowed to be taken into consideration. Indeed, even though debates about affirmative action often focus on the issue of race, at present more white women have benefited from affirmative action programs than racial minorities, not because programs favor them over minorities but because there are more white women in the country.

An understanding of *Plessy v. Ferguson* helps to place in perspective today's debates about affirmative action. The heritage of *Plessy* makes many people in the United States suspicious of racial classifications of any sort. Nonetheless, advocates of affirmative action do not agree with Harlan that the Constitution is color-blind. Unlike the *Plessy* majority, but like Harlan and Tourgée, they believe that the law can be used affirmatively to overcome the effects of racial prejudice. That belief puts them in the ironic position of maintaining the legal principle underlying *Plessy* and confirmed in *Bakke* that racial classifications can be constitutional if they are reasonable and promote the public good. To be sure, the public good they champion is quite different from the one desired by architects of Jim Crow laws. It is not to separate races but to bring about professional communities that are representative of the diversity of the population they serve. To the objection that affirmative action guidelines are unreasonable because they generate reverse discrimination, supporters distinguish between affirmative action classifications and those that stigmatize a particular group. In contrast, opponents, for the most part, argue that the goals of affirmative action do not justify the means, that any consideration of race violates the principle that people should be judged on their own terms, not on the basis of the group to which they belong.[6] It is, therefore, opponents of affirmative action who claim the legacy of Harlan's *Plessy* dissent and argue for a color-blind Constitution.

Proponents counter that a color-blind Constitution is a noble goal to work for but that, in a country that is not yet color-blind, it should remain aspiration, not fact. If the history of the Constitution did not include the recognition of slavery, *Dred Scott,* and *Plessy,* proponents argue that perhaps now we would be ready for a color-blind standard. But inheriting a constitutional and national history that has used race to stigmatize various groups, they do not want to fall prey to the error committed in the *Civil Rights Cases.* Writing for the majority, Justice Joseph P. Bradley made the perfectly reasonable claim that a time must come when a black citizen should stop being the "special favorite of the law, and when his

---

[6] Some opponents of affirmative action do not argue against racial classifications. They simply disagree with the reasonableness of existing classifications. But they are in the minority.

rights as a citizen or a man are to be protected in the ordinary modes by which other men's rights are to be protected."[7] But clearly that time had not come a mere eighteen years after the abolition of slavery. Indeed, the Court's decision in the *Civil Rights Cases* served to delay the time when blacks could achieve an equal place in United States society after suffering from a history of more than two hundred years of slavery. Not wanting to repeat the errors of the past, proponents of affirmative action feel that to impose a color-blind standard too hastily would be to delay the realization of conditions in which that standard could serve the interests of justice in all cases. From this perspective it is imperative, as Justices Brennan, White, Marshall, and Blackmun argue in *Bakke,* that we not "let color blindness become myopia which masks the reality that many 'created equal' have been treated within our lifetimes as inferior both by the law and by their fellow citizens."[8]

Opponents respond that the only way to eliminate racism is to stop taking race into account. If proponents worry that imposing a formally neutral standard of color-blindness will undercut the demands of justice by ignoring the historical and present conditions of people of color, opponents claim that those conditions result from people failing to maintain a color-blind standard. To be sure, advocates of affirmative action believe that its racial classifications are necessary to promote the public good, but the authors of the legislation supported in *Plessy* and the order demanding the relocation of Japanese American citizens during World War II used the same logic. Worried that any principle allowing race to be taken into account has the potential for abuse, opponents urge the adoption of a standard that has no exceptions. To this argument Justice Blackmun responded, "In order to get beyond racism, we must first take account of race. . . . We cannot — we dare not — let the Equal Protection Clause perpetuate racial supremacy."[9]

Thus, at the heart of the argument for affirmative action lies a paradox, just as at the heart of the argument against Jim Crow laws lay the paradox that "separate but equal" could not be equal. But the argument for the truth of the paradox in *Brown* relied on empirical evidence in the past to demonstrate the harmful effects of segregated schools. In contrast, the paradox in *Bakke* is future-oriented. Since the future, unlike the past, is incapable of generating empirical evidence, those believing in the *Bakke* paradox must ask other citizens to trust them that adhering to *Bakke*'s standards will bring about a situation in which a color-blind

[7]109 U.S. 3 at 25 (1883).
[8]438 U.S. 265 at 327 (1978).
[9]438 U.S. 265 at 407 (1978).

standard is finally appropriate. Nonetheless, debates over affirmative action poignantly illustrate how our vision of the future is conditioned by our understanding of the past.

Indeed, as we have seen, the metaphor of the color-blind Constitution so important for those debates first appeared in Supreme Court history in Harlan's *Plessy* dissent. As we have also seen, Harlan takes the metaphor from Tourgée's brief to the Court. What is not widely known is that Tourgée first used the metaphor in an 1880 novel. But at that time he did not use color-blindness as a positive quality that keeps people from discriminating. Instead, he used it as a defect that did not allow people to see the actual condition of freedmen. Describing how the freedman had been granted legal rights, the narrator complains, "Right he had, in the abstract; in the concrete, none. Justice would not hear his voice. The law was still color-blinded by the past."[10] Tourgée's literary use of the metaphor indicates that he recognized how color-blindness could become a myopia keeping the law from acting affirmatively to help improve the concrete conditions of those whom society had historically disadvantaged. Thus Tourgée brought together competing uses of a metaphor whose meaning continues to be debated today. We remain in the wake of *Plessy*.

[10]Albion W. Tourgée, *Bricks without Straw* (New York: Fords, Howard, and Hulbert, 1880), 35. Although legal scholar Andrew Kull, in *The Color-Blind Constitution* ([Cambridge: Harvard University Press, 1992], 119–20), is unaware of this quotation, it confirms his observation that Tourgée, in his own time, supported versions of affirmative action that recognized race as a legal category, a stand that Kull contrasts with his own interpretation of Justice Harlan's position. When Tourgée first began his press campaign against Jim Crow laws, he noted, "[W]e shall see whether justice is still color-blind or National citizenship worth a rag for the defense of right or not" (*Daily Inter Ocean,* October 17, 1891, 4).

Members of the Court

The beliefs of the nine justices sitting on the Supreme Court can determine the outcome of a case. One reason Tourgée delayed moving Plessy's case through the courts was that he hoped for a more favorable makeup on the ultimate Court. In an October 31, 1893, letter to Louis A. Martinet, who along with Rodolphe Desdunes was a member of the New Orleans committee that challenged the Louisiana law, he revealed how carefully he calculated the possibility of winning a five-to-four majority:

> When we started the fight there was a fair show of favor with the Justices of the Supreme Court. One, at least, had come to regret the "Civil Rights Cases" who had been most strenuously for them. There are now four men on the court who are not fully committed by participation in those cases. If Hornblower is confirmed there will be five.
>
> Of the whole number of Justices there is but one who is known to favor the view we must stand upon.
>
> One is inclined to be with us legally but his political bias is strong the other way.
>
> There are two who may be brought over by the argument.
>
> There are five who are against us. Of these one may be reached, I think, if he "hears from the country" soon enough. The others will probably stay where they are until Gabriel blows his horn.[1]

It is not possible to know with certainty which justices Tourgée aligned with which positions. The justice who was rethinking his ruling on the *Civil Rights Cases* was most likely Samuel Blatchford, who left the Court in 1893. "Hornblower" is William B. Hornblower, a New York

[1] Quoted in Otto H. Olsen, ed., *Thin Disguise* (New York: Humanities Press, 1967), 78.

Left: Official portrait of the members of the 1896 Supreme Court that decided the *Plessy* case. From left to right: Edward Douglass White, Henry Billings Brown, Horace Gray, Stephen Johnson Field, Chief Justice Melville Weston Fuller, John Marshall Harlan, David Josiah Brewer, George Shiras Jr., Rufus Wheeler Peckham.

lawyer nominated by newly elected Democrat Grover Cleveland to take Blatchford's seat. His nomination was defeated in the Democrat-controlled Senate because of opposition from New York Democratic Senator David B. Hill, who was upset with Cleveland for getting the presidential nomination, which he wanted. Cleveland then nominated another New York lawyer, Wheeler H. Peckham, who was rejected but whose brother would be named to the Court in 1895. Finally, Edward Douglass White, a Democrat from Louisiana, was approved to fill the vacant seat. If Tourgée was counting on winning over Hornblower, he must have been devastated by White's appointment. A former member of the Confederate army, White had identified himself with the southern Redeemers, who were intent on "redeeming" the South from Reconstruction and from rule by northern carpetbaggers and blacks.

The justice Tourgée could count on for support was clearly Harlan. The one inclined to go along legally, if not politically, may have been Justice Howell E. Jackson, a Democrat from Tennessee, appointed by the lame-duck Republican President Benjamin Harrison in early 1893. Knowing that a Democrat-controlled Senate would not confirm a lame-duck appointment of a Republican, Harrison went with Jackson. At first Tourgée was outraged at the appointment and wrote an editorial entitled "Ben Harrison a Traitor Too." But Jackson did win black support. Whether Tourgée had reevaluated his judgment of Jackson by the fall of 1893, when he wrote the letter, is unclear. Nonetheless, there is evidence that Jackson fit the portrait Tourgée painted. For instance, although a southern Democrat, he had, as a district judge, overturned a lower court decision and upheld a conviction under the 1870 Civil Rights Act. The case did not involve African Americans, but Tourgée may well have seen Jackson establishing an important legal position. Jackson, however, died in 1895 and was replaced by the conservative New York Democrat Rufus Wheeler Peckham.

One can only guess who Tourgée thought could be won over by argument. Perhaps he counted on Hornblower, who never made it to the Court. He might also have had in mind two new Republicans: George Shiras Jr. and Henry Billings Brown, who eventually wrote the majority opinion but years later somewhat reconsidered his position. If Tourgée hoped to win over two of these three by argument, the third was probably the one he thought might be influenced by public opinion. Another possibility is David Josiah Brewer, who had not been on the Court for the *Civil Rights Cases* and who came from a missionary family with a strong antislavery tradition. But Brewer was a nephew of Stephen Field, who along with Horace Gray had ruled in the *Civil Rights Cases* and was certain to oppose the argument for Plessy. Likewise, Melville W. Fuller, the Democratic chief justice, was an almost certain opponent.

Tourgée miscalculated when he asserted that as of October 31, 1893, five justices on the Court would not be committed because of their participation in the *Civil Rights Cases*. With the confirmation of Blatchford's replacement, there would be six. The three who were on the Court in 1883 at the time of the *Civil Rights Cases* were Harlan, Field, and Gray. Short sketches of the justices on the Court in 1896 follow.[2]

Stephen Johnson Field (1816–1899)

Born in Haddam, Connecticut. Nominated by Abraham Lincoln (Republican). Took seat in 1863.

Although nominated by the Republican Abraham Lincoln, Field was a Democrat with political aspirations. He came from a remarkable New England family. An older brother was David Dudley Field, a noted legal figure who advocated codification of the law. Younger brothers included Cyrus West Field, who promoted the first Atlantic cable, and Henry Martyn Field, a Presbyterian minister and author of numerous travel books (see the selection on p. 101). One of his sisters was the mother of Justice David Josiah Brewer. Graduating from Williams College after spending two and a half years in the Middle East with his sister and her minister husband, Field joined his brother David in a New York law practice until he moved to California in late 1849. He was known for opinions that favored commercial interests; he wrote the lower-court precedent for the opinion in *Santa Clara County v. Southern Pacific Railroad Company* (1886), which gave corporations Fourteenth Amendment rights granted to "persons." He was much more hesitant about using the Fourteenth Amendment to protect the rights of African Americans. He dissented in two cases that upheld their rights to serve on juries: *Strauder v. West Virginia* (1880) and *Ex parte Virginia* (1880). He did, however, protect the rights of Chinese when in a circuit court decision he ruled that children born in the United States of Chinese aliens were United States citizens under the Fourteenth Amendment. His opinion was confirmed by the Supreme Court in *United States v. Wong Kim Ark* (1898). In 1896 at the time of *Plessy*, he was almost eighty years old and in failing health, and he sometimes fell asleep during hearings. Under pressure, he resigned in 1897.

[2] For fuller portraits, see Melvin I. Urofsky, ed., *The Supreme Court Justices: A Biographical Dictionary* (New York: Garland, 1994).

John Marshall Harlan (1833–1911)

Born in Boyle County, Kentucky. Nominated by Rutherford B. Hayes (Republican). Took seat in 1877.

A southern Whig, Harlan was a former slave owner. Dissatisfied with both the Democratic and Republican Parties, he joined the Know-Nothing Party, which had strong anti-immigrant and anti-Catholic programs. He fought for the North in the Civil War, freeing his slaves before its end. He was against Lincoln's reelection in 1864 and opposed the Thirteenth Amendment, but he campaigned hard for Ulysses S. Grant in 1868 and began to change a number of his political views, especially on the need to protect the rights of freedmen. When Rutherford B. Hayes became president in March 1877, he sent Harlan along with four other special commissioners to Louisiana to negotiate the dispute over its 1876 state election. In part as a reward for his services, he was appointed to the Court by Hayes. Harlan was often at odds with the majority and became known as the "Great Dissenter." He dissented when in 1883 the Court declared unconstitutional much of the Civil Rights Act of 1875. He did, however, concur in *Pace v. Alabama* (1883), which upheld an Alabama law that punished interracial couples more harshly than couples of the same race for indulging in fornication and adultery. He was the lone dissenter in *Plessy.*

Horace Gray (1828–1902)

Born in Boston, Massachusetts. Nominated by Chester A. Arthur (Republican). Took seat in 1882.

Gray was born into a very rich family. After studying at Harvard Law School, he worked in private practice and was also reporter to the Massachusetts supreme judicial court when Lemuel Shaw, who is cited in the *Plessy* case, was chief justice. In 1864 Gray became the youngest man appointed to his state's highest court. Nine years later, noted for his prodigious scholarship and knowledge of legal history, he was named its chief justice. As a young man he had joined the antislavery Free-Soil Party, and in 1857 he wrote a devastating criticism of the historical evidence used to justify Roger Taney's proslavery decision in *Dred Scott.* He did, however, join the majority in the *Civil Rights Cases.* A firm believer in precedent, he would not have gone against the Court's interpretation of the Thirteenth and Fourteenth Amendments in that decision.

Melville Weston Fuller (1833–1910), Chief Justice

Born in Augusta, Maine. Nominated by Grover Cleveland (Democrat). Took seat in 1888.

Fuller attended Bowdoin College and Harvard Law School and then moved to Chicago. He was active in Democratic Party politics and supported Stephen A. Douglas in his race against Abraham Lincoln. He was not a strong supporter of the North in the Civil War and did not serve in the Union army. During the war he even supported a state constitutional amendment denying blacks the right to vote, and he denounced the Emancipation Proclamation. When the Democrat Cleveland nominated him, Republicans drew attention to his conduct in the Civil War. Their attempt to delay his confirmation until the next election, which was indeed won by a Republican, failed. Fuller took his seat as chief justice on October 8, 1888. He was a conservative in economic matters, but he did show some sensitivity to the rights of minorities when he dissented in *Fong Yue Ting v. United States* (1893), a decision that gave the United States the right summarily to deport resident Chinese aliens. As chief justice, Fuller determined who wrote the opinion of the Court.

David Josiah Brewer (1837–1910)

Born in Smyrna, Asia Minor (modern Turkey). Nominated by Benjamin Harrison (Republican). Took seat in 1889.

The son of missionaries with strong antislavery roots, Brewer became one of the Court's intellectual leaders for economic conservatism. His mother was the sister of Justice Stephen J. Field. Dissenting in *Budd v. New York* (1892), Brewer proclaimed, "The paternal theory of government is to me odious" and warned that the Court's decision brought the world of Edward Bellamy's *Looking Backward* closer to reality. Brewer was a strong proponent of the Tenth Amendment and advocated keeping states free from federal interference. One of his most famous opinions was *In re Debs* (1895), in which the Court unanimously upheld an injunction against workers in the Pullman strikes. Having missed the arguments before the Court, he did not participate in the *Plessy* decision.

Henry Billings Brown (1836–1913)

Born in South Lee, Massachusetts. Nominated by Benjamin Harrison (Republican). Took seat in 1891.

Educated at Yale and Harvard, Brown moved to Detroit where he worked and lived. In 1875 Ulysses S. Grant appointed him to the federal district court in eastern Michigan. His specialty was admiralty and patent law, and he wrote most of the Supreme Court's opinions in those areas while on the bench. He was considered a moderate to conservative member of the Court. He dissented in its five-to-four decision in *Pollock v. Farmers' Loan & Trust Co.* (1895) to invalidate the income tax. He usually supported a state's right to assert its police powers. For instance, writing for the majority in *Lawton v. Steele* (1894), he affirmed that "[t]he state may interfere wherever the public interests demand it, and in this particular a large discretion is necessarily vested in the legislature to determine, not only what the interests of the public require, but what measures are necessary for the protection of such interests."

George Shiras Jr. (1832–1924)

Born in Pittsburgh, Pennsylvania. Nominated by Benjamin Harrison (Republican). Took seat in 1892.

Shiras graduated from Yale and came to the Court from private practice. Tending to side with the majority, he did not establish an independent voice. He gained some notoriety a year before the *Plessy* decision when it was reported that he switched his vote to invalidate the income tax in the *Pollock* case. Shiras wrote two important 1896 opinions. In *Swearinger v. United States* he spoke for a five-justice majority in refusing to uphold the conviction of a populist editor accused of violating a federal obscenity law in one of his political editorials. He also wrote for a unanimous Court when in *Wong Wing v. United States* it declared unconstitutional a provision that allowed a United States commissioner to sentence illegal Chinese aliens to hard labor prior to deportation.

Edward Douglass White (1845–1921)

Born in La Fourche Parish, Louisiana. Nominated by Grover Cleveland (Democrat). Took seat in 1894.

White was a southern gentleman, a Jesuit-trained Roman Catholic who attended Georgetown University until the Civil War interrupted his studies. Like John Marshall Harlan, he came from a family of southern Whigs. He joined the Confederate army but was captured shortly thereafter. After the war he was active in Louisiana politics as a member of the Democratic Party. An unverified report linked him to the Ku Klux Klan during his Louisiana days. When Harlan served on the special commission sent to Louisiana to resolve disputed 1876 election results, White was a spokesperson for a Louisiana delegation and clashed with the Kentuckian. In 1910 President William Howard Taft would appoint him chief justice. He is remembered as a vigorous exponent of the "rule of reason" doctrine, which limited the Sherman Antitrust Act to banning only "unreasonable" restraints on trade by corporations. He was also the architect of the Supreme Court's policy on territories acquired as the result of the Spanish-American War. Influenced by Roman law, he gave those territories a special status. Until they were incorporated into the United States, they were, according to article IV of the Constitution, governed by Congress. Bill of Rights protections did not, however, apply to them.

Rufus Wheeler Peckham (1838–1909)

Born in Albany, New York. Nominated by Grover Cleveland (Democrat). Took seat in 1895.

Born into one of upstate New York's oldest and most prominent families, Peckham made his career as a corporate lawyer. He became a prominent spokesperson for the doctrine of "substantive due process," which allowed the Court to declare state laws regulating abuses by businesses unreasonable violations of the Fourteenth Amendment's protection of life, liberty, and property. His most famous decision was *Lochner v. New York* (1905), which declared unconstitutional a state law limiting the work week of bakers to fifty hours. According to Peckham, the law violated the Fourteenth Amendment by depriving workers of the right to earn property by contracting out their labor. Peckham's logic was anticipated in a dissent that he made in *People v. Budd* (1889) while a member of the New York court of appeals.

Chronology of Events Related to *Plessy* (1849–1925)

1849

In *Roberts v. City of Boston*, Lemuel Shaw, chief justice of Massachusetts' highest court, declares that racially segregated schools in Boston do not violate the Massachusetts constitution's guarantee of equality under the law.

1857

In the *Dred Scott* case the United States Supreme Court denies United States citizenship to all African Americans, free and enslaved.

1861

The Civil War begins.

1862

March: Homer A. Plessy is born free in New Orleans of Creole parents.

1863

January 1: In the Emancipation Proclamation President Lincoln frees all slaves in the rebellious southern states. The proclamation does not apply to border states and territories under the control of the Union army.

1865

February: Congress proposes the Thirteenth Amendment, which prohibits slavery.

April 8: Lee surrenders to Grant.

April 14: President Lincoln is assassinated.

April 15: Andrew Johnson is sworn in as president.

May 29: Presidential Reconstruction begins.

November 24: Mississippi passes the first black code limiting the rights of African Americans.

December: The Thirteenth Amendment is ratified by the states.

December 24: The white supremacist organization the Ku Klux Klan is founded in Tennessee.

1866

April 9: The 1866 Civil Rights Act implies United States citizenship for African Americans and guarantees certain rights.

June 16: Congress proposes the Fourteenth Amendment, which implies citizenship and certain rights for all African Americans.

1867

March 1: By this date ten southern states have rejected the Fourteenth Amendment.

March 2: Congress passes the first Reconstruction Act over President Johnson's veto. It divides the South into military zones and requires ratification of the Fourteenth Amendment as a condition for a state's readmission to the Union.

1868

February 22: Congress marks George Washington's birthday by beginning impeachment proceedings against President Johnson.

March 16: The vote to remove Johnson from office fails by one vote.

July 28: The Fourteenth Amendment is ratified by the states.

November 3: Ulysses S. Grant is elected president.

1869

February 27: Congress proposes the Fifteenth Amendment, making it unconstitutional to deny someone the right to vote on the basis of race. Despite protests by women, discrimination on the basis of sex is not banned.

1870

The Fifteenth Amendment is ratified by the states.

1872

November 4: Grant is reelected president.

1873

April 14: In the *Slaughter-House Cases* the Supreme Court gives a restricted interpretation of the Thirteenth and Fourteenth Amendments.

1875

March 1: A lame-duck Congress passes a more inclusive civil rights bill than the 1866 bill.

1877

March 5: Rutherford B. Hayes is inaugurated president, following a disputed election that was resolved by Congress. Reconstruction ends.

April 24: The last federal troops are returned to their barracks in the South.

1880

November 2: James A. Garfield, a strong supporter of African American rights while in Congress, is elected president.

1881

July 2: President Garfield is shot. He dies on September 19.

July 4: Booker T. Washington presides over the opening of Tuskegee Normal and Industrial Institute in Alabama.

September 20: Chester A. Arthur is sworn in as president.

1883

October 15: In the *Civil Rights Cases* the Supreme Court declares the 1875 Civil Rights Act unconstitutional.

1884

November 4: Grover Cleveland is elected the first Democratic president since the Civil War.

1885

In *Century Magazine*, George Washington Cable and Henry Grady debate the responsibility of the nation to African Americans in the wake of the *Civil Rights Cases.*

1886

In *Santa Clara County v. Southern Pacific Railroad Company* the Supreme Court rules that a corporation is a legal person and thus is protected by the Fourteenth Amendment.

1888

Homer Plessy marries Louise Bourdenave.

November 6: The Republican Benjamin Harrison is elected president.

1890

Louisiana passes a "Jim Crow" law mandating "equal but separate" accommodations on railroads for "whites" and "coloreds."

1891

September 1: Prominent African Americans in New Orleans form a committee to challenge the state's Jim Crow law.

October 10: The committee officially names Albion W. Tourgée its legal representative.

1892

February 24: Daniel F. Desdunes is arrested in Louisiana for riding in a white car on an interstate trip.

June 7: Homer Plessy is arrested in Louisiana for riding in a white car on an intrastate trip.

July 9: In Desdunes's case, Justice John Howard Ferguson of Louisiana declares unconstitutional Jim Crow laws on interstate travel.

November 8: Cleveland is elected president again.

November 18: Charges against Plessy are upheld by Justice Ferguson of Louisiana.

1893

In *Ex parte Plessy* the Louisiana supreme court upholds Ferguson's ruling against Plessy.

1895

September 18: Booker T. Washington delivers his "Atlanta Exposition Speech."

1896

May 18: In *Plessy v. Ferguson* the U.S. Supreme Court upholds the constitutionality of Louisiana's equal-but-separate law.

1925

March 1: Homer Plessy dies in New Orleans.

Questions for Consideration

1. Although Homer Plessy could pass as "white" and had only one-eighth African blood and seven-eighths European blood, he was officially "colored" under Louisiana law. How did Plessy's racial mixture complicate efforts to mandate "separate but equal" facilities? What does that mixture tell us about how society determines racial identity? If Plessy looked "white," what role does skin color ultimately have in determinations of race?

2. What were the goals of Radical Reconstruction? Why did they fail, and how did their failure create the conditions for the *Plessy* case? Try to imagine how United States society would be different if Radical Reconstruction had succeeded and if in the *Civil Rights Cases* the Supreme Court had upheld the constitutionality of the 1875 Civil Rights Act.

3. Why was the debate over the 1866 Civil Rights Act and the Fourteenth Amendment so passionate? How did the issue of states' rights and the distrust of the federal government intersect with the issue of race?

4. The Fifteenth Amendment prohibited states from depriving someone the right to vote on the basis of race. Many advocates of women's rights criticized the amendment for not prohibiting discrimination on the basis of sex as well. If you had participated in the debates, would you have withheld support of the amendment until it protected the interests of women?

5. The Supreme Court ruled that the Louisiana separate-but-equal law did not violate Homer Plessy's Fourteenth Amendment rights. But in *Santa Clara County v. Southern Pacific Railroad Company* (1886) it ruled that corporations, as legal "persons," have some Fourteenth Amendment protections. What are the implications of juxtaposing these two cases?

6. In the majority opinion in *Plessy,* Justice Brown stated that the crucial Fourteenth Amendment question was whether the Louisiana law was a reasonable use of a state's police powers. According to Brown, "In determining the question of reasonableness [the state legislature] is at liberty to act with reference to the established usages, customs and traditions of the people, and with a view to the promotion of their comfort, and the preservation of the public peace and good order." What do you think of his definition of reasonableness? Can you offer a different definition? Would your definition have altered the outcome of the *Plessy* case?

190

7. Justice Brown claimed that the "underlying fallacy" of Plessy's argument was the "assumption that the enforced separation of the two races stamps the colored race with a badge of inferiority. If this be so, it is not by reason of anything found in the act, but solely because the colored race chooses to put that construction upon it." In terms of strict logic, was Brown correct? Was there any language in the law that explicitly treated the "colored race" as inferior? If according to the law "whites" and "coloreds" were treated equally, how would you have mounted an argument to refute Brown's claim? Did his claim have an "underlying fallacy"?

8. According to Brown, Plessy's argument assumed "that social prejudices may be overcome by legislation, and that equal rights cannot be secured to the negro except by an enforced commingling of the two races." In contrast, he asserted that "[i]f the two races are to meet upon terms of social equality, it must be the result of natural affinities, a mutual appreciation of each other's merits and a voluntary consent of individuals." Do you agree with Brown that the elimination of racial prejudice must come from the "voluntary consent of individuals," not through legal measures? If you agree, yet believe that he made the wrong decision in *Plessy,* how can you distinguish your beliefs from his? If you disagree with him on this issue, how would you respond to the argument that legislative efforts to force people to change their beliefs can backfire by creating resentment over government interference in the private consciences of individuals?

9. What do you think of Justice Harlan's reference to the Chinese in his dissent? How does it complicate explanations of race in the United States in "black and white" terms?

10. Compare the styles of argumentation used by John Tyler Morgan the politician, Frederick L. Hoffman the statistician, Henry M. Field the minister, and Booker T. Washington the educator. Which do you find most effective? Least effective? Why? What role did religion play in their various solutions to the "race question"? Which of their positions was closest to that of the Plessy majority? How do their arguments help explain the majority's opinion that the Louisiana law was a reasonable use of a state's police powers?

11. What would have been the effect of basing social policy on Hoffman's "scientific" data?

12. What is the meaning of Washington's metaphor of the hand? Why, given Washington's argument about the role of blacks in the South, is the hand an appropriate image? What do you think of it as a metaphor for a multicultural nation? How is this metaphor different from that of the melting pot? Of the salad bowl?

13. What is the relation between W. E. B. Du Bois's description of double-consciousness and the logic of the *Plessy* majority? Compare Du Bois's description of "the strivings of the Negro people" with the portrayal of African Americans in the selections by Morgan, Hoffman, Field, and Washington.

14. What was Charles W. Chesnutt's response to Justice Bradley's argument in the *Civil Rights Cases* that a time has to come when an African American citizen must stop being the "special favorite of the law, and when his rights as a citizen or a man are to be protected in the ordinary modes by which other men's rights are protected"? What is your response to Bradley's argument? Do you believe that the time he described had been reached at the time of the *Civil Rights Cases* (1883)? Had it been reached by the time of *Plessy* (1896)? Has it been reached today?

15. Compare Washington's, Du Bois's, and Chesnutt's arguments. Which do you find most effective? Why?

16. How did the Court in *Brown v. Board of Education* (1954) argue that "separate but equal schools" are inherently unequal? What is the precise relation among *Plessy, Brown,* and *Regents of the University of California v. Bakke* (1978)?

17. What are the different ways to interpret the "color-blind" metaphor? Do you believe that United States society is color-blind today? Do you believe that it should aim to be color-blind? Would declaring the Constitution color-blind at the time of *Plessy* have made today's society more or less color-blind? Would declaring the Constitution color-blind today make a future society more or less color-blind?

18. Knowing the makeup of the *Plessy* Court, how would you have adjusted your argument to try to convince the justices to rule in Plessy's favor?

19. Join with others to reenact the Supreme Court hearing on *Plessy,* some taking the side of Plessy, some the side of the state of Louisiana, and some the role of the Supreme Court justices. If possible, repeat your reenactment with people switching roles. What is the difference between reading about the case and participating in a reenactment of it?

Selected Bibliography

WORKS ON PLESSY V. FERGUSON

Aleinikoff, T. Alexander. "Re-Reading Justice Harlan's Dissent in *Plessy v. Ferguson*: Freedom, Antiracism, and Citizenship." *University of Illinois Law Review* 1992 (1992): 961–77.

Fiss, Owen M. *Troubled Beginnings of the Modern State, 1888–1910.* Vol. 8 of Holmes Devise, *History of the Supreme Court of the United States.* New York: Macmillan, 1993.

Lofgren, Charles A. *The "Plessy" Case: A Legal-Historical Interpretation.* New York: Oxford University Press, 1987.

Medley, Keith Weldon. "The Sad Story of How 'Separate but Equal' Was Born." *Smithsonian*, February 1994, 105–17.

Olsen, Otto H. *Carpetbagger's Crusade: The Life of Albion Winegar Tourgée.* Baltimore: Johns Hopkins University Press, 1965.

———, ed. *The Thin Disguise: "Plessy v. Ferguson."* New York: Humanities Press, 1967.

WORKS ON THE LEGAL, SOCIAL, AND HISTORICAL BACKGROUND

Belz, Herman. *Emancipation and Equal Rights: Politics and Constitutionalism in the Civil War Era.* New York: Norton, 1978.

Berger, Raoul. *Government by Judiciary: The Transformation of the Fourteenth Amendment.* Cambridge: Harvard University Press, 1977.

Beth, Loren P. *John Marshall Harlan: The Last Whig Justice.* Lexington: University of Kentucky Press, 1992.

Cable, George Washington. "The Freedman's Case in Equity." *Century Magazine* 29 (1884–85): 409–18.

Chesnutt, Charles W. *The Marrow of Tradition.* Boston: Houghton Mifflin, 1901.

Collins, Charles Wallace. *The Fourteenth Amendment and the States.* Boston: Little, Brown, 1912.

Desdunes, Rodolphe Lucien. *Our People and Our History.* Trans. Sister Dorothea Olga McCants. 1911. Reprint, Baton Rouge: Louisiana State University Press, 1973.

Du Bois, W. E. B. *Black Reconstruction in America: An Essay toward a History of the Past Which Black Folk Played in the Attempt to Reconstruct Democracy in America, 1860–1880.* New York: Russell and Russell, 1935.

————. *The Souls of Black Folk*. 1903. Reprint, New York: Penguin, 1989.

Fairman, Charles. *Reconstruction and Reunion, 1865–1888*. Vol. 6 of Holmes Devise, *History of the Supreme Court of the United States*. New York: Macmillan, 1971.

Franklin, John Hope. *Reconstruction after the Civil War*. Chicago: University of Chicago Press, 1960.

Fry, Joseph A. *John Tyler Morgan and the Search for Southern Autonomy*. Knoxville: University of Tennessee Press, 1992.

Gotanda, Neil. "A Critique of 'Our Constitution Is Color-Blind.' " *Stanford University Law Review* 44 (1991): 1–68.

Grady, Henry W. "In Plain Black and White." *Century Magazine* 29 (1885): 909–17

Haller, John S. Jr. *Outcasts from Evolution: Scientific Attitudes of Racial Inferiority, 1859–1900*. Urbana: University of Illinois Press, 1971.

Hovenkamp, Herbert. "Social Science and Segregation before *Brown*." *Duke Law Journal* 85 (1985): 624–72.

Hyman, Harold M., and William M. Wiecek. *Equal Justice under Law*. New York: Harper and Row, 1982.

Kaczorowski, Robert. *The Politics of Judicial Interpretation: The Federal Courts, Department of Justice, and Civil Rights, 1866–1876*. Dobbs Ferry, N.Y.: Oceana Publications, 1985.

Karst, Kenneth L. *Belonging to America: Equal Citizenship and the Constitution*. New Haven: Yale University Press, 1989.

Kull, Andrew. *The Color-Blind Constitution*. Cambridge: Harvard University Press, 1992.

Levy, Leonard W., and Douglas L. Jones. *Jim Crow in Boston*. New York: DaCapo Press, 1974.

Litwack, Leon F. *Been in the Storm So Long: The Aftermath of Slavery*. New York: Knopf, 1979.

Logan, Rayford W. *The Betrayal of the Negro from Rutherford B. Hayes to Woodrow Wilson*. New York: Collier, 1965.

Nelson, William E. *The Fourteenth Amendment: From Political Principle to Judicial Doctrine*. Cambridge: Harvard University Press, 1988.

Olsen, Otto H., ed. *Reconstruction and Redemption in the South*. Baton Rouge: Louisiana University Press, 1980.

Soifer, Aviam. "Protecting Civil Rights: A Critique of Raoul Berger's History." *New York University Law Review* 54 (1979): 651–706.

————. "Status, Contract, and Promises Unkept." *Yale Law Journal* 96 (1987): 1916–59.

tenBrock, Jacobus. *Equal under Law*. New York: Collier, 1965.

Tourgée, Albion W. *Bricks without Straw*. New York: Fords, Howard, and Hulbert, 1880.

————. *Pactolus Prime*. New York: Cassell and Company, 1890.

Urofsky, Melvin I., ed. *The Supreme Court Justices: A Biographical Dictionary*. New York: Garland, 1994.

Washington, Booker T. *Up from Slavery*. New York: Doubleday Page, 1901.

Washington, Booker T., W. E. Burghardt Du Bois, Paul Laurence Dunbar, Charles W. Chesnutt, et al. *The Negro Problem*. New York: James Potts, 1903.

Woodward, C. Vann. *Origins of the New South, 1877–1913*. Baton Rouge: Louisiana University Press, 1951.

———. *The Strange Career of Jim Crow*. 3rd ed. New York: Oxford University Press, 1974.

Index